ISAIAH

ISAIAH

an exposition by
W. A. CRISWELL

ZONDERVAN
PUBLISHING HOUSE   OF THE ZONDERVAN CORPORATION
GRAND RAPIDS, MICHIGAN 49506

ISAIAH: AN EXPOSITION
Copyright © 1977 by The Zondervan Corporation
Grand Rapids, Michigan

Second printing   1978

Library of Congress Cataloging in Publication Data

Criswell, Wallie A
    Isaiah: an exposition.

    1. Bible. O.T.   Isaiah—Sermons.   2. Baptists
—Sermons.   3. Sermons, American.   I. Title.
BS1515.4.C74   224'.1'066   77-24267
ISBN 0-310-22870-0

To
CRIS CRISWELL
and the Class of 1977, the first
graduating class of the First Baptist Academy,
a lighthouse of intellectual endeavor and
spiritual undergirding for our children
who are the hope and future
of tomorrow.

CONTENTS

FOREWORD

There is a vast difference between a sermon written out word for word and a sermon preached extemporaneously from the pulpit to a large audience. These expositions of Isaiah are delivered sermons, spoken without notes, and designed first for hearers. There is, therefore, repetition to be found in them which would not be found in a written message. In reading, one can go back and reread what may not have been clear, but in speaking the preacher must sense in his soul that the people understand what he is saying as he goes along. This causes him often to repeat what has already been said or explained.

Through the years I have learned something that has helped me greatly in my study and preparation for sermons. It is this: a book of messages on a book of the Bible is the finest commentary I could ever hope to find on that portion of Scripture. I pray that this volume on Isaiah will enrich both the preacher's and teacher's library.

The delivered messages were blessed of God to the people who heard them in our church. May the Holy Spirit no less bless them to the hearts of those who now read them.

My deepest, sincerest gratitude is herewith expressed to those who copied the sermons from tape recordings and who corrected them for grammatical errors. In the fury of preaching the pastor will often forget whether the subject was plural or singular!

May God bless the eyes that look upon these pages.

W. A. *Criswell*
First Baptist Church
Dallas, Texas

ISAIAH

1

The Prophet Isaiah

The vision of Isaiah the son of Amoz, which he saw concerning
Judah and Jerusalem in the days of Uzziah, Jotham, Ahaz, and
Hezekiah, kings of Judah. (Isa. 1:1)

As we begin our study of Isaiah we are astonished at how little we
know of the man himself. Actually, we must say that we know little
about any of the world's greatest men. In thinking of the myriad-
minded Shakespeare, the unsurpassed genius produced by the
English-speaking world, we discover that we do not even know
how to spell his name because there is contradiction about the way
he spelled his name. There are knowledgeable scholars who even
deny that he ever lived; some of them attribute his dramas to
Christopher Marlowe; others say that Francis Bacon wrote them.
We know practically nothing of the great genius Shakespeare. We
know even less of Dante, the incomparable Italian poet. Absolutely nothing for certain can be researched about the finest poet of
the ancient world, Homer — where he was born, how he lived, or
how his writings evolved. It is amazing how little we know of the
world's finest writers.

So it is with the prophets of the Bible. In looking through the

Scriptures we find portraits and presentations of mighty characters such as Abraham, Jacob (Israel), or Joseph, but when we study the prophets Amos, Hosea, or Isaiah, we discover practically no information about these men.

There must be a reason for it and it could be that in the providence of God He hid the man in the mist. He shrouded his form and figure so that the voice might be heard. We are to listen to the word of God and are not to behold the man who delivered it.

Thus, as we begin our study of Isaiah, we do not know much about him, but what little we know is unusually significant.

ISAIAH THE MAN

First, Isaiah was a man of the city. He was born in the city, he labored in the city, and he loved the city. His long ministry of possibly fifty years or more was spent in the city. From the period 750 B.C. to 700 B.C. the court preacher Isaiah delivered his prophecies and his messages in the city. His figures, his references, and his outstanding poetic imagery are all drawn from urban life.

The prophet Amos was a man of the country, and his figures of speech are from the field and the flock. But the figures of speech that we read in Isaiah are taken from city life. He was the court preacher, the city minister.

Isaiah was the first in a long line of famous city preachers. He was a Jeremiah of Anathoth and Jerusalem, a Paul of Ephesus, Corinth, and Rome, an Ignatius of Antioch, a John Chrysostom of Constantinople, a Savanarola of Florence, a John Calvin of Geneva, a John Knox of Edinburgh, a Spurgeon of London, a Phillips Brooks of Boston, a Thomas deWitt Talmage of Brooklyn, a Dwight L. Moody of Chicago, or a George W. Truett of Dallas. Isaiah was the first of a line of magnificent, history-changing preachers.

He was a man of unusual cultivation and culture; an aristocrat in birth, in bearing, and in speech. Tradition says that his father, Amoz, was a brother of Amaziah the king, who was the father of Uzziah the king. This could explain why, in the sixth chapter of the prophecy, when he saw the great vision in the days of the death of King Uzziah, the young man was so deeply stricken and grieved.

He was at home in the highest circles of government. He had ready access to the king. He knew the priesthood intimately and was no less conversant with the life of the upper classes. He moved with grace and understanding among the great, the sovereign, and the leaders of the land.

Isaiah grew up in a day of affluence and prosperity. King Uzziah of Judah and Jeroboam II of Israel brought their people to the highest achievements of economic and political prosperity. They even rivaled the power and glory of the united kingdom under David and Solomon. And, of course, attendant to the affluence, riches, and power of the nation were the vices that inevitably accompany them. Isaiah lived to see the degeneration of the people and of the nation.

When we read the Bible and examine the background against which Isaiah lived, we think of America. How good God has been to our people and with what affluence and wealth He has blessed us! And yet the very source of our degeneration, promiscuity, violence, and rebellion lies in our riches and our wealth. I doubt whether there is a knowledgeable man today but who would say that one of the things wrong with the young people of our generation is that they have never known anything but abundance and wealth.

ISAIAH STANDS TALL IN THE MIDST OF THE DECAY OF THE NATION

So it was in the days of Isaiah. He lived to see the nation's wealth plundered and its affluence used as a means of the decimation and degeneration of the people. Because of this, Isaiah went about dressed in a garment of haircloth as did Elijah and John the Baptist, calling the people to repentance. For three years Isaiah walked through the streets of Jerusalem dressed only in a loincloth; he was dressed like a slave, barefoot and unclothed, that he might demonstrate the prophecy of the Word of God which spoke of a coming servitude and captivity.

ISAIAH'S FAMILY IS USED BY GOD

The family of Isaiah was a part of his message and prophetic ministry to the people. He used a term of endearment in referring to his wife as "the prophetess"; not that she delivered oracles of God, but the word "prophetess" was Isaiah's way of saying Mrs. Pastor or Mrs. Preacher. His sons were themselves messengers of the prophecy that Isaiah delivered. For example, he named his firstborn son Shear-jashub, which means "a remnant shall return." When the judgment of God fell upon the nation and the people, He would spare a small remnant.

Isaiah had another son named Maher-shalal-hash-baz, which means "hastening to the prey, speeding to the spoil," which was a prophecy of the coming of the bitter and hasty Assyrians who would destroy the northern kingdom and the cities of Judah and would shut up Hezekiah and Jerusalem as in an iron vise.

Thus, the family of Isaiah was itself a part of the prophetic ministry of the man of God.

Isaiah's Death As Tradition Repeats It

How did Isaiah die? Universal tradition says that he was sawed in pieces. In Hebrews 11:37 there is mention of a hero of faith who was put to death this way. Tradition says that the hero in the passage in Hebrews is Isaiah. The Mishnah, part of the Jewish Talmud, says that Isaiah was martyred, slain by the wicked King Manasseh. Justin Martyr speaks of Isaiah being sawed in pieces with a wooden saw.

In about A.D. 150 a Jewish apocalypse was written entitled *The Assumption of Isaiah,* and Isaiah's martyrdom by being sawed in two is told in that apocalypse. Throughout the tradition of the death of Isaiah he is said to have been murdered by wicked Manasseh.

Isaiah — the Greatest Poetic Genius

Isaiah was the most accomplished poetically inspired genius the world has ever produced. There are no limits to the poetical sublimity Isaiah reaches as he declares the message of almighty God. He is an artist with words, a master with language, and an orator far beyond a Demosthenes. Celestially he uses his perorations, his descriptions, and his poetic imagery. He employs every form of poetic speech: alliteration, parable, interrogation, dialogue, metaphor, simile, paronomasia (a play upon words). He rises to heights of poetry beyond what we could think human speech could bear.

In a version of the Bible other than the King James, we see that most of his prophecy is written in beautiful poetic form — it has rhythm, figure, imagery, and style. Isaiah uses a rich vocabulary beyond any other who ever spoke in the Word of God.

For example, in Ezekiel there are 1,535 different words. Jeremiah has 1,653 different words. In all of the Psalms there are 2,170 different words. But Isaiah uses 2,186 different words! His language, his figures of speech, and his poetic genius are raised by inspiration to a divine and celestial fire.

No wonder that in Jerusalem there is a beautiful monument called the Shrine of the Book. What book? The Shrine of the Book is shaped like a dome, and when one goes inside it, he sees a gigantic, circular glass case which displays a fourteen-feet long parchment of the entire Book of Isaiah copied by the Essenes in about 150 B.C.

Isaiah was the evangelical messenger of the Old Testament. He was the apostle Paul of the Old Covenant. He was the man who stood alone and proclaimed the incomparable gospel of the grace of the Son of God before the gospel itself. His name means "the Lord of our salvation." His theme was justification by faith, salvation by trusting God alone. His message was delivered in beautiful evangelical form and language. It is as though the prophet Isaiah stood in the shadow of the Son of God as He walked through Galilee, Judaea, Perea, and finally to Calvary. He was a man of the life, ministry, and saving message of the divine Redeemer.

If a man stands in the pulpit to preach a sermon during the Christmas season, he will read from Isaiah, "Behold, a virgin shall conceive, and bear a son, and shall call his name Immanuel" (7:14). If a man presents a message on Good Friday, he could preach from Isaiah 53:5, "He was wounded for our transgressions, he was bruised for our iniquities: the chastisement of our peace was upon him; and with his stripes we are healed." If a pastor delivers a

Wednesday night lecture on the theology of atonement, he may use as a background the prophetic words of Isaiah, "[God] shall see of the travail of his soul, and shall be satisfied." If a man stands in the name of God to proclaim the golden age that is yet to come, he can use as the background of his message the celestial visions of the prophet Isaiah who saw new heavens and a new earth and who beyond the grave cried, "O death, where is thy sting? O grave, where is thy victory?" (1 Cor. 15:55).

ISAIAH DESCRIBES THE TRUE GOLDEN AGE

He is the mighty prophet of the millennium, the messianic messenger of the old covenant. Isaiah pictures by heavenly revelation the millennial age that is yet to come. Herein is an astonishing fact, for all the ancient philosophers and poets spoke of the golden age as long since past.

Plato, for example, describes the golden age of mankind in the form, context, and place of an island named Atlantis, which was located beyond the gates of Hercules, beyond the Straits of Gibraltar in the vast expanse of the Atlantic Ocean, and which is now submerged. In the civilization and life of the people who lived on that continent of the long ago, Plato found the golden age of mankind long since past.

Every ancient poet of the Greco-Roman world spoke of the golden age as being a time of innocence and bliss in the story of mankind long ago.

But Isaiah lifted up his voice and in words inspired from God described the golden age that is yet to come — the millennial age in which God will come down, when the skies will be rent asunder, and the Prince of Glory will reign in person upon this former wicked and stolid earth, but which will then be cleansed and purified, a place of beauty, holiness, and righteousness! As Isaiah describes the beautiful, millennial, golden age that is yet to come, he says that it will be inherited by a remnant. Not all will be saved, says Isaiah; not all will come to a knowledge of the truth. Not all will enter into the kingdom, but there will be some. Some will be saved; some will turn in faith to the Lord; some will be plucked out of the burning fire and the entire remnant will be called the people of the Lord. Isaiah says that the remnant will have a king over them who is of the line of David. He will be born of a virgin. He will be endowed, empowered, and filled with the Holy Spirit of God and He will reign in beauty, justice, and righteousness.

The spirit and the imagery of the messianic millennial kingdom is found throughout the Word of God. It is found in the Protevangelium in Genesis — "seed of the woman." As the days passed its rising glory is increasingly seen in Moses, in David, and in Solomon, but it is only when we read Isaiah that we see the beauty of His person, the expressed image of His glory, and the marvelous, incomparable kingdom over which He will some day rule and reign.

WILL ISAIAH'S PROPHECIES COME TO PASS?

What must we think about the glorious prophecies of Isaiah? Can we believe them? Will this dull and sinful earth ever see anything so resplendent as the majestic King, the Messiah of the millennial reign come down? Will our eyes ever look upon the Redeemer? Will we ever share in that ultimate and final kingdom? If we lie in the dust of the ground, will we also feel the stirring of a resurrection, a quickening of a new life? Spoken into immortality and glory — could such a thing ever be?

All one has to go on is this: The same prophet who described in minute detail the first coming of the Lord — His birth in the womb of a virgin, His ministry among people who sat in darkness and in the region of death, His kindness in healing the sick, in ministering to the poor — the same prophet, who as clearly as if he stood on Calvary that awesome day, described the suffering and atoning death of the Son of God. He is the same prophet who described the glorious return of that same Messiah in wonder, in holiness, in power, and in beauty. If I can believe that Isaiah described the first coming of our Lord seven hundred fifty years before He walked the face of the earth in the days of His flesh, can I not also believe that the same prophet no less saw by divine inspiration the returning King who will set up His millennial kingdom in the earth and His subjects will be those who love, worship, and believe in the Lord?

With anticipation a child of God should lift up his face waiting for the dawning of our final millennial redemption!

When I read through the prophet Isaiah I find that when the prophet describes destruction and despair, he speaks in the same breath of the glory of the Lord. In one moment Isaiah portrays death, disease, loss, and the helplessness of people who have no other choice but to face slavery and captivity, but in the next moment he says, "Comfort ye, comfort ye my people. . . . Speak ye comfortably to Jerusalem." And then Isaiah describes the glories of the kingdom yet to come and avows "and all flesh shall see it together." The superlative language he uses to describe the millennial kingdom is treasured in our hearts by promise forever:

> And there shall come forth a rod out of the stem of Jesse, and a Branch shall grow out of his roots . . . But with righteousness shall he judge the poor. . . . The wolf also shall dwell with the lamb, and the leopard shall lie down with the kid . . . and the lion shall eat straw like the ox. . . . They shall not hurt nor destroy in all my holy mountain: for the earth shall be full of the knowledge of the LORD, as the waters cover the sea. (Isa. 11:1-6)

When God creates the new heavens and a new earth, He shall reign, whose name is "The Lord our Righteousness."

2

God and Government

The vision of Isaiah the son of Amoz, which he saw concerning Judah and Jerusalem in the days of Uzziah, Jotham, Ahaz, and Hezekiah, kings of Judah. (Isa. 1:1)

By studying the political and national life of the kings mentioned in Isaiah 1:1 we shall be able to understand the background against which Isaiah delivered his message.

Uzziah

Uzziah reigned for fifty-two years. He was an able and gifted administrator as well as a military strategist. With Jeroboam II, the king of Samaria, and Uzziah, the king of the southern kingdom of Judah, the nation was brought back to the glorious position and prosperity it knew under the united kingdom of David and Solomon. Uzziah prospered in everything he did. He did so as long as Zechariah the prophet lived.

There are twenty-eight different Zechariahs in the Bible and when we think of this Zechariah, we are likely to think of the prophet who wrote the next to the last book in the Old Testament. This is not he. That Zechariah returned with Zerubbabel from the

21

Babylonian captivity. This Zechariah is an unknown prophet, and the only thing we know about him is that he had a tremendous influence for good upon Uzziah.

As long as Zechariah lived, Uzziah served the Lord faithfully and well. But when Zechariah died in Uzziah's old age, the king turned from the Lord. It is tragic that a man would give his life to God, then in his old age turn away from the faithful ministry of God and seek to arrogate unto himself the services that belonged only to the appointed priests. Azariah, the high priest, and eighty of his fellow priests begged Uzziah not to do this, but the stiff-necked, hard-hearted, and incorrigible king continued in his purpose to set aside the ministry of the priest and to do this service himself. When he did so, he was stricken with leprosy and for the remainder of his reign and life he lived separate and apart — the life of a leper.

However, it was during the prosperous reign of Uzziah that the young Isaiah grew up. And it was in the year of the death of Uzziah that Isaiah saw the glorious vision recorded in the sixth chapter of his book and began his prophetic ministry.

JOTHAM

Uzziah had a son named Jotham, who was co-regent with him. Jotham was a noble man and a good king. He was able, like his father, and he continued the great prosperity by which God had blessed the nation. He was a devout man of the Lord and extended the courts of the temple. Doubtless Amos and Hosea, prophets of the northern kingdom, and Micah of the southern kingdom, along with Isaiah had a salubrious effect upon Jotham. As Jotham began his reign, Isaiah began his prophetic ministry. Jotham was followed by Ahaz. Without a thorough understanding of Ahaz and his times, we can never fully understand Isaiah and the word he brought from the Lord.

AHAZ

The little kingdom of southern Judah was surrounded by many nations: on the east was Joab and Edom, to the south was the ancient kingdom of the pharaohs, to the west were the city states of

Philistia, and to the north was the unfriendly state of Israel, which often in the Bible is called Ephraim. To the northeast was Damascus, the capital of Syria, and to the ultimate north, covering the horizon of history from side to side, was the growing, gigantic empire of Assyria with its famous capital on the Tigris River, Nineveh. There in oriental splendor reigned one who called himself the king of kings, in whose eyes the little kinglets of Judah and Samaria were but as grasshoppers.

This king of Assyria numbered his hosts by the myriads. His chariots and his horses covered the land like locusts. Their onrush was like the flooding of a giant ocean. Four times in Isaiah's lifetime did the terrible and irresistible force of the Assyrians overrun Judah. The behemoth of Assyria was that winged, man-headed bull of Ashur who had wings for swiftness, a man's head for intelligence, and the form of a bull for strength. This behemoth of Assyria was an ogre to the Jews. They lived in daily terror of the merciless and cruel invasion of the Assyrians.

The Assyrians finally destroyed forever the northern kingdom of Israel. They wasted the cities of Judah and shut up the city of Jerusalem as a man would close a hammer in a vise. Deliverance could come only by the intervention of God.

How is it that Assyria became involved in the political and national life of Judah? It came through King Ahaz. You see, Pekah, the king of Israel in Samaria, and Rezin, the king of Syria in Damascus, formed a conspiracy to dethrone Ahaz, to overrun Judah, and to set up a puppet government there. That confrontation and conflict is called the Syro-Ephraimite War. Ahaz, instead of turning to God and trusting in the Lord, decided to find help in some other source.

At that time Isaiah the prophet of God came before Ahaz and said:

> Take heed, and be quiet; fear not, neither be fainthearted for the two tails of these smoking firebrands, for the fierce anger of Rezin with Syria, and of the son of Remaliah. (7:4)

Thus the prophet Isaiah described them and said to Ahaz:

> Ask thee a sign of the Lord thy God; ask it either in the depth, or in the height above.

> But Ahaz said, I will not ask, neither will I tempt the LORD.
> (7:11,12)

But Ahaz had already decided to find help from some other source and replied he would not be presumptuous to tempt God to ask for a sign. Then it was that the prophet delivered the great messianic prophecy:

> Behold, a virgin shall conceive, and bear a son, and shall call his name Immanuel. (7:14)

Looking beyond the spiritless, spineless, weak, and vascillating king he saw the glorious Messiah in His coming sovereignty and grace. But to Ahaz he said:

> For before the child shall know to refuse the evil, and choose the good, the land that thou abhorrest shall be forsaken of both her kings. (7:16)

Ahaz had already decided to find help from some other source. What did he do? To whom did he turn? Ahaz turned to Tiglath-pileser III, the ruthless and merciless king of Assyria (2 Kings 16:7).

Tiglath-pileser was one of the great conquerors of all time, like Alexander the Great or Julius Caesar. It did him nothing but good to have the opportunity to extend the Assyrian Empire over all the south through Palestine. Therefore, Tiglath-pileser came willingly. He was the one who designed and devised the deportation of conquered provinces, a practice which brought indescribable heartache to the conquered people who were removed from their homes. That is the Tiglath-pileser to whom Ahaz made appeal for help — not to God, but to the Assyrian king. He was far more impressed by the power of Assyria than he was by the power of God.

So with gladness and with eagerness Tiglath-pileser came and the Assyrians destroyed not only the northern kingdom of Samaria forever, not only Damascus and Syria, but he also destroyed the cities of Judah. Had it not been for the intervention of God, Assyria would have destroyed Jerusalem, the Holy City, and the temple itself. It was Ahaz who invited Tiglath-pileser to come.

What has that to do with us? you might ask. I would like to say it is as pertinent and of as much concern to us as the headlines we read in the newspaper today.

Let us go back to World War II. God was favoring our Allied Forces as an answer to prayer, and was giving victory to us. General Patton with his tanks had crossed the Rhine and had nothing between his victorious American forces and Berlin and all Germany except the beautiful contour of the land with its pleasant valleys and hills. But our government directed him to stop. As a result, Berlin and Germany were delivered into the hands of the Communists when we were already there in victory. The same thing happened to Bulgaria, Romania, Czechoslovakia, and Albania. In later years we allowed China and North Korea to become communistic. And now, in recent years we delivered Laos, Cambodia, Thailand, and South Vietnam into the hands of the Communists. The result is that one-third of the world's population and two-thirds of the world's land mass is under the hands of those merciless and cruel rulers.

There has never been a challenge to the Christian gospel that can compare with the ruthless, revengeful attitude of the atheistic Communists. So far as we know, they have destroyed the churches and the congregations of China. So far as we know, many other countries have only an underground of the faithful. The people are oppressed. They live in despair and have no one to help them. That is exactly what happened to Judah under Ahaz. As a sycophant of Tiglath-pileser, Ahaz journeyed to Damascus to meet him, brought back into Jerusalem the idolatry he saw there, closed the temple, desecrated the house of God, and burned his own children in the valley of Hinnom as sacrifices to the god Moloch. Thus did Ahaz bring the glory of God's people down to the dust of the ground.

HEZEKIAH

Ahaz was followed by Hezekiah. Is it not remarkable how a bad man often will have a good son? Good king Hezekiah began his reign at twenty-five years of age and reigned twenty-nine years. He was a man like David, a man after God's own heart. The first thing

Hezekiah did was to call the people to revival, repentance, and reformation. He opened the doors of the temple, the house of God. He cleansed the temple and invited the remnant of northern Israel to come and celebrate the Passover with them, the first Passover that had been observed in many generations. When the Assyrian Sennacherib came, as inevitably he would, he destroyed the cities of Judah, surrounded Jerusalem on every side, and called upon King Hezekiah to surrender. Hezekiah took the letter from Sennacherib demanding abject surrender and spread it upon the altar in the house of the Lord. Thereupon the prophet Isaiah was sent with this message from the Lord to the king:

> Therefore thus saith the LORD concerning the king of Assyria, He shall not come into this city, nor shoot an arrow there, nor come before it with shield, nor cast a bank against it.
>
> By the way that he came, by the same shall he return, and shall not come into this city, saith the LORD.
>
> For I will defend this city, to save it, for mine own sake, and for my servant David's sake. (2 Kings 19:32-34)

In that one night an angel passed over the hosts of Sennacherib, and when the dawn broke 185,000 Assyrian corpses were counted (2 Kings 19:35). Thus does God spare and thus does God save and thus does God answer by fire. Trusting the mighty arm of the Lord for deliverance, Hezekiah saved his people.

Then something happened that brought disaster to the nation.

> In those days was Hezekiah sick unto death. And Isaiah the prophet the son of Amoz came unto him, and said unto him, Thus saith the LORD, Set thine house in order: for thou shalt die, and not live.
>
> Then Hezekiah turned his face toward the wall, and prayed unto the LORD,
>
> And said, Remember now, O LORD, I beseech thee, how I have walked before thee in truth and with a perfect heart, and have done that which is good in thy sight. And Hezekiah wept sore.
>
> Then came the word of the LORD to Isaiah, saying,
>
> Go, and say to Hezekiah, Thus saith the LORD, the God of David thy father, I have heard thy prayer, I have seen thy tears: behold, I will add unto thy days fifteen years.
>
> And I will deliver thee and this city out of the hand of the king of Assyria: and I will defend this city. (Isa. 38:1-6)

What happened in that fifteen years? Two things: first, Merodach-baladan, the upcoming young sovereign from Babylon, was getting ready to destroy Nineveh, the capital of Assyria, when he heard of the recovery of Hezekiah. So he sent an ambassador to Hezekiah ostensibly to congratulate him on his recovery. Actually, his intent was to form a conspiracy against the sovereign of Nineveh (2 Kings 20:12). Is it not strange how good men, great men, godly men often are weak men? The ambassador flattered Hezekiah; and Hezekiah opened his treasures, his heart, the city, and the temple to these emissaries of Merodach-baladan from Babylon.

> Then came Isaiah the prophet unto king Hezekiah, and said unto him, What said these men? and from whence came they unto thee? And Hezekiah said, They are come from a far country, even from Babylon.
> And he said, What have they seen in thine house? And Hezekiah answered, All the things that are in mine house have they seen: there is nothing among my treasures that I have not shewed them.
> And Isaiah said unto Hezekiah, Hear the word of the LORD.
> Behold, the days come, that all that is in thine house, and that which thy fathers have laid up in store unto this day, shall be carried into Babylon: nothing shall be left, saith the LORD.
> And of thy sons that shall issue from thee, which thou shalt beget, shall they take away; and they shall be eunuchs in the palace of the king of Babylon. (2 Kings 20:14-18)

All this happened because, in answer to prayer, Hezekiah recovered and fell a prey to the flattery of the emissary.

During the added fifteen years of Hezekiah's life Manasseh was born to Hezekiah. Manasseh reigned fifty-five years and of all the kings who ever lived, there was none so vile and wicked as Manasseh. It was because of his sins that God destroyed Judah and sent the people into Babylonian captivity. One of the recurring refrains in the Holy Scriptures is God's judgment upon Judah because of Manasseh.

> But they hearkened not: and Manasseh seduced them to do more evil than did the nations whom the LORD destroyed before the children of Israel.
> And the LORD spake by his servants the prophets, saying,
> Because Manasseh king of Judah hath done these abominations,

and hath done wickedly above all that the Amorites did, which were before him, and hath made Judah also to sin with his idols:

Therefore thus saith the LORD God of Israel, Behold, I am bringing such evil upon Jerusalem and Judah, that whosoever heareth of it, both his ears shall tingle.

And I will stretch over Jerusalem the line of Samaria, and the plummet of the house of Ahab: and I will wipe Jerusalem as a man wipeth a dish, wiping it, and turning it upside down.

And I will forsake the remnant of mine inheritance, and deliver them into the hand of their enemies; and they shall become a prey and a spoil to all their enemies;

Because they have done that which was evil in my sight, and have provoked me to anger, since the day their fathers came forth out of Egypt, even unto this day.

Moreover Manasseh shed innocent blood very much, till he had filled Jerusalem from one end to another; beside his sin wherewith he made Judah to sin, in doing that which was evil in the sight of the LORD. (2 Kings 21:9-16)

Notwithstanding the LORD turned not from the fierceness of his great wrath, wherewith his anger was kindled against Judah, because of all the provocations that Manasseh had provoked him withal.

And the LORD said, I will remove Judah also out of my sight, as I have removed Israel, and will cast off this city Jerusalem which I have chosen, and the house of which I said, My name shall be there. (2 Kings 23:26,27)

Surely at the commandment of the LORD came this upon Judah, to remove them out of his sight, for the sins of Manasseh, according to all that he did;

And also for the innocent blood that he shed: for he filled Jerusalem with innocent blood; which the LORD would not pardon. (2 Kings 24:3,4)

The tremendous prophecy of Jeremiah proclaims:

Then said the LORD unto me, Though Moses and Samuel stood before me, yet my mind could not be toward this people: cast them out of my sight, and let them go forth.

And it shall come to pass, if they say unto thee, Whither shall we go forth? then thou shalt tell them, Thus saith the LORD; Such as are for death, to death; and such as are for the sword, to the sword; and such as are for the famine, to the famine; and such as are for the captivity, to the captivity.

> And I will appoint over them four kinds, saith the Lᴏʀᴅ: the sword
> to slay, and the dogs to tear, and the fowls of the heaven, and the
> beasts of the earth, to devour and destroy.
> And I will cause them to be removed into all kingdoms of the
> earth, because of Manasseh the son of Hezekiah king of Judah, for
> that which he did in Jerusalem. (Jeremiah 15:1-4)

When was Manasseh born? Because of whose wickedness did God destroy Judah and Jerusalem and the holy temple? Manasseh was born during the fifteen years God gave to Hezekiah.

What does this mean to us? I believe that when we pray, we should pray: "Lord God, I do not know what is best. But You know what is best. I do not understand sometimes, and I cannot see the end of the way; so, Lord, I am not trying to impose my will on yours: You choose, Lord. This is how I would like for it to be done; however Lord, not my will, but Thine be done."

I remember a mother who prayed over her dying son and the Lord answered her prayer and the boy lived but was later electrocuted in the state penitentiary at Huntsville for murder and robbery. How much better it would have been to have prayed, "Lord, if the boy can live and honor You, or if it is God's will that he be translated to heaven, Your will be done." Or again, "Lord, am I to die? If You can give me length of days, help me to serve and honor You in every breath I breathe. But Lord, if it honors You that I die, then, Master, give me dying grace. Your will be done."

There are some things that we know are God's will. It is God's will that all men be saved. It is God's will that all men come to repentance. Therefore, when I pray for a man to be saved, I am praying according to God's will.

> And this is the confidence that we have in him, that, if we ask any
> thing according to his will, he heareth us:
> And if we know that he hear us, whatsoever we ask, we know that
> we have the petitions that we desired of him. (1 John 5:14,15)

When we pray according to what we know to be God's will, then we must be importunate in it. But there are many things about which I can pray without wisdom. "Lord, should I live fifteen years?" It might not be best. "Then, Lord, stand by my side when the day of translation comes." There are a thousand things in our daily lives about which we pray. However, we ought always to pray in the spirit and in the intercession, "Lord, not my will; You know best." God always gives what is best for those who leave the choice to Him. It would have been a different world for Judah and for Jerusalem had Manasseh never been born and had Merodach-baladan never sent his flattering emissary. All of this would never have come to pass had Hezekiah been translated when Isaiah was sent to him saying, "Set thy house in order." Lord, give us the spirit of humility and of looking up to heaven.

3

The Doctrine of the Remnant

> Except the LORD of hosts had left unto us a very small remnant,
> we should have been as Sodom, and we should have been like unto
> Gomorrah. (Isa. 1:9)

The Greek Septuagint translation of "remnant" is *sperma*,
"sperm, seed." "If the Lord had not left to us a little seed," just a
little band of faithful followers, we would have been utterly destroyed, completely annihilated, as Sodom and Gomorrah.

The doctrine of the remnant is found throughout the prophecy
of Isaiah. We read:

> And it shall come to pass in that day, that the LORD shall set his
> hand again the second time to recover the remnant of his people,
> which shall be left, from Assyria, and from Egypt, and from Elam,
> and from Shinar, and from Hamath and from the islands of the sea.
> (11:11)

> And there shall be an highway for the remnant of his people,
> which shall be left, from Assyria; like as it was to Israel in the day that
> he came up out of the land of Egypt. (11:16)

> And it came to pass, when king Hezekiah heard it, that he rent his
> clothes, and covered himself with sackcloth, and went into the
> house of the LORD.

31

> And he sent Eliakim, who was over the household, and Shebna the scribe, and the elders of the priests covered with sackcloth, unto Isaiah the prophet the son of Amoz.
>
> And they said unto him, Thus saith Hezekiah, This day is a day of trouble, and of rebuke, and of blasphemy: for the children are come to the birth, and there is not strength to bring forth.
>
> It may be the LORD thy God will hear the words of Rabshakeh, whom the king of Assyria his master hath sent to reproach the living God, and will reprove the words which the LORD thy God hath heard: wherefore lift up thy prayer for the remnant that is left. (37:1-3)

We see it again:

> And the remnant that is escaped of the house of Judah shall again take root downward, and bear fruit upward:
>
> For out of Jerusalem shall go forth a remnant, and they that escape out of mount Zion: the zeal of the LORD of hosts shall do this. (37:31,32)
>
> Hearken unto me, O house of Jacob, and all the remnant of the house of Israel, which are borne by me from the belly, which are carried from the womb:
>
> And even to your old age I am he; and even to hoar hairs will I carry you: I have made, and I will bear; even I will carry, and will deliver you. (46:3,4)

We find throughout the Bible the doctrine of the faithful band, the bold remnant of God. For example:

> Esaias also crieth concerning Israel, Though the number of the children be as the sand of the sea, a remnant shall be saved:
>
> And as Esaias said before, Except the Lord of Sabaoth had left us a seed, we had been as Sodoma, and been made like unto Gomorrha. (Rom. 9:27,29)

Again we read:

> And the dragon was wroth with the woman, and went to make war with the remnant of her seed, which keep the commandments of God, and have the testimony of Jesus Christ. (Rev. 12:17)

The doctrine of the remnant — the little holy band that is left in a darkened and destroyed world.

Isaiah begins his message from the Lord describing the sin and iniquity of the people and the inevitable judgment and visitation from heaven that always follows:

> Hear, O heavens, and give ear, O earth: for the LORD hath spoken, I have nourished and brought up children, and they have rebelled against me.
>
> The ox knoweth his owner, and the ass his master's crib: but Israel doth not know, my people doth not consider.
>
> Ah sinful nation, a people laden with iniquity, a seed of evil-doers, children that are corrupters; they have forsaken the LORD, they have provoked the Holy One of Israel unto anger, they are gone away backward.
>
> Why should ye be stricken any more? ye will revolt more and more: the whole head is sick, and the whole heart faint.
>
> From the sole of the foot even unto the head there is no sound-ness in it; but wounds, and bruises, and putrefying sores: they have not been closed, neither bound up, neither mollified with oint-ment.
>
> Your country is desolate, your cities are burned with fire: your land, strangers devour it in your presence, and it is desolate, as overthrown by strangers.
>
> And the daughter of Zion is left as a cottage in a vineyard, as a lodge in a garden of cucumbers, as a besieged city.
>
> Except the LORD of hosts had left unto us a very small remnant, we should have been as Sodom, and we should have been like unto Gomorrah. (Isa. 1:2-9)

So severe is the judgment from God that Isaiah avows that had it not been for God's intervention, and had not God called out a small remnant, they would have been completely de-stroyed.

TWO DOCTRINES ARE PRESENTED IN THE BOOK OF ISAIAH

As the prophet delivers from God the message of inevitable judgment, he also presents a voice of hope and salvation. There are two doctrines that run throughout the Book of Isaiah which are like silver linings to dark and ominous clouds. One says that the people who sit in darkness have seen a great light, and the light has shined upon them that sit in the valley of the shadow of death. However the earth may be judged and destroyed, and however the nation may be lost in despair, yet God has a faithful remnant. They are purged and renovated, and they become the foundation for a new society, a new culture, a new government, and a new kingdom. This is the doctrine of the remnant.

The other doctrine presented by Isaiah is the doctrine of the coming King and the coming kingdom. As we proceed through the book we shall see that he presents the doctrine in glowing literature beyond what man has written, heard, or seen.

Isaiah frequently leaps from despair to hope, from threat to promise, from earth to heaven, from destruction to salvation. We see this illustrated in his presentation of the doctrine of the remnant. Let us look at several truths about this doctrine.

First, the hope and salvation of the world lies in that faithful little group. The world cannot be destroyed as long as they live in our midst.

Do you remember the story of the angel visitors to Sodom? They warned Lot to flee for his life and when Lot delayed, the angels cast him out of the city saying, "Haste thee, escape thither; for I cannot do any thing till thou be come thither" (Gen. 19:22). As long as righteous Lot was in the city of Sodom, the fire, brimstone, and judgment could not fall. As long as the remnant is here, the world cannot be destroyed.

In Matthew 24:22 we read, "And except those days should be shortened, there should no flesh be saved: but for the elect's sake those days shall be shortened." It is the elect who bring reprieve, hope, and salvation to the world.

The mighty word from God in Revelation 7:3 is addressed to the four angels who hold the four winds of destruction, "Saying, Hurt not the earth, neither the sea, nor the trees, till we have sealed the servants of our God in their foreheads." It is they who bring hope and salvation to the world. God's way through the ages is that His work and will are carried out through a small minority, through the remnant.

For example, when the Midianites consumed the land of Israel like locusts, God raised up Gideon who called the men of Israel to war against the invading force of the Midianites but only 32,000 responded. When the Lord looked down upon the small army of 32,000 men, He said, "The people are yet too many" (Judg. 7:4). The Lord told Gideon to tell all the faint-hearted to go home, and

22,000 men turned their backs and left. God looked down on the remaining 10,000 and told Gideon to take them down to the edge of the water to drink.

> So he brought down the people unto the water: and the LORD said unto Gideon, Every one that lappeth of the water with his tongue, as a dog lappeth, him shalt thou set by himself; likewise every one that boweth down upon his knees to drink.
> And the number of them that lapped, putting their hand to their mouth, were three hundred men: but all the rest of the people bowed down upon their knees to drink water. (Judg. 7:5,6)

It was God's plan and will that Gideon have only 300 men out of the 10,000 to do His work.

There were twelve tribes in Israel of which ten were carried away and completely destroyed. Two tribes were left and were carried away into captivity. Finally, a small remnant returned with Zerubbabel, Joshua the high priest, Nehemiah the governor, and Ezra the scribe.

GOD CHOOSES A SMALL REMNANT TO DO HIS WORK

The same pattern of choosing a faithful few to do God's work is seen in the life of our Lord. Thousands of people gathered around Him in Capernaum having been fed by the loaves and fishes from His gracious and omnipotent hand. They listened to every word He spoke, but when the message was finished, the people departed, and the Lord said to the Twelve, "Will ye also go away?" (John 6:67). Acts 1:15 states that there were only about 120 disciples who assembled in the upper room after Jesus had ascended into heaven. Seemingly, God chooses to do His work by means of a small remnant, but the remnant is always there.

In the days of the Flood, Noah found grace in the eyes of the Lord. Abraham, the father of the faithful, the friend of God, lived in the days of universal idolatry. During the time of that awesome apostasy stood Elijah, the champion of Jehovah. When the Jews were carried into Babylonian captivity, a little band of them returned with Zerubbabel and Joshua.

And so through the ages and centuries there is always the faithful remnant. Martin Luther stood in the midst of ecclesiastical darkness and said, "Here I stand, so help me God; I can do no other." In the days of sadness and oppression, the faithful little pilgrim band brought their church and their faith to the shores of the new America.

ONLY A REMNANT SHALL BE SAVED

When we come to the end of the age, to the consummation of the program of God — there will be the faithful remnant.

"Except the LORD of hosts had left unto us a very small remnant, we should have been like unto Gomorrah." At the end of the age, how will it be? In Luke 18:8 God says, "Nevertheless when the Son of man cometh, shall he find faith on the earth?" In the days of the Flood, how many were there — only eight of Noah's family. In the days of universal idolatry there was only one. In the days of the apostasy there were 7,000. In the days of the carrying away into Babylonia there were 42,000 in the remnant. When the Lord had finished His ministry in the earth and had been crucified by those who rejected Him, there were only 120 left to believe. When the Lord comes, will He find faith in the earth? How many will be included in the Rapture when the Lord calls out of the earth His elect? So far as I can understand as I study the Word of God, there will be but a small remnant of the faithful when Jesus comes again.

Having spoken at one of our state conventions, I was called by a newspaper reporter who said: "I hear you are predicting that unless there is an intervention from God, the day is fast approaching when Christianity will be practically obliterated from the face of the earth. What do you mean?" I replied: "Do you have a pencil? Let us make a graph. Write down that 185 years ago, 25 percent of the world's population was evangelical Christian. Today it is less than 8 percent. By 1980 it will be less than 4 percent. By the year 2000 it will be less than 2 percent. On the graph, follow the decline. What will the percentage of evangelical Christians be in the twenty-first century after the year 2000? It will decrease to almost nothing."

What is the message of Isaiah? In the first chapter the prophecy states that because of the sins and iniquities of the people, the judgment of God would fall and the people would be as Sodom and Gomorrah, utterly obliterated were it not that God would intervene and leave a small remnant. Isaiah's message is a word of encouragement:

> Comfort ye, comfort ye my people, saith your God.
> Speak ye comfortably to Jerusalem, and cry unto her, that her warfare is accomplished, that her iniquity is pardoned: for she hath received of the LORD's hand double for all her sins. (40:1,2)

Isaiah was instructed to name his firstborn son Shear-jashub, "a remnant shall return." This is the doctrine of the Lord Jesus Christ for our encouragement. The seed falls by the wayside and the birds of the air pick it up. The seed falls among thorns and briars which choke it to death. But the doctrine of the remnant states that some of it will fall on good ground and there bear fruit unto God.

In Paul's teachings we find these words of comfort:

> Wot ye not what the scripture saith of Elias? how he maketh intercession to God against Israel, saying,
> Lord, they have killed thy prophets, and digged down thine altars; and I am left alone, and they seek my life.
> But what saith the answer of God unto him? I have reserved to myself seven thousand men, who have not bowed the knee to the image of Baal. (Rom. 11:2-4)

Someone once said to Charles Spurgeon: "So you believe that some will not believe, accept, and be saved no matter what you do, no matter how much you preach, no matter how much you work. What a despairing doctrine!" Spurgeon replied: "Nay, not so. I know they will not all believe, repent, turn, and be saved. But I know that some will listen, some will open their hearts, some will repent, and some will be saved."

This is the comfort God gives His children in the doctrine of the remnant. Darkness, unbelief, and rejection will be in the world, but some will always be saved. God's remnant will always be called out. This is the doctrine of the Holy Spirit. In 1 Peter 1 the Holy Spirit calls and we feel His moving voice in our heart. In Ephesians 1 the Holy Spirit seals our name, written in heaven before we were born, before we were conceived, and God knew us from afar. His grace touched us, spoke to us, and led us to turn from our sins and look in faith to the blessed Jesus.

The truth of this doctrine can be observed in any city, in any state, in any nation. The gospel will be presented to millions of people. Many of them will not listen, will not turn, or will not believe, but some will. The Holy Spirit in His elective grace will bring some.

The doctrine of the remnant can be applied to every area of our life. For example, a man works hard and everything that he makes belongs to him. And yet the man, out of love for God, will take what he has and give it to the Lord. An unbeliever will scoff at such a man and say: "What idiocy, what foolishness; why, everything that he has belongs to him. He can spend it on himself. Look at him. Instead he gives it to his God. How foolish can a man be?" You see, he does not know, he has not felt, he has not been called. A man works for something and he possesses it. It is all his. Then he falls in love and thereafter he will take everything and divide it with his sweetheart. It is like a couple who have almost everything. Then they will get on their knees and pray, "Oh, God, give to us a precious little baby and we will raise the child in the love and nurture of the Lord all the days of its life." Thereafter they will divide all they possess with the child.

There is a joy unspeakable in bringing to God all we have and everything we are.

4

The Great Invitation

> Come now, and let us reason together, saith the LORD: though your sins be as scarlet, they shall be as white as snow; though they be red like crimson, they shall be as wool. (Isa. 1:18)

When we open God's Scriptures we find that they are filled with marvelous invitations. In the Book of Exodus Moses stood in the midst of the camp and cried, saying: "Who is on the LORD'S side? let him come unto me" (32:26). In the Book of Isaiah we read:

> Ho, every one that thirsteth, come ye to the waters, and he that hath no money; come ye, buy, and eat; yea, come, buy wine and milk without money and without price. (55:1)

These words are found in Ezekiel:

> As I live, saith the Lord GOD, I have no pleasure in the death of the wicked; but that the wicked turn from his way and live: turn ye, turn ye from your evil ways; for why will ye die, O house of Israel? (Ezek. 33:11)

Matthew 11:28 presents a picture of the pleading Christ: "Come unto me, all ye that labour and are heavy laden, and I will give you rest."

I heard the voice of Jesus say,
"Come unto me and rest;
Lay down, thou weary one, lay down
Thy head upon My breast."

I came to Jesus as I was,
Weary and worn and sad;
I found in Him a resting place,
And He has made me glad.

In the Gospel of John we read:

Philip findeth Nathanael, and saith unto him, We have found
him, of whom Moses in the law, and the prophets, did write, Jesus
of Nazareth, the son of Joseph.
And Nathanael said unto him, Can there any good thing come
out of Nazareth? Philip saith unto him, Come and see. (1:45,46)

These words we read in 2 Corinthians:

Now then we are ambassadors for Christ, as though God did
beseech you by us: we pray you in Christ's stead, be ye reconciled to
God (5:20)

We read in the Book of Revelation:

And the Spirit and the bride say, Come. And let him that heareth
say, Come. And let him that is athirst come. And whosoever will,
let him take the water of life freely. (22:17)

A Most Amazing Invitation

The greatest of all invitations in its magnitude is the one in
Isaiah, "Come now, and let us reason together, saith the LORD:
though your sins be as scarlet, they shall be as white as snow;
though they be red like crimson, they shall be as wool." The
magnificent fact about this text is that God should condescend to
reason with a man whom He made. You see, religion and revelation are not illogical or magical. The religion of God, the faith of
Jesus Christ, the revelation of the Book, is of all things rational and
right. There is nothing more powerful than the moral foundation
upon which God has spoken to man in His word, "Come now, and
let us reason together, saith the LORD."

We read in ancient Roman history of a man named Felix who

married an adulteress by the name of Drusilla. In the providences of God, as revealed in Acts 24, Paul, God's preacher, was brought before that Felix. He had been appointed procurator of the province of Judaea by the Roman Caesar. Tacitus, the Roman historian, describes Felix as being greedy, vicious, vile, evil, and lustful. When he invited Paul to stand before him, Felix probably thought he would be entertained for an hour with a strange, far-out, oriental religion. But the Bible says that when Paul stood before Felix he reasoned of righteousness, temperance, and judgment to come. As Paul spoke of this reasonable, rational, morally founded word of God, the Bible says that Felix trembled.

Of all things that are right and rational, the religion of God is most so. God says that "Thou shalt not commit adultery" and says why. Adultery is a sin that breaks up marriage, orphans children, and dissolves the home. It is a sin beyond any other that destroys and dissolves the human soul and the personal life. The religion of God is reasonable.

God calls as witness to His reasonable faith the great moral foundations of the universe. In the passage we are discussing God says that it is stupid for a man to leave God out of his life: it is stupidity beyond that of an ox or an ass.

> Hear, O heavens, and give ear, O earth: for the LORD hath spoken, I have nourished and brought up children, and they have rebelled against me.
> The ox knoweth his owner, and the ass his master's crib: but Israel doth not know, my people doth not consider. (Isa. 1:2,3)

In Isaiah 5:13 we read:

> Therefore my people are gone into captivity, because they have no knowledge.

What Isaiah is saying is that the people do not think. When a man puts God out of his life, dismisses Him from His business, and forgets Him in his dreams and visions, God says that the man is more stupid than an ox and not as bright as an ass. You see, God confronts man whether he likes it or not, and He intrudes into a man's life whether he wants it or not. It is as impossible for a man's mind to keep out the idea of God as it is for the tides of the sea to keep from washing up onto the shore. As God upheaves the oceans, He upheaves a man's soul.

In Seattle there was a successful atheistic lawyer. He had built a palatial home overlooking beautiful Lake Washington and the Cascades beyond. One night he awakened from sleep and sensed that his little girl was standing by his bed looking quietly and intently into his face in the early dawn. She was so tiny standing there in her little white nightgown with her curly, black hair falling over her shoulders. The father pretended to remain asleep. After the little girl looked at her father intently for awhile, she quietly turned around and stood before the large picture window facing the Cascades and the dawn of the eastern sun. As the girl watched the sunrise over the beautiful mountains, she began to bow back and forth and to say sweetly in childlike innocence and humility: "Good morning, God. Good morning, God." The lawyer buried his face in his pillow and cried, "O God, that I could see You, that I could know You, that I could find You." Through the quiet, humble innocence and simplicity of his little girl, he found the Lord. God intrudes into a man's life. He cannot escape it.

The Closing Argument: God's Pardon

The entire first chapter of Isaiah is a court scene. The Lord brings an arraignment against His people, saying, "I have nourished and brought up children, and they have rebelled against me" (Isa. 1:2). Instead of worshiping God and giving glory to Him, they have given their souls to everything else in the world and have let God out. God calls them to trial, and verse 18 is the end of the case. Another way to translate it is, "Come now, and let us conclude the reasoning, says the Lord." And the Lord's reproach turns into pardon. His hurt and disappointment turn into love and forgiveness. "Though your sins be as scarlet, they shall be white as snow; though they be red like crimson, they shall be as wool."

You see, a man and his faith is not a man facing a Mosaic legislation. It is not a man facing a church, an organization, or a denomination. It is between a man and God alone. The Lord says, "I am their father. I have nourished and brought up children."

And the Lord's attitude toward us is in the loving, tender manner of someone who sired us and supports us. It is the same spirit we read about in the story of the prodigal son when the father waits, hopes, and prays.

Is it not amazing that God should plead and reason with a man? Our religious experience is a personal confrontation with God. It is like the apostle Paul. All the things he writes about in his thirteen epistles — reconciliation, atonement, all the things that go into making us right with God — all is an overflow from the scene on the road to Damascus when Jesus stopped him in the way, and Saul, falling at His feet, cried, "Lord, who art thou?" and Jesus replied, "I am Jesus whom thou persecutest." Before there is prayer, worship, theology, and any of the services of God, there first must be this confrontation, this getting right with the Almighty.

What is the situation between man and his God? It is that our sins separate us from Him. Later on in his prophecy Isaiah, quoting the Lord, states:

> Behold, the LORD's hand is not shortened, that it cannot save; neither his ear heavy, that it cannot hear:
> But your iniquities have separated between you and your God, and your sins have hid his face from you, that he will not hear. (59:1,2)

Thus, before a man can serve, worship, or pray to God, he must first get right with Him.

How does a man find himself accepted in the presence of the Lord? "Though your sins be as scarlet, they shall be white as snow; though they be like crimson, they shall be as wool." What can wash away my sins? Who can forgive a man's iniquity? Who can write his name in the Book of Life? No one forgives sin but God. All of the ceremonies in the world cannot wash away our sins. All of the ablutions, baptisms, masses, and rituals in the world cannot cleanse a man from the stain of sin in his soul. A man is saved, cleansed, and forgiven in the love and mercy of God.

How does God take a man when he is like scarlet and make him as snow? That is the gospel of the Good News. God does that in the sacrifice of the cross, in the blood and suffering of Jesus Christ. Our Lord gives us the right to stand in His presence, accepts us as beloved sons and daughters; pure, sanctified, whole, forgiven, washed, and clean. God saves us through Jesus Christ.

I once heard of a father and his son who were watching a parade in London of red-coated British soldiers. The father was looking through the window watching the parade of the soldiers pass by. The little boy, watching the same parade, exclaimed to his father, "Daddy, look at their beautiful white uniforms!" The father replied; "Son, they are not white. They are scarlet, red." "No," said the boy, "look, they are white, pure white." The father in astonishment looked closer and then saw what had happened. Around the window out of which they were viewing the parade was a band of red glass. The little boy, being unable to stand high enough to look through the clear pane, was watching the parade through the red glass. When one looks at red through red, it is pure white. God does this with our sins. The Lord looks at us through the blood, and when He looks at us in the love and mercy of Jesus Christ for us, He sees us clean and pure and forgiven. "These are they which came out of great tribulation, and have washed their robes, and made them white in the blood of the Lamb" (Rev. 7:14).

What can wash away my sin?
Nothing but the blood of Jesus;
What can make me whole again?
Nothing but the blood of Jesus.

Oh! precious is the flow
That makes me white as snow;
No other fount I know,
Nothing but the blood of Jesus.

The reasonable thing for any man to do is to give his soul to God, and to dedicate his life to Him. He should open his heart, his home, his business, and the future to the Lord.

5

In the Last Days

> The word that Isaiah the son of Amoz saw concerning Judah and Jerusalem.
>
> And it shall come to pass in the last days, that the mountain of the LORD's house shall be established in the top of the mountains, and shall be exalted above the hills; and all nations shall flow unto it.
>
> And many people shall go and say, Come ye, and let us go up to the mountain of the LORD, to the house of the God of Jacob; and he will teach us of his ways, and we will walk in his paths: for out of Zion shall go forth the law, and the word of the LORD from Jerusalem.
>
> And he shall judge among the nations, and shall rebuke many people: and they shall beat their swords into plowshares, and their spears into pruninghooks: nation shall not lift up sword against nation, neither shall they learn war any more.
>
> O house of Jacob, come ye, and let us walk in the light of the LORD. (Isa. 2:1-5)

Earlier we saw that the first chapter of Isaiah was the background against which Isaiah delivered his prophetic message. Without an understanding of that background we cannot enter into the depths of the meaning of the word of God that was delivered through him. Isaiah began:

45

> The vision of Isaiah the son of Amoz, which he saw concerning
> Judah and Jerusalem in the days of Uzziah, Jotham, Ahaz, and
> Hezekiah, kings of Judah. (1:1)

Isaiah grew up under Uzziah, a good king and an able administrator, a man of wonderful consecration and genius. During his reign the borders of the land were extended. Uzziah won back the port of Elath on the Red Sea, built a navy, and established a substantial merchandising trade with the Far East. His policies were blessed of God as he walked in humility before Jehovah.

Uzziah was followed by a worthy son named Jotham who inherited the abilities and followed the national policies of his father. The kingdom was greatly blessed under Jotham's reign as it was under that of his father. The people lived in prosperity and peace. The hand of the Lord was with them.

It was during those days that Isaiah lived as a young man and was called to be a messenger of the Lord.

In one of those strange and inexplicable providences of life, Jotham was followed by a son who, of all men, was unable, unworthy, unfit, and ungodly. Ahaz, as a very young man, came to the throne from a harem. He was a spoiled and petulant child. He governed with the ignorance and superstition of an untaught woman. The country suffered and decayed as a result. Isaiah describes the fallen people:

> As for my people, children are their oppressors, and women rule
> over them. O my people, they which lead thee cause thee to err, and
> destroy the way of thy paths. (Isa. 3:12)

The glorious, magnificent kingdom of Judah that Isaiah knew under Uzziah and Jotham fell in disintegration into a leper's grave. Isaiah described it:

> For Jerusalem is ruined, and Judah is fallen: because their tongue
> and their doings are against the Lord, to provoke the eyes of his
> glory. (Isa. 3:8)

Isaiah Possessed Illimitable Love for His Country

Such tragedy to overwhelm the holy city and the sacred nation brought untold sadness and sorrow to the heart of the young patriot. Isaiah loved the city of Jerusalem and his country. What Athens was to Demosthenes, what Rome was to Caesar, what Florence was to Dante, Jerusalem was to Isaiah. To see the city and nation fall into disaster and destruction brought unspeakable grief to his heart.

And Isaiah says this was done to provoke the eyes of [the Lord's] glory." What a strange phrase, "to provoke the eyes of [the Lord's] glory. You see, the Book of Isaiah begins, "The vision of Isaiah the son of Amoz, which he saw concerning Judah and Jerusalem." To us the word "saw" is simply the past tense of the verb "see," but the meaning of the word "saw" as Isaiah used it in Hebrew means "to split, to cleave, and to see through and beyond." And this is the vision that came to the prophet as he beheld before him the weak, vascillating, and wicked king Ahaz.

Isaiah Stands Before King Ahaz

As Isaiah stood before Ahaz he remembered that Ahaz in a time of exigency had turned to Tiglath-pileser, the cruel and merciless king of Assyria. No less than five times were the bitter and ruthless soldiers, mercenaries of the winged bull of Ashur, let loose on the kingdom of Judah. Isaiah lived in dread of that awesome, monstrous, and ravaging power. Now Isaiah stands before Ahaz, who has secretly made a covenant inviting Tiglath-pileser to come down into Judah, and he pleads with the king. He asks him to trust in the Lord, to look to God in returning and in rest, and to allow Him in quietness and confidence to be his strength. But Ahaz refused. Isaiah states:

> Moreover the LORD spake again unto Ahaz, saying,
> Ask thee a sign of the LORD thy God; ask it either in the depth, or in the height above.
> But Ahaz said I will not ask, neither will I tempt the LORD. (7:10-12)

It was when the hypocritically pious Ahaz spoke these words that Isaiah saw above and beyond the weak and vascillating king; he saw a vision of the coming of the Lord:

> Therefore the LORD himself shall give you a sign; Behold, a virgin shall conceive, and bear a son, and shall call his name Immanuel. (7:14)

Isaiah, looking over fallen Jerusalem and ravaged Judah, saw the vision of the Lord in the last days:

> And it shall come to pass in the last days, that the mountain of the LORD'S house shall be established in the top of the mountains, and shall be exalted above the hills; and all nations shall flow unto it.
>
> And many people shall go and say, Come ye, and let us go up to the mountain of the LORD, to the house of the God of Jacob; and he will teach us of his ways, and we will walk in his paths: for out of Zion shall go forth the law, and the word of the LORD from Jerusalem.
>
> And he shall judge among the nations, and rebuke many people: and they shall beat their swords into plowshares, and their spears into pruninghooks: nation shall not lift up sword against nation, neither shall they learn war any more. (2:2-4)

Isaiah was looking over and beyond the disintegrated and destroyed nation to the coming kingdom of the majesty, righteousness, and glory of the Lord.

In a like manner I fear for our beloved America. There is a judgment of God that is beginning to visit America that spells the downfall of our beloved country.

CURRENCY, CRIME, AND COMMUNISM —
AMERICA'S MOST THREATENING FOES

There are three major factors that contribute to the foreboding that I feel for America's future. First is the currency, the economic life of our people. Today money is backed by nothing. Our great economic strength has been drained and sapped until our currency is supported by nothing.

The President of the United States announces to Congress that the budget of the United States government will be $52 billion in debt. The economists predict that it will be closer to $100 billion in one year. We have a tendency to speak as though a billion dollars was almost nothing. What does such a debt mean? It means that the economic life of our nation is floundering.

There is no institution under God's heaven that can live with fiscal irresponsibility. One may say that he loves his wife and loves his home, but if he does not solve the monetary problems of the home, it does not matter how much he loves her, for their home is headed for destruction. If a bank does not have a sound fiscal policy, it is headed for bankruptcy.

The same truths apply to the government of the United States of America. We have a philosophy in America that says a person has the right to a dole, a hand-out. There are instances in which as many as three generations are living on welfare. If one asks them to take a job they refuse because it is easier to live on welfare from the government than it is to work.

Every time a piece of money is printed it ought to represent labor. When money is printed without labor and without a representation of the wealth increase of the nation, we have inflation, that is, the ultimate destruction of the people, the government, and the economic system. The day may come in America when a loaf of bread will cost a wheelbarrow full of bills.

The second threat to America's future is crime. Any nation can have just as much crime as it chooses to have. There can be no crime at all or the country can be drowned in crime — it is up to the nation. How much crime do we want?

In New York City I can remember when Times Square was a gathering place for thousands of Americans. When one would think of America he would think of Times Square. People were out until the early hours of the morning walking unafraid in liberty and freedom.

Go there now. It is deserted, filthy, and ragged. What has happened? Times Square today is a rendezvous for murderers, muggers, robbers, and violent men — the pusher, the dopester, the pimp, and the prostitute. People do not go there because they are afraid.

One of my friends recently moved to New York City and on the way to school his son was mugged and beaten. The father went to the police and was told: "You do not understand life in New York City. You must always keep your son supplied with mug money.

He must always have $2 or $3 in his pockets for the muggers so that when he is attacked he will have something to give them and they will not beat him up. If he does not have mug money, they will beat him up."

The police do not say: "By the grace of God, this is enough. We cannot have our teenagers mugged as they go to school. This must stop." No, the word of the police is, "Keep your son supplied with mug money so that when he is attacked he has money to give the robber." This is America.

I once listened to a discussion between a group of people and a police chief in one of the large cities of America. The people asked him: "Why do you not do something about these x-rated movies in our neighborhoods? Why do you not close them?" He said: "We have tried again and again. We raid the movie theaters, confiscate the film, and close them up. The theater owners take it to the courts and we have never yet won a case. We lose every one of them. The lower courts present the case to the Supreme Court where the movies are shown and the Supreme Court says, 'We cannot define pornography.' The courts refuse to help rid the filth, dirt, and lust that are sweeping America like a fire."

When I think of the Supreme Court of the United States, the Chief Justice, and his eight fellow justices, I think of the words of the apostle Paul:

> And for this cause God shall send them strong delusion, that they should believe a lie. (2 Thess. 2:11)

This is happening in America today.

The third foe that threatens America's future is communism. Recently I heard a United States senator say: "We have caused the blood bath in Indo-China, in southeast Asia." I heard another United States senator announce, "What we should do is invite back to Cambodia the Communist prince who was expelled when he was delivering his country to the Communists." What will that senator say when the same thing happens to the Philippines, to the islands of the Pacific, or to the islands of the Caribbean? Could it even happen in Cuba only ninety miles from our shores? I can remember as though it were yesterday when Castro was wined and

dined all over America. This is modern America. If there is any
will in us to resist the encroachment of communism, I have not
been able to find it.

I wonder what would happen if the Communists took over
Mexico and we would have a border with them for more than a
thousand miles. The Soviet Union has enough nuclear-powered
submarines right now to cut the lifeline of the United States for oil,
minerals, or anything else vital to our existence. It almost seems as
though our future is being decided not by our government but by
the men in the Kremlin.

Then, what does one do? Over, above, and beyond the destruction of our economic life, the increasing floodtides of violence,
blood, and crime, is the victory of the coming of the Lord. He will
never fail. These are but signs of His soon return.

> My hope is built on nothing less
> Than Jesus' blood and righteousness;
> I dare not trust the sweetest frame,
> But wholly lean on Jesus' name.
>
> On Christ the solid Rock, I stand —
> All other ground is sinking sand.

If you want a foundation upon which to build your home, your
life, and our nation, build it on Christ. Over and beyond the
despair and weakness of a national government and a judicial
system that can find no answer to the awesome needs of our
people, Isaiah saw the glory of the Lord and the coming kingdom
of Christ our Savior.

6

The Prophetic Call

In the year that king Uzziah died I saw also the Lord sitting upon a throne, high and lifted up, and his train filled the temple.

Above it stood the seraphims: each one had six wings; with twain he covered his face, and with twain he covered his feet, and with twain he did fly.

And one cried unto another, and said, Holy, holy, holy, is the LORD of hosts: the whole earth is full of his glory.

And the posts of the door moved at the voice of him that cried, and the house was filled with smoke.

Then said I, Woe is me! for I am undone; because I am a man of unclean lips, and I dwell in the midst of a people of unclean lips: for mine eyes have seen the King, the LORD of hosts.

Then flew one of the seraphims unto me, having a live coal in his hand, which he had taken with the tongs from off the altar:

And he laid it upon my mouth, and said, Lo, this hath touched thy lips; and thine iniquity is taken away, and thy sin purged.

Also I heard the voice of the Lord, saying, Whom shall I send, and who will go for us? Then said I, Here am I; send me.

And he said, Go, and tell this people, Hear ye indeed, but understand not; and see ye indeed, but perceive not.

Make the heart of this people fat, and make their ears heavy, and shut their eyes; lest they see with their eyes, and hear with their ears, and understand with their heart, and convert, and be healed.

Then said I, Lord, how long? And he answered, Until the cities be wasted without inhabitant, and the houses without man, and the land be utterly desolate,

And the LORD have removed men far away, and there be a great forsaking in the midst of the land.

But yet in it shall be a tenth, and it shall return, and shall be eaten: as a teil tree, and as an oak, whose substance is in them, when they cast their leaves: so the holy seed shall be the substance thereof. (Isa. 6:1-13)

GOD'S UNUSUAL SERAPHIM

In this text we see the first and only time that seraphim are mentioned in the Bible. The singular form of the Hebrew word *seraph* is made plural by adding *im*, *seraphim*. The same ending is used to make the singular word *cherub* plural, *cherubim*.

Seraphim are unusual, possibly one of the highest orders of angels. Seraphim, like archangels, although mighty and exalted, yet serve God in deep humility. Each seraph covered his face with two of his wings in deep humility before God, and with two of his wings he was swift to carry out the mission of the Lord. They voiced their worship of God to each other in a threefold cry, "Holy, holy, holy." I would think that refers to the three in the Godhead.

Holy, holy, holy,
  Lord God Almighty!
Early in the morning
  Our song shall rise to Thee;
Holy, holy, holy!
  Merciful and Mighty!
God in Three Persons,
  Blessed Trinity!

So these seraphim offer their praise as they minister before God and as they bow before the Lord. The sight of that vision must have been incomparably glorious.

THE LORD HIGH AND LIFTED UP

Do you know where Isaiah saw the glory of the Lord high and lifted up? In a sanctuary, the holy temple of Jerusalem. That is the place where proud Pompey entered as a heathen in desecration in

63 B.C. Pompey with his Roman legions swept up from the east and took Judah and made it a part of the Roman Empire, a province under the Roman Caesar. He captured Jerusalem and with it the holy temple of God. Pompey entered the court of the Gentiles, continued through the court of Israel, proceeded through the court of the women, entered the court of the priests, and stood before the door of the sanctuary itself. When it became apparent that he was to enter the holy place where only the priests went to minister before the Lord, the Jewish people fell on their faces by the thousands before the Roman general and begged him not to desecrate the holy temple of God. In despicable contempt the general walked into the holy place where the seven-branched lampstand, the table of shewbread, and the golden altar of incense were, where Uzziah was struck with leprosy when he dared to perform the office which was granted to the priest alone. Not only did Pompey enter the holy place, but he seized the veil that separated the holy place and the holy of holies and with contempt he pulled it aside and stalked into the innermost sanctuary of God. He looked around, came back out, and remarked: "It is empty. There is nothing there but darkness." Pompey did that in the place where Isaiah saw the Lord high and lifted up.

It takes the eyes of the soul to see God, ears of the heart to hear God. To those who are blind, He does not exist. To those who are deaf, He does not speak. To those who have eyes to see, ears to hear, and a heart to feel, God is present in glory before us forever.

Feeling Sinful Before God

In Isaiah's vision he felt himself sinful and unworthy:

> Then said I, Woe is me! for I am undone; because I am a man of unclean lips, and I dwell in the midst of a people of unclean lips: for mine eyes have seen the King, the Lord of hosts. (Isa. 6:5)

Any man who stands in the presence of God will find himself overcome with a flood of unworthiness and uncleanliness sweeping over him.

Our first parents felt this unworthiness when they hid themselves from the presence of the Lord because they were naked and ashamed as He walked and talked with them in the garden. Moses felt it when at the burning bush he hid his face from the presence of the Lord. Manoah felt it when the angel came to announce the birth of their son Samson and went up to heaven in a fire of glory. Manoah cried, "We shall surely die, because we have seen God" (Judg. 13:22). Job felt it when he said, "I have heard of thee by the hearing of the ear: but now mine eye seeth thee. Wherefore I abhor myself, and repent in dust and ashes" (Job 42:5,6). Peter felt it when he cried before the Lord, "Depart from me; for I am a sinful man" (Luke 5:8). Paul felt it when, blinded by the glory of the light, he was led by the hand into Damascus. John felt it when, seeing the glorified Jesus, he fell at the Lord's feet as one dead. Any time a man feels he is worthy, good, or righteous, he has not seen the Lord. He has never been in the presence of God, for the closer a man comes to God, the more sinful and unworthy he feels.

> Woe is me! for I am undone; . . . for mine eyes have seen the King, the LORD of hosts.
> Then flew one of the seraphims unto me, having a live coal in his hand. . .
> And laid it upon my mouth, and said, Lo, this hath touched thy lips; and thine iniquity is taken away, and thy sin purged. (Isa. 6:5-7)

The coal was taken from the altar of sacrifice at the cross where atonement is made and where blood is shed. And in the shedding of blood there is remission of sin. In the cross of Christ we have forgiveness, atonement, and salvation. From the cross, the altar, Isaiah finds that his heart is purified and his lips are cleansed.

THE HEAVY MESSAGE

Then Isaiah hears the voice of the Lord and volunteers to be God's servant and messenger. What message shall he bring? Is it to be one of triumph and victory? No, it is the opposite, "And he said, Go, and tell this people, Hear ye indeed, but understand not; and see ye indeed, but perceive not" (Isa. 6:9). Their eyes are blinded and their ears are deaf lest they hear; and their heart is hardened lest they be converted and be saved. Isaiah said, "Lord, how long?"

And the Lord answered, "Until the cities be wasted without inhabitant, and the houses without man, and the land be utterly
desolate, And the Lord have removed men far away, and there be a
great forsaking in the midst of the land" (Isa. 6:11,12). What an
unusual but sad assignment!

I think that is one of the reasons why Isaiah's vision is given in
the sixth chapter and not in the first chapter of his prophecy. Why
doesn't Isaiah begin with his call as Jeremiah does or as Ezekiel
does? Because the first five chapters are so tragically sad, and the
sixth chapter is placed here so that Isaiah might explain why his
message was so tragic. His commission was to bear a message of
judgment and sorrow to the people. The Word of God tells us that
there is never a time when this world is swept into the kingdom,
never any hour, when those who preach the gospel of Christ will
be able to convert the world. The world increasingly becomes
violent and wicked, filled with war, conflict, and bloodshed.

In reading the Book of Revelation I believe we have seen the age
pass from the Philadelphian church of the open door to the last
age, the Laodicean age of apostasy. When I was a youth every
country on the face of the earth was open to the missionary. We
could send all the missionaries to China, India, or any other
nation that we pleased. Since that time I have seen nation after
nation close the door to the missionary. Thousands of people
are not allowed to hear the preaching of the gospel of the grace of
God.

Not only that, but we are seeing more and more of the world
plunge into atheistic, Communistic darkness. It is a cause of
infinite fear and trembling to me. Once a nation falls into the
hands of the Communists it is almost certain that it will never be
able to extricate itself from it. Communism is like a curse, a death,
a judgment, and it grows each day.

There is another reason why I think the sixth chapter of Isaiah is
where it is and not at the beginning of the book. I believe it is an
introduction to the great book of Immanuel, chapters 7 through
11. In the hour of darkness, tragedy, and loss brought about by the
death of Uzziah, every hope for the future was dashed to the

ground. Uzziah was a mighty monarch, a great administrator, and under him the kingdom came to the glory it knew under David and Solomon. It was in the catastrophe of the death of Uzziah and in the awesomeness of the message God gave him to deliver, that Isaiah lifted up his eyes and saw the Lord of hosts, the king of glory, high and lifted up, with his train of shekinah light filling the earth.

THE DOCTRINE OF THE REMNANT

As the vision closes it presents the doctrine of the remnant. In it there shall be those who love and serve God, and out of the stump of the olive tree which was cut down God will raise up a people and a kingdom that shall glorify our Lord forever. In speaking of death Job said in hope:

> And though after my skin worms destroy this body, yet in my flesh shall I see God:
> Whom I shall see for myself, and mine eyes shall behold, and not another. . . . (Job 19:26,27)

The grave may swallow us up, the hunger of hell may reach out for us, the whole earth may be plunged into impenetrable darkness, the nations of the earth may decay, and government may fall, but above it all, reigning in sovereign grace and glory is the King of our souls, the Hope of our hearts, and the Savior of the world.

Isaiah 7 is the beginning of the great book of Immanuel, ". . . a virgin shall conceive, and bear a son, and shall call his name Immanuel" (v. 14). In Isaiah 9:6 we find, ". . . and his name shall be called Wonderful, Counsellor, The mighty God, The everlasting Father, The Prince of Peace." Looking ahead to the eleventh chapter we read: "The wolf also shall dwell with the lamb, and the leopard shall lie down with the kid; and the calf and the young lion and the fatling together; and a little child shall lead them. They shall not hurt nor destroy in all my holy mountain . . ." (vv. 6,9a). Everyone will know the Lord, and His knowledge and love will fill the earth as waters cover the sea. The Lord says that when these things come to pass, "Lift up your heads; for your redemption draweth nigh" (Luke 21:28b).

From what I can read in the Holy Book I think the world is drawing toward the great consummation, toward the battle of Armageddon. Today's submarines with their nuclear warheads and the faster-than-sound bombers built to deliver multi-headed atomic missiles of death and destruction are ominous indications that we are moving toward the great consummation of the Lord. But we are not to be discouraged. We are not to tremble in foreboding or in fear, for this is the beginning of God's visitation, God's redemption, God's coming, God's peace, God's glory, God's kingdom, and in it you and I and all who love the Lord shall have a beautiful, triumphant, and worthy part.

What hope, what blessing, what encouragement! This message of God from the throne of grace is delivered through His prophets and His holy apostles for our comfort and encouragement in any day and any hour. The Lord still lives and the earth belongs to Him.

7

The Volunteer

Also I heard the voice of the Lord, saying, Whom shall I send,
and who will go for us? Then said I, Here am I; send me. (Isa. 6:8)

There is no finer expression, beauty of language, sublimity of
thought, or glorious revelation than this one found in the sixth
chapter of Isaiah. In it is delineated the call of the prophet. This is
the most detailed of any instance we have where a man has been
called of God to the prophetic ministry. The young Isaiah relates
how it happened in the first eleven verses of his sixth chapter.

Isaiah's vision of God seems to be a departing and fading reality
in our generation. To so many God belongs to the days of the
Roman and Greek mythologists. He is not real anymore. To
many, He is either dead, or He does not exist. To others He is
uncaring, unresponsive, and unknowing. But not to Isaiah. He
was real to him and his eyes looked upon the Lord in His glory. In
the presence of the great God he felt so unworthy. The nearer a
man draws to God the more sinful he feels. The farther a man is
from God the more he looks upon himself as being good and
acceptable. To illustrate this we can look at a woman's wash
hanging on the line in the backyard. It looks white and clean, but

when the snow falls the wash looks gray and dirty against the pure whiteness of the snow. So it is with a man's life. He may be proud of how upstanding he is, but against the purity of the holiness of God he looks dirty and sinful.

Isaiah heard the voice of God calling for a volunteer and he replied, answering with his life, "Here am I; send me." Here is a man who feels himself so unclean and so unworthy in the presence of the great God, and the Lord cleanses him by an atoning grace, by the sacrifice of Christ. The man feeling himself so unworthy and sinful is not told by God, "Take a bath, put on fine clothes, and you will be just right." Nor does God say to him: "Get a better education and you will be prepared. Employ a program of self-improvement and you will be properly endowed for the great work of the Lord." Don't you wish it could be that way? But God says it doesn't work that way. Fig leaves do not cover a man's nakedness. It takes blood. And in the shedding of blood there is atonement and remission of sins. Having had the experience of needing God and having been regenerated by the Spirit of the Lord, Isaiah heard the voice of God saying, "Whom shall I send, and who will go for us?" And he answered, "Here am I; send me."

Those Who Are Saved Will Hear the Call of God

Every regenerated child of God has heard the call of God. If a man has met the Lord, and if the Holy Spirit has touched his heart and his lips, he will hear God's call. If a man has a vision of God he will hear a call of God in his heart. That call can come in many ways. It can come through a vision of angels as when Jacob saw the ladder and the angels ascending and descending. Or it could be in a burning bush experience as when Moses heard the voice speaking to him out of the unconsumed bush. Or it could come as a call in the night, "Samuel, Samuel." It could be a still, small voice as with Elijah, or the anointing of a prophet like David. It could be an invitation to be a fisher of men, like the call to Peter. It could be a burning in the heart like the experience of Cleopas. It could be a meeting of Jesus on the Damascus road like Saul of Tarsus had. Or it could be a vision of the glorified, risen, ascended, Jesus as that seen by the sainted apostle John on the Isle of Patmos. But any time, anywhere you see a vision of God you also will hear the voice of the Lord calling you.

A Man Will Volunteer

Everyone who has had an experience with God feels that call in his or her heart and will volunteer. The Bible says that the call is the need and the need is the call. Let me illustrate that from the Bible.

One day when David was a boy tending his father's sheep, his father called him from the sheepfold and said, "Son, take this food and bring it to your brothers who are soldiers in the army of Jehovah." The boy went down to the army of Israel and saw across the vale of Elah the armies of the blaspheming, uncircumcised Philistines. Every day a giant from the Philistine army, named Goliath, walked down the hill, looked into the faces of the armies of God, and said: "I dare you to come out, you cowards. You do not have a God who is able and mighty to deliver. He is a coward, too, and you are just like Him." He blasphemed the name of Jehovah God and he belittled the people of the Lord. They cowered in the dust before the giant.

The boy David had never before heard a man curse God. He had grown up tending his sheep and playing his harp, singing songs of praise to God. He was astonished to see God's people cower in the dust of the ground. He looked around and said, "Isn't there anyone who will challenge this infidel?" Not one answered him. So little David said, "I will go." Astonished, the people exclaimed: "You are an unshaven, ruddy-faced teenager. How can you meet a giant like that with his armor and a spear as big as a weaver's beam?" David replied: "One time when I was tending my father's sheep, God helped me deliver my flock out of the jaws of a bear. Another time a lion attacked and God helped me deliver the flock from the lion. The Lord God who delivered me from the bear and the lion is the same Lord God who will deliver me from this giant, Goliath." The call is the need, the need is the call, and the young man volunteered.

Consider Nehemiah when his brother came back from Judaea and described the destruction in Jerusalem with her walls leveled and her gates burned with fire. The Prime Minister of the Persian Empire wept openly and offered himself before the king to be used of God to rebuild the gates and walls of the Holy City. The call is the need and the need is the call.

This is seen also in the life of the apostle Paul coming down to Troas:

> And a vision appeared to Paul in the night; There stood a man of Macedonia, and prayed him, saying, Come over into Macedonia, and help us.
> And after he had seen the vision, immediately we endeavoured to go into Macedonia, assuredly gathering that the Lord had called us for to preach the gospel unto them. (Acts 16:9,10)

He just saw a man of Macedonia saying, "Help us." So Paul turned his face westward instead of eastward and our forefathers became Christians. This is the Spirit of God working in His people.

It is amazing how the spirit of people made in the image of God can rise in a need or an emergency. Not long after World War II, I was in Europe standing in a long line before an immigration desk crossing over from Folkestone, England, to Boulogne, France. While the line slowly moved I noticed the British woman in front of me with the name Emma Jenson on her passport. She had a little girl with her, and since the line was moving slowly, I began to visit with that British woman. Her little girl had lived most of her life in an air-raid shelter. The mother said: "My husband, my daughter, and I were managing quite well during the war. But just a few days before the awful conflict closed a rocket bomb burst over our home. My husband was killed and everything we had was destroyed." She pulled back the heavy hair of her child where across the forehead and back over her head was a dark, deep scar. She said, "I nursed our little girl to life and health." When I told her how sorry I was she said: "No, do not sympathize with me. There are thousands who have been hurt and injured worse than I. I am doing well. In the goodness of God only one thing was spared in our home, a typewriter. I got a job at Cambridge University typing for a professor of law. After I put my daughter to bed at night I type through the early hours of the morning and make a living

supporting myself and our little child." That is the human spirit —
in the face of a need or a call to rise and shine.

THE VOLUNTEER WILL HAVE A HEAVY, DIFFICULT ASSIGNMENT

So it is in the household of faith. Lord, now that I have given my
life to You, now that I have volunteered, what would You have me
to do? And the Lord assigns a difficult and heavy assignment. It is
never easy. Any time the Lord calls, and a child of God hears the
voice of God and volunteers, the assignment will always be hard
and difficult. And you would think it would be one of success. You
deliver the message, the world will hear, they will turn, and they
will be saved. They will all be in the kingdom. But it is often the
opposite. The darkness grows darker and the earth becomes more
pagan and lost. In an agony we cry, "O God, how long?" And the
Lord replies, "Until there is not an inhabitant in the land."

I remember a time when I was to preach to the National
Association of Evangelicals. Before I brought the message, they
presented the tragedy of our missions in Vietnam. First they
showed a picture of a monument in Vietnam dedicated to our slain
missionaries. In the picture on each side of the monument stood a
Vietnamese pastor. The man showing the picture said: "Both of
those pastors have just been martyred. They have laid down their
lives for Christ before the oncoming Vietcong and hordes of the
north." Then a doctor told his story. He described how the Communist legions came down from the north, first through the
highlands and then through the coastal cities and the awful destruction and death that followed in the wake of the invading
soldiers. Then they revealed to us lists of the names and families of
the missionaries who are either now martyred, have been taken
captive, or have disappeared from view. After the presentation we
stood up and in silent prayer asked God's blessing and presence in
that tragic and unhappy land. Would you not think that in the face
of such death, destruction, and tragedy Christians would quit?
How long? Until there is not an inhabitant left in the land.

The idea to quit did not enter Isaiah's mind. He was doing God's
work, delivering God's message. There is no failure in the Al-

mighty. It is unusual how the Christian faith is put together. It used to be said that the blood of the martyrs is the seed of the church. It is the sacrifice, the tears, the devotion, the pouring out of the crimson of life that gives it power.

I once heard of a man, representing an affluent denomination, who visited a university campus making an appeal for young men and women from the university to go to Africa as missionaries. Being from an affluent and historical denomination he said: "Come, young people, come. There will be a fine salary for you. There will be an adequate pension for you. There will be an American compound in which you can live, one stocked with American food. You will be provided with an automobile. There will be everything you will need. Come to Africa and represent our Lord." Only three people responded to his appeal. Later, another missionary from a poorer communion came to the same university campus. The mission representative stood up and said: "Young men and young women, come. It is a dark assignment. We live in disease and in death, but come." And when he made the invitation to sacrifice their lives to disease, to suffering, and to death, the altar was crowded with young men and young women offering their lives to God. This is an unusual characteristic about the Christian faith. Make it easy, soft, and affluent and it dissolves before our eyes. But if the Christian service has sacrifice in it, life unto death and death unto life, then it lives, it is vibrant, and it has power. People are saved by the offering of the love of Jesus by God's spokesmen who are filled with His Holy Spirit and who give their all to His service.

Here am I, Lord; send me. Use me, Lord, to pour my life out for Thee, to serve Thee, to magnify Thee. We will not be discouraged; we will not lose heart.

8

The Sign of the Virgin Birth

> Therefore the Lord himself shall give you a sign; Behold, a virgin
> shall conceive, and bear a son, and shall call his name Immanuel.
> (Isa. 7:14)

Embedded in the prophecy of Isaiah is what is called the Book of
Immanuel, that is, chapters 7, 8, and 9. Chapter 7 begins:

> And it came to pass in the days of Ahaz the son of Jotham, the son
> of Uzziah, king of Judah, that Rezin the king of Syria, and Pekah
> the son of Remaliah, king of Israel, went up toward Jerusalem to war
> against it, but could not prevail against it. (v. 1)

That is the background of the Book of Immanuel. Ahaz was the
son of a noble and gifted father who himself was the son of a great
and mighty king. There was no greater administrator than Uzziah
the king of Judah and his son Jotham. But how such a sorry son
could be born to so noble a father and grandfather, I do not know.
The worst king to sit on a throne was wicked Ahaz.

AHAZ ASCENDS TO THE THRONE OF DAVID

The deeds of Ahaz as king were idolatrous: he filled the city with
graven images, he revived the worship of Moloch in the Valley of

Hinnom, and there he burned his own son in the fire. At one of the most critical junctures in the history of Judah wicked Ahaz sat on the throne of the kingdom.

Rezin the king of Syria and Pekah the king of Samaria resolved in confederation to remove Ahaz and to set up a puppet on the throne of Judah amenable to their will. In the face of that terrible threat to the house of David and to the people of Judah, King Ahaz, instead of turning to Jehovah God for help, strength, and wisdom to know what to do, privately and secretly delivered his kingdom and his people to Tiglath-pileser, the cruel and merciless king of the Assyrian empire. It is upon this occasion that God sent Isaiah to confront Ahaz and to plead that he not find refuge in the Assyrians but that he find strength and hope and help in Almighty God. Beginning at verse 3 in chapter 7 we have the first confrontation of Isaiah before Ahaz:

> Then said the LORD unto Isaiah, Go forth now to meet Ahaz, thou, and Shear-jashub thy son, at the end of the conduit of the upper pool in the highway of the fuller's field;
> And say unto him, Take heed, and be quiet; fear not, neither be fainthearted for the two tails of these smoking firebrands, for the fierce anger of Rezin with Syria and of the son of Remaliah. (vv. 3,4)

But Ahaz had already made up his mind that he was going to offer his kingdom and his people into the hands of Tiglath-pileser. What an awesome thing for a man of God to do!

Nineveh was the site of the magnificent oriental palace of Tiglath-pileser. There he reigned, as he described himself, as "the king of kings." His hosts were numbered by the myriads. His horses and chariots covered the earth like locusts. When they overran a nation it was like the overflowing tides of an ocean. The winged bull of Ashur was a veritable scourge and ogre of the whole world, and now he was to be so to Judah and the people of God.

THE APPEAL OF ISAIAH THE PROPHET

When Isaiah stood before Ahaz and made the appeal found in Isaiah 7:3,4, we learn from 2 Kings and 2 Chronicles that Ahaz had already given himself and his people to Tiglath-pileser. He had sent an ambassador to the Assyrian king saying, "I am your slave." Can you imagine a man doing that? Having closed the temple of the Lord and having substituted graven worship in its place, Ahaz plundered the temple of its silver and gold and sent it to Tiglath-pileser in tribute.

The second time God sent Isaiah to stand before Ahaz we read he came with a glorious offer from heaven saying that God would deliver the city. Standing before Ahaz the king, Isaiah said:

> Ask thee sign of the Lord thy God; ask it either in the depth, or in the height above.
> But Ahaz said, I will not ask, neither will I tempt the Lord (Isa. 7:11,12)

It was then in the face of that pious, hypocritical reply that the great prophet replies:

> Therefore the Lord himself shall give you a sign; Behold, a virgin shall conceive, and bear a son, and shall call his name Immanuel.
> Butter and honey shall he eat, that he may know to refuse the evil, and choose the good.
> For before the child shall know to refuse the evil, and choose the good, the land that thou abhorrest shall be forsaken of both her kings. (Isa. 7:14-16)

There are two ideas in the word of the Lord to Ahaz, one which I plainly understand, the other which I had to study to understand.

The second part of the sign I can easily understand. "Ahaz, a child is going to be born. Before the child is old enough to eat butter and honey or to know good from evil the two kings that terrify you [referred to by the Lord in Isa. 7:4 as 'the two tails of . . . smoking firebrands'] will be dead." Did that come to pass? Within three years Rezin the king of Syria had been slain by Tiglath-pileser. Within the same period of time Pekah the king of Aamaria had been slain by Hoshea, his successor, and the last king of the northern kingdom. I can understand that part of the sign easily. The first part is a little different.

> Behold, a virgin shall conceive, and bear a son, and shall call his name Immanuel.

How is it that a sign that came to pass seven hundred fifty years later could be a sign to Ahaz? The answer became apparent to me as I studied. The prophet Isaiah was telling Ahaz that he, the king, was afraid that Rezin of Syria and Pekah of Samaria were coming down to destroy the people of God and to destroy the house of David. But God, according to Isaiah, had a different view. Let us listen to the word of the Lord. What Isaiah is saying is suggested in his change of pronouns. When he says, "Ask thee a sign of the LORD," it is singular and is addressed to Ahaz. When Ahaz refused, then Isaiah changed the pronoun. The "you" becomes plural. Isaiah addresses the whole house of David. He addresses Judah and the people of God, and he is addressing all who will ever call on the name of the Lord: "Hear now the word of the Lord. God Himself shall give you a sign and this is the sign: You are afraid that God will allow Rezin of Syria and Pekah of Samaria to destroy the house of David, to destroy his throne, and to destroy the people of God. Listen to the words of the Lord and listen to the sign that God shall give." Then God remembers the covenant promise He made to David:

> He shall build an house for my name, and I will stablish the throne of his kingdom for ever. (2 Sam. 7:13)

God remembers that Davidic covenant. There will never be a king who is able to destroy the throne that God has promised to His Son who will reign and will be seated upon the throne of His father David. That Son is in God's remembrance of His promise in Genesis:

> And I will put enmity between thee and the woman, and between thy seed and her seed; it shall bruise thy head, and thou shalt bruise his heel. (Gen. 3:15)

Isaiah says that God is remembering His covenant He made with Judah when God said through Jacob:

> The sceptre shall not depart from Judah, nor a lawgiver from between his feet, until Shiloh come. (Gen. 49:10)

The king who shall sit upon the throne shall be called "God is with us" and shall be born of a virgin, the sign, the meaning of the virgin birth. That is what God said and what He did.

After Isaiah delivered this Immanuel prophecy he seemingly was filled with a flood tide of holy words from heaven. They are recorded in Isaiah 7:17-22 and 8:22. They are all prophecies of terror. It is an awesome judgment:

> The LORD shall bring upon thee, and upon thy people, and upon thy father's house, days that have not come, from the day that Ephraim departed from Judah; even the king of Assyria.
>
> And it shall come to pass in that day, that the LORD shall hiss for the fly that is in the uttermost part of the rivers of Egypt, and for the bee that is in the land of Assyria.
>
> And they shall come, and shall rest all of them in the desolate valleys, and in the holes of the rocks, and upon all thorns, and upon all bushes.
>
> In the same day shall the Lord shave with a razor that is hired, namely, by them beyond the river, by the king of Assyria, the head, and the hair of the feet: and it shall also consume the beard.
>
> And it shall come to pass in that day, that a man shall nourish a young cow, and two sheep;
>
> And it shall come to pass, for the abundance of milk that they shall give he shall eat butter: for butter and honey shall every one eat that is left in the land. (Isa. 7:17-22)
>
> And they shall look unto the earth; and behold trouble and darkness, dimness of anguish; and they shall be driven to darkness. (Isa. 8:22)

Ahaz delivered his people into the hands of Tiglath-pileser who destroyed the northern kingdom, Samaria, and carried away forever into dispersion and captivity the ten tribes. Not only did the Assyrians destroy the northern kingdom but in the lifetime of Isaiah alone, the bitter, merciless Assyrians overran Judah four times. Had it not been for the intervention of God when the Assyrians came, the whole nation would have been utterly destroyed.

In the ninth chapter Isaiah suddenly bursts into one of the most glorious prophecies in human speech:

> Nevertheless the dimness shall not be such as was in her vexation, when at the first he lightly afflicted the land of Zebulun and the land

of Naphtali, and afterward did more grievously afflict her by the way of the sea, beyond Jordan, in Galilee of the nations.

The people that walked in darkness have seen a great light: they that dwell in the land of the shadow of death, upon them hath the light shined.

Thou hast multiplied the nation, and not increased the joy: they joy before thee according to the joy in harvest, and as men rejoice when they divide the spoil.

For thou hast broken the yoke of his burden, and the staff of his shoulder, the rod of his oppressor, as in the day of Midian.

For every battle of the warrior is with confused noise, and garments rolled in blood; but this shall be with burning and fuel of fire.

For unto us a child is born, unto us a son is given: and the government shall be upon his shoulder: and his name shall be called Wonderful, Counsellor, The mighty God, The everlasting Father, The Prince of Peace.

Of the increase of his government and peace there shall be no end, upon the throne of David, and upon his kingdom, to order it, and to establish it with judgment and with justice from henceforth even for ever. The zeal of the LORD of hosts will perform this. (Isa. 9:1-7)

WHAT SHALL WE SAY OF THIS PROPHECY?

What do you think about that? "Behold, a virgin shall conceive, and bear a son, and shall call his name Immanuel. . . . and his name shall be called Wonderful, Counsellor, The mighty God, The everlasting Father, The Prince of Peace." Do you believe that? Those who follow the strange ideas of modern theology say that this is nothing but oriental hyperbole and poetic imagery. "Impossible," they say. "No such thing could ever be. Jesus might be a wonderful man but He is not the wonderful Counselor. He might be a glorious prophet but He is not the mighty God. He might be a marvelous leader but He is not the everlasting Father, the Prince of Peace." Unanimously the entire skeptical and liberal world avows, "No!"

"Yes!" says Matthew:

> Now all this was done, that it might be fulfilled which was spoken of the Lord by the prophet, saying,
> Behold, a virgin shall be with child, and shall bring forth a son,

and they shall call his name Emmanuel, which being interpreted is, God with us. (Matt. 1:22,23)

"Yes!" says John:

> In the beginning was the Word, and the Word was with God, and the Word was God.
>
> And the Word was made flesh, and dwelt among us, (and we beheld his glory, the glory as of the only begotten of the Father,) full of grace and truth. (John 1:1,14)

"Yes!" says Paul:

> . . . of his dear Son: . . .
> Who is the image of the invisible God, the firstborn of every creature. (Col. 1:13b,15)

A critic might come to you and say, "Tell me honestly, if a seventeen-year-old girl came to you being pregnant and said, 'My child has no earthly father; my child is conceived by God,' would you believe her?"

I certainly would, if the birth of that child had been predicted since the dawn of creation; if every prophet who ever lived foretold His glorious coming; if when He died the third day He was raised from the dead; and if after His ascension into heaven there were millions of people who laid down their lives in His name. If it were that child, yes! For you see, this is the intrusion of God in human history and in human life. The virgin birth of our Lord is of the same piece as is His resurrection. When I read in God's Word that He came down and assumed human form and flesh that He might die for our sins, when I read that in love He died for us on the cross, when I see that He was raised from the dead for our justification, when I have the experience of praying to Him in heaven, and when I feel the assurance, comfort, and strength that He is coming again to be King and Lord over the whole earth, I sense that the word is all of one piece, and it is all of God.

All of the things that happened in history worked together for His coming. In the fullness of time He came. The whole earth was filled with expectancy that out of the East should arise a great messianic deliverer. Tacitus and Suetonius, the Roman historians, speak of it. Those who came from afar said to King Herod in Jerusalem: "We have seen His star in the east and we have come to worship Him. Where is He?" The whole earth was filled with expectancy of a coming Lord. In the fullness of time, just as the prophet announced 750 years before, He came.

If He was not born of a virgin, God in the flesh, if He was conceived like the rest of us, then when He died, He died for His own sins. He is not my Savior; He could not be. He had to die for His own sins just as all of us die for our sins; He died as one among us. He may have been a good man, a great man, maybe the greatest man. He may have been a brilliant man, maybe the finest philosopher and sage who ever lived, but if He was born like the rest of us, He was born a sinner possessing a propensity and affinity for sin we cannot deny. A man may say, "I will be perfect," yet the drag of sin will pull him down. But God gives the promise in the Garden of Eden that the seed of the woman shall crush Satan's head. God gives the promise that David shall have a son who will sit upon his throne forever. God gives the promise that the name of that coming One shall be the mighty God and the everlasting Father. God gives the promise that His name is Immanuel, God with us. As God He is able to bear all our sins in His own body on the tree. Where sin abounded, grace abounded much more. This is our Savior who in our stead suffered for our sins that we might find forgiveness in God and life everlasting in His wonderful name.

This is the evangel to be announced, to be heralded, to be preached to the whole world, "Christ is come to save men's souls." That is why they named Him Jesus, Savior, because He would save His people from their sins. He is Christ our living Lord.

> All hail the power of Jesus' name!
>   Let angels prostrate fall;
> Bring forth the royal diadem,
>   And crown Him Lord of all.
>
> Ye chosen seed of Israel's race,
>   Ye ransomed from the fall,
> Hail Him who saves you by His grace,
>   And crown Him Lord.of all.

9

The Foundation of the Faith

And when they shall say unto you, Seek unto them that have familiar spirits, and unto wizards that peep, and that mutter: should not a people seek unto their God? for the living to the dead?

To the law and to the testimony: if they speak not according to this word, it is because there is no light in them. (Isa. 8:19,20)

When we read the text in Isaiah 8:19,20 we would think that the prophet was speaking to us today. One of the surest signs of the emptiness of the unbelief and infidelity of the American people is that they are turning in large numbers to astrologers, sorcerers, soothsayers, wizards, fortune tellers, and necromancers, many of whom say they are able to bring up the dead to speak to us. Few great newspapers in America today would dare publish an edition without a column on astrology. This is a sign of the spiritual poverty of America. When we turn from the true God we automatically turn to false, sterile, and barren gods. It was also so in the days of Isaiah.

One of the great intellectuals of all times was Lord Francis Bacon, a philosopher of tremendous insight, an essayist and author of unusual gifts. One time Lord Bacon held a Bible up above his head and said, "Thus God speaks."

73

In the Pentateuch the phrase "Thus saith the Lord" is repeated 700 times. In the entire Bible the phrases "Thus saith the Lord," "And God said," or "The word of the Lord came" are repeated not only 700 times in the Pentateuch, but in the entire Bible they are used more than 4,000 times. The Old Testament is cited 320 times in the New Testament by word and text, and the Old Covenant is referred to many more times. This is the Word of God. "If [men] speak not according to this word, it is because there is no light in them."

The foundation for our faith is not superstition, soothsaying, wizardry, or necromancy, but it is the revealed true light from heaven bound up in these sacred pages. The Bible is the great unique. It is like Christ Himself. There is none like Him. Even the Lord identified Himself with His Word. Both are called the Word of God, the incarnate Word, the spoken Word, and the written Word.

The Bible is gloriously unique. It reveals to us the ages past. Man had not witnessed the creation for he had not yet been brought into being. We know of the aeons and the ages past because they are revealed to us by the Lord in this sacred Book. The Lord God who opened for us the ages of the past is the same Jesus who opened for us the vista of the millennia of the future. It is nothing for God to tell us what happened thousands of years ago or what will happen thousands of years in the future. It is all present with Him. The Lord from the beginning, seeing the end, outlined for us the movement of human history. We read on this sacred page the great consummation of the age. God reveals it to us in this holy Book.

God Speaks to Us Now

Not only in the revelation of the past and not only in the glorious vistas of the future does God speak to us, but He also speaks to us now. The message from His Book is one of life, strength, light, and encouragement now. In the beautiful passage in the fifty-fifth chapter of Isaiah we find:

> For as the rain cometh down, and the snow from heaven, and

returneth not thither, but watereth the earth, and maketh it bring
forth and bud, that it may give seed to the sower, and bread to the
eater. (v. 10).

The showers that fall from heaven turn into flowers, into wheat
fields, into beautiful meadows and pastures, and into orchards that
are fruitful as only God can make them. So the Word of God
comes down to us from heaven watering our souls and bringing
blessing and fruit to us. The change that the Holy Scriptures bring
to human life and human destiny is glorious beyond compare.

It is so meaningful how God's Word can change human life. In
the Fiji Islands a black native was reading God's Book. A French
infidel was watching him and finally came over to him and said,
"So you are reading the Bible," and the infidel ridiculed the black
native. The black native turned to the French infidel and said: "Do
you see that boiling pot over there? Were it not for this Book you
would be in that pot." What a glorious change the Word of God
makes in human life!

When I was in seminary I had a lovely student pastorate at the
White Mound Baptist Church in Coryell County. In that church I
had a godly deacon who could pray the angels down. When he was
called upon he would always kneel on his knees and just talk to
God as though they were the best of close friends. One day
someone gave him a Bible written in Spanish. He did not know
what to do with it. He couldn't read a word. Then he thought: "I
have tenant farmers on my place, a Mexican family. I will give the
Bible to them." So he placed the Bible in the hands of the farmer.
A day passed and a week. A week passed and a month. Then the
tenant farmer came to the deacon and said: "My family and I have
been reading the Bible and we have been saved. We want to be
baptized like it says in the Book." The deacon brought it to me and
said, "What shall I do?" I said, "Deacon, have them come to the
church, make a public confession of faith and glory, and be
baptized. Praise the Lord!" They did and I baptized all of them.
Some time later as I went on Saturday to my little church parish I
was met by the deacon. He said: "Pastor, something sad has
happened. The house of my Mexican tenant farmer has burned

down and they have lost everything except for one thing, and they want me to take you to the little house where they are temporarily sheltered to show you something." So the deacon took me to the temporary home where the family was housed. The Mexican tenant farmer came out of the house carrying in his hand that Bible that was badly burned. Placing it in my hand he said, "Pastor, I dashed into the burning house to rescue just one thing — this Word of God." That is God — God speaking in His Word, God treasuring up for us His heavenly blessed presence and promise.

> We've traveled together, my Bible and I,
> Through all kinds of weather, with smile or with sigh!
> In sorrow or sunshine, in tempest or calm!
> Thy friendship unchanging, my lamp and my psalm.
>
> We've traveled together, my Bible and I,
> When life has grown weary, and death e'en was nigh.
> But all through the darkness of mist or of wrong,
> I found there a solace, a prayer, and a song.
>
> So now who shall part us, my Bible, and I?
> Shall 'isms', or schisms, or 'new lights' who try?
> Shall shadow for substance, or stone for good bread,
> Supplant thy sound wisdom, give folly instead?
>
> Ah, no, my dear Bible, exponent of light!
> Thou sword of the Spirit, put error to flight!
> And still through life's journey, until my last sigh,
> We'll travel together, my Bible and I.

Recently a man of my church passed away. For years he had been a producer of plays on Broadway in New York. He married a beautiful woman in my church, came to Dallas to live, and was won to Christ in our church. He grew in grace with us, redeeming the time. One day, to my great sorrow, he suffered a heart attack and died. When I buried him I stood at the casket and looked down on his still and silent face. His wife had placed his Bible on his breast in his hand. I said to her, "That is a beautiful thing." She said: "Yes, after he was saved he read the Bible day and night. He would put a little Testament in his pajama pocket when he went to bed. He would prop it up by the mirror when he shaved in the morning. In the funeral parlor when I looked on his face his hands seemed so empty, so I went home and got his Bible." He was buried with the Word of God on his breast.

Years ago, a marvelous Christian named John Wanamaker lived in Philadelphia. He had become a successful merchant prince with beautiful specialty department stores in New York and in Philadelphia.

He had the fortune of being appointed Postmaster General of the United States. One day he was speaking to a group of businessmen and was talking about investments. The great Christian churchman said, "I want to tell you the greatest investment I ever made in my life." They expected him to refer to the property on which he had built the block-long store in Philadelphia or to a lucrative investment in stocks or bonds. No, John Wanamaker said, "When I was a boy, I worked hard, saved my money, and I bought a Bible for $2.75." To him this was "the greatest investment I ever made."

JESUS PREACHED WITH AN OPEN BIBLE IN HIS HAND

When we study the life of Jesus we find that our Lord preached from the Bible. When He went to Nazareth where He had been brought up, He went to church as His custom was. We read that He went to the synagogue, from the book of the prophet Isaiah. He turned to the sixty-first chapter, He read the passage, and then said, "This day is this scripture fulfilled in your ears." Luke, who writes the story of our Lord, records in his twenty-fourth chapter,

> And beginning at Moses and all the prophets, he expounded unto them in all the scriptures the things concerning himself. (v. 27)

And as though that were not enough, the beloved physician writes yet again,

> And he said unto them, These are the words which I spake unto you, while I was yet with you, that all things must be fulfilled, which were written in the law of Moses, and in the prophets, and in the psalms, concerning me.
> Then opened he their understanding, that they might understand the scriptures. (24:44,45)

Notice that the Lord expounded unto them all things "in the law of Moses." The Jews divided the Bible (and every Hebrew Bible is exactly alike) into three parts: (1) the Torah, the book of Moses, (2) the prophets, and (3) the Hagiographa, the holy writings. The largest book in this section is the Psalms. The Lord says that He found the exposition of God's Word in the whole Bible — not just a part of it.

I think of Spurgeon who preached through the Bible. His great collection of sermons are the best commentaries on the Word of God in the English language. Someone said to Spurgeon, "Mr. Spurgeon, your sermons sound all alike." And Spurgeon said: "That is right. Wherever I pick my text I make a beeline to the cross." The whole Book exhibits and lifts up our Lord. When a man expounds the Word of God he presents the blessedness of the revelation and promise of the Father in the Son.

In Acts 8 Philip the evangelist preached Jesus to the Ethiopian treasurer. In Acts 10, standing before the household of Cornelius, Simon Peter says,

> To him give all the prophets witness, that through his name whosoever believeth in him shall receive remission of sins. (v. 43)

Standing on the Word of God we find our faith and our foundation today. We are a people of the Book. The apostle Paul in his first letter to his son in the ministry, Timothy, said,

> Till I come, give attendance to reading, to exhortation, to doctrine. (4:13)

In 2 Timothy we read the glorious passages that I use so often in speaking to conferences and preachers,

> All scripture is given by inspiration of God, and is profitable for doctrine, for reproof, for correction, for instruction in righteousness. (3:16)

> I charge thee therefore before God, and the Lord Jesus Christ, who shall judge the quick and the dead at his appearing and his kingdom,
> Preach the word. (4:1,2a)

Not in a thousand years would I be able to understand why so many preachers stand in their pulpits and preach out of the *Reader's Digest, Christian Century, Newsweek, Time,* or out of the editorial pages of the paper when they could stand like a powerful king and expound the Word of God. What a preciousness is this blessed Book!

Many years ago, on the streets in Lyons, France, a rich merchant named Peter Waldo was saved. He began to witness on the streets of the cities of southern Europe. He gathered around him men who later were called Waldensians. On the streets they sang and preached Jesus. Being a rich merchant Waldo took all his fortunes and paid for the printing of little Bibles which he gave to the people in their own language. Here is a poem of one of the Waldensian merchants who is opening his silks to a queenly lady:

> Oh lady fair, I have yet a gem
>   Which purer lustre flings,
> Than the diamond flash from the jewelled crown
>   On the lofty brow of kings.
>
> A wonderful pearl of exceeding price
>   Whose virtue will not decay,
> Whose light shall be as a spell to thee
>   And a blessing on thy way.
>
> The cloud went off from the Pilgrim's brow
>   As a small, meager book
> Uncased with gold or gem of cost,
>   From his flowing robes he took.
>
> Here, lady fair, is the pearl of price;
>   May it prove as much to thee.
> Nay, keep thy gold, I ask it not;
>   For the Word of God is free.

God gave the Word to us freely and He wrote its sacred pages in blood. He watered His holy Word in tears, He bathed it in suffering and sacrifice, and He handed it down to us by the hands of the angels.

Thus to believe and receive the Word of God is to believe and to receive the Word of Christ.

10

The Shoulders of Jesus

For unto us a child is born, unto us a son is given: and the government shall be upon his shoulder: and his name shall be called Wonderful, Counsellor, The mighty God, The everlasting Father, The Prince of Peace.

Of the increase of his government and peace there shall be no end, upon the throne of David, and upon his kingdom, to order it, and to establish it with judgment and with justice from henceforth even for ever. The zeal of the LORD of hosts will perform this. (Isa. 9:6,7)

Has it ever dawned on you that you can tell the story of the whole Bible from the shoulders of men?

In Genesis 9:23 we read that two of the sons of Noah, Shem and Japheth, placed a garment upon their shoulders, and walked backward to cover the nakedness of their drunken father, Noah. Ham had looked unabashed upon his father's shame, but the other sons covered Noah's nakedness and his drunken shame with the garments from their shoulders. For this modesty the descendants of Shem and Japheth were to be blessed forever.

When Abraham dismissed Hagar and Ishmael from his home, he laid upon Hagar's shoulders bread and water.

When Eliezer in Mesopotamia sought to find a bride for Isaac, he stood at the well and saw a beautiful damsel come with a pitcher of water on her shoulders.

In the story of the Exodus of God's people out of the darkness of Egypt, they stood ready that Passover night each one bearing on his shoulder the kneading trough.

When the Spirit of God fell upon Aholiab and Bezaleel, through them He made garments of glory and of beauty for Aaron the high priest. On each shoulder was an onyx stone engraved with the names of the children, the tribes of the people of God.

When the Lord instructed Moses as to how the people were to perform the service of the tabernacle He ordered that all of the accouterments were to be placed upon wagons except the ark of the covenant, the golden altar of incense, the seven-branched lampstand, and the golden table of shewbread. These were to be borne on the shoulders of the children of Kohath. When the Philistines put the ark upon a wagon and Uzzah touched it, the wrath of God smote him, for the ark was to be carried sacredly upon the shoulders of men.

In the Book of Joshua we read that a representative from each of the tribes where the Jordan parted was to pick up a stone on his shoulder and deposit it in Canaan's land. This was to represent the visitation of God from heaven.

In the story of Samson, the strong man bore upon his shoulders the gates of Gaza, carrying them all the way to Hebron. Having been presented as a spectacle of the impotence of Jehovah God in the house of Dagon, Samson prayed, "Lord, just this one time stand with me." Samson bowed his shoulders and pulled down the temple of the false god.

The story of Samuel begins in the account of the kings with the presentation of Saul, the first king of Israel. When the prophet presented him the people noticed that he stood taller than any man in the land of Israel.

Throughout the Bible one can tell the story of the omnipotent God with the shoulders of men. In coming to the prophet Isaiah and going beyond my text to Isaiah 22 we read that because of

Shebna's pride and iniquity, God has disowned and discharged him. He was in disfavor with the Almighty. God said, "I have given the leadership of the kingdom to Eliakim, the son of Hilkiah. I will lay the key of the house of David upon his shoulder."

THE GOVERNMENT UPON HIS SHOULDERS

God said that in Eliakim He would lay the key of the kingdom of David. I suppose in that time it meant something similar to what I saw when I once was delivering the address at the commencement of a college. Preceding me as I walked into the auditorium was a young man with a mace, which was a sign of the dignity, significance, and power of the occasion. The key of the house of David must have been something like that, a sign of the power and authority of the kingdom.

When I read, "For unto us a child is born, unto us a son is given: and the government shall be upon his shoulder: and his name shall be called Wonderful, Counsellor, The mighty God, The everlasting Father, The Prince of Peace," I feel that there is a marvelous significance in that reference to the shoulder of Jesus. God will some day lay on the shoulders of Jesus the entire government and administration of the universe. What a vast change it is from the god of this world, Satan, to the administration and sovereignty of Christ! As in Isaiah 22, when God took the administration from Shebna and gave it to godly Eliakim, so the prophecy avows that some day God will take the government of the universe from the god of this world, Satan, and give it to Christ. How drear is the portrayal of the life of this world under the prince of darkness! Satan has sown the world with tears, suffering, and death. The world is nothing other than one great planet for the burying of God's created people. Death is everywhere reigning supreme. Suffering, trial, tears, disappointment, frustration, and hurt are everywhere. The prophecy says the day is coming when the government of the world will be seized from the hands of Satan, and placed in the hands of the Lord God. We will have a new King, a new government, and it will be in the hands of the Lord God Christ. There will be no more death. The dead shall be raised from the heart of the earth. All of us shall be immortalized, translated, in a moment, in the twinkling of an eye, at the last trump. God will make us kings and priests under the Lord.

Many caricatures of the life to come like to picture us on a cloud with a halo, wings, and a harp. But how untrue for God has shown us that in the life to come we will be intensely active.

In Luke 19 we read:

> And he said unto him, Well, thou good servant: because thou hast been faithful in a very little, have thou authority over ten cities.
> And the second came, saying, Lord, thy pound hath gained five pounds.
> And he said likewise to him, Be thou also over five cities. (vv. 17-19)

When God recreates the whole universe, all of the heavens, the starry spheres, the Milky Way, this planet, it will be full of the most intense life. Its government shall rest upon His shoulders. Our capital city will be the New Jerusalem. From that capital city we shall go out to administer the whole creation of God, but we shall live in the New Jerusalem.

The Great Lord and King Is Our Friend and Savior

Someone said, "I hope my address is by some glory square on a hallelujah boulevard where I can see the King in His glory come in and out, walking before the people." Can it be that we will be able to look upon the great King? Can it be that He would know us, that He would speak to us? Can it be that He will call me by my name? Yes, it will be so, for He is Jesus — our friend and Savior.

> The golden sun and the silvery moon,
> And all the stars that shine,
> Were made by His omnipotent hands,
> And He's a friend of mine.
>
> When He shall come with trumpet sound,
> To head the conquering line,
> The whole world will bow before His feet,
> And He's a friend of mine.

It is unimaginable that the Lord God and King of the whole

universe should be the same Lord Jesus who died for us. The shoulders that bear the government of the universe are the shoulders that bore the cross to Calvary. His heart has not changed. He is the same.

In Revelation we read a description of the immortalized, glorified Christ:

> And in the midst of the seven candlesticks one like unto the Son of man, clothed with a garment down to the foot, and girt about the paps with a golden girdle.
> His head and his hairs were white like wool, as white as snow; and his eyes were as a flame of fire;
> And his feet like unto fine brass, as if they burned in a furnace; and his voice as the sound of many waters.
> And he had in his right hand seven stars: and out of his mouth went a sharp two-edged sword: and his countenance was as the sun shineth in his strength. (1:13-16)

Even His feet were beyond the brilliance that one could look upon. Yet when John fell at His feet as dead, the Lord reached forth His hand and put it on his shoulders. I would think the Lord had done that a hundred times as He talked to John. Maybe He laid His hand on John's shoulders as He pointed to the world in giving the Great Commission for the evangelization of all the people. Maybe He did that in encouraging John in an hour of disappointment and despair. Maybe He lovingly touched him as they walked through a wheat field or down a road. It was the same Lord Jesus who put His hand on the shoulders of John. His heart has not changed.

His sympathy and compassion for us is the same. The same shoulders that bear the government, in loving compassion bear us up in sympathy, pity, forgiveness, and understanding. He said, "I am the Good Shepherd." He said, "There were ninety and nine safe in the fold and one was lost." He searched for it until He found it. The Bible tells us:

> And when he hath found it, he layeth it on his shoulders, rejoicing.
> And when he cometh home, he calleth together his friends and

neighbours, saying unto them, Rejoice with me; for I have found
my sheep which was lost. (Luke 15:5,6)

Why was His heart not full of judgment against the lost sheep?
He could have said: "You senseless and stupid sheep! Do not you
know better than to drift away from the flock? Do not you know
you will be lost?" Instead He searched for the lost sheep until He
found it. Then He put it on His shoulder rejoicing.

OUR SYMPATHETIC AND UNDERSTANDING LORD JESUS

Our Lord is sympathetic and full of kindness and understanding
when people err and sin. The same shoulders that carry the weight
of the government of heaven bear us in deepest sympathy and
understanding.

I lived through something like that which so moved me. I have a
practice of talking to all the children who come into the church.
An appointment is made, the parents bring the children to me,
and I talk to them about the Lord, the church, and about being
baptized. Somehow I did not know the background of one of the
children who was coming. As the child sat by the mother, I began
to talk to the child. To my chagrin and exasperation the child
could not answer. You see, the children are given a six-week's
course and they are taught the answers in the book on joining the
church. The child stumbled and could not answer. I thought it
was a waste of time that they should make an engagement for the
child to see me and not be prepared. The mother moved close to
the child and, in the sweetest way, the tenderest tone, and the
gentlest manner, began to talk to the little child about what I was
asking. Then I realized that the child was retarded. I did not know
it. The mother did not say, "You stupid moron, why can you not
answer these simple questions the pastor asks?" The mother instead talked to the little child. As I looked I could not help but see
the Spirit of God working through the sweet mother. In how many
ways do we show ourselves unknowing. God does not find it in His
heart to be judgmental, but He in kindness helps and encourages
us. He lays it on His shoulders, lovingly and tenderly.

11

His Name Is Wonderful

> For unto us a child is born, unto us a son is given: and the
> government shall be upon his shoulder: and his name shall be called
> Wonderful, Counsellor, The mighty God, The everlasting Father,
> The Prince of Peace. (Isa. 9:6)

We are told that there are 256 different names the Bible accords
to Jesus our Lord. It is as though one name could not express the
infinite virtue and worth of His marvelous life. We have already
read about one of them in Isaiah 7:14, "Immanuel." In Isaiah 9 we
read about other names. "And his name shall be called Wonderful, Counsellor, The mighty God, The Everlasting Father, The
Prince of Peace." In this chapter we choose to expound one of His
names. "His name shall be called Wonderful," that is, a someone
who is transcendently glorious above all that we could ever know
or see.

A "wonder" would refer to something out of the ordinary,
something unusual and uncommon. Had you been present to see
Israel walk through the parted waters of the Red Sea dry shod, you
would have said, "That is wonderful." Had you been standing by
Joshua, the captain of the hosts of the armies of Israel when he
commanded the sun and the moon to stand still over the Valley of

Ajalon, you would have said, "It is wonderful." Had you stood on Mount Carmel in the days of Elijah when in answer to a man's prayer, fire fell from heaven and consumed the wood, the sacrifice, and the altar, and licked up the water and dust in the trench, you would have said, "It is wonderful."

Wonderful in His Preexistence

To us who look with eyes of faith to the Lord Jesus Christ, He is Wonderful. "His name shall be called Wonderful." He is wonderful in His preexistence. All of us were created when we were born. God fashioned our physical frame in the womb of our mothers, then He breathed into us the breath of life and we became a living soul. We were created; we began our existence upon our birth. Not so with the Lord Jesus. "In the beginning was the Word, and the Word was with God, and the Word was God. . . . All things were made by him and without him was not any thing made that was made." Christ was preexistent.

In John 12 the sainted apostle identifies the Lord Jesus as the Jehovah of the Old Testament. In the New Testament His name is Jesus; in the Old Testament His name is Jehovah. He is the wonderful God of the Old Covenant and of the New. In the Gospel of John the apostle quotes the Lord as saying "before Abraham was, I am" (8:58). He is a marvelous man, but He is also the glorious Counselor. He is a great teacher, but He is also the mighty God. He is a marvelous leader, but He is also the everlasting Father. He is an incomparable example for us, but He is also Immanuel, God with us. He is wonderful in His preexistence. He is no less wonderful in His incarnation.

Wonderful in His Birth

The apostle Paul wrote that in the fullness of time God sent forth His Son. How full of meaning is that sentence. All history moved for that great, final moment of destiny when the world's Savior should come upon the earth.

In the Diaspora the Jew had carried the book of the Law, the Old Testament, and his synagogue everywhere he went. The Greeks had taught the entire civilized world a common language in which they could listen to the story of the grace of the Lord. The Romans had laced the entire civilized world with roads and highways over which the emissaries of Christ could proclaim the Good News of the gospel of Jesus. The whole world moved toward the moment of His coming. When He was born all of the stars seemed to be lowered like golden lamps to the earth and the heavens were resplendent with the presence of God. The spheres were singing in expectation and glory of what should happen that evening in Bethlehem. Then when the child was born, the angels who had been practicing from the dawn of creation flung upward to God their glorious salutations and down over the earth their marvelous benediction. The child of promise had been born! It is wonderful! A star guided the wise men from the east and the poor humble shepherds felt welcome to kneel down and worship before the babe in a manger. The whole story of the Lord Jesus is wonderful!

Wonderful in His Life

The beginning of His life is like the story of the great consummation at the end of His life. All of the events of His life fit beautifully together. His birth was wonderful. His resurrection was wonderful. He was wonderful in all His life. Pontius Pilate said, "I find in him no fault at all." He lived a sinless life, pure and chaste as the very Son of God.

His ministry was no less beautiful and precious. Sometimes a man can be known by his enemies more than by his friends. Do you know what our Lord's enemies said about Him? "He is a friend of sinners." Not only that, but His enemies said: "He does good on the Sabbath day. He heals the blind, He restores withered hands, and He cleanses the leper." Thus His enemies castigated Him. Not only that, but His enemies said that the Lord claimed God as His Father. Even what His enemies said about Him makes Him wonderful.

His preaching ministry was everywhere blessed. The common people heard Him gladly, that is, they understood His language and rejoiced in His message. And no less did His healing and teaching ministries bring hope and heaven to their hearts.

WONDERFUL IN HIS DEATH

The Lord was wonderful in His death, not only that He died for the sins of the people, but it also was a wonderful thing how God did it. It was the purpose of God that the Lord be exposed when He died. He could have died for us in secret, but this was not the purpose of God. When the Lord died He was to be exposed to the whole world. Thousands were to see Him. He was crucified near the city gates where a great highway went by, and at a time when there were hundreds of thousands of pilgrims gathered in the city of Jerusalem. He was raised up above the earth toward the sky where all might see Him. God's purpose in the death of our Lord was that the whole world might know it. The Lord was not crucified in a cathedral between two golden lampstands but in a place and on a hill where the whole earth could see it and marvel before it. Should some choose not to look, the Lord closed down the sun and shook the earth that all people might know He was dying. It was God's purpose that the Lord should be publicly exposed, and we cannot expose the Lord too much. We cannot brag about Jesus too much. We cannot glorify the Lord too much. We cannot lift Him up too high. We cannot preach Him too fervently or too zealously.

WONDERFUL IN HIS RESURRECTION

He is wonderful in His resurrection. The Lord taught His disciples that on the third day He would be raised from the dead. When the third day came was there an apostle who went to the tomb to see if He had been raised? Not one. They did not believe it. It was impossible to them that one should be raised from the dead. When He was raised there was only a woman there who had come to prepare her Lord for final burial. Is it not unbelievable how He appeared when He was raised from the dead? One would have thought He would have gone to Pilate who had condemned Him, to Herod who mocked Him, to the Sanhedrin who tried Him, or to the people who cried for His blood. No; He appeared to a humble woman named Mary who had come to anoint His body with spices. He appeared to the little band of disciples and to James His brother in the flesh that He might win His family to the faith. Finally, He appeared to the persecutor Saul of Tarsus. The Lord reveals Himself to us who look in faith to Him, who love Him.

There is something about all of this I cannot understand. To us who believe, our Lord is marvelous, but to those who do not believe, He is nothing or less. O Master, how thankful I am that You have chosen me to look in faith to You, that You chose my name to be inscribed in the Book of Life, that You moved upon my heart in faith and I received You as a Savior. Lord, I am so thankful that You revealed Yourself to me.

WONDERFUL IN HIS PRESENT MINISTRY

He is wonderful in His present ministry of intercession. There could be no more glorious verse than that found in Hebrews:

> Wherefore he is able also to save them to the uttermost that come unto God by him, seeing he ever liveth to make intercession for them.

He is our Representative at the right hand of the Majesty on high to see to it that we make the gates of heaven some day. Will we fall by the wayside? Will Satan yet destroy us? Will we finally sin unto damnation and perdition? Never! He is there to be our representative, our mediator, our pleader, our counselor, our great lawyer and defender. His ministry is one of intercession for us. Anyone can come boldly to the throne of grace and lay bare before the Lord the prayers of his soul. So I say, Come. God is exposed now. The veil of the temple has been rent in two. There are no walls and hidden sanctuaries. God is not removed far from us. He is as close as our hands and feet. Come. Tell Him all about what you have in your heart.

That does not mean that He gives me everything for which I ask. He always gives me what is best. God will always give the best to those who leave the choice to Him. He hears us, He blesses us, and He answers our prayers. He will talk to us as our best friend and partner if we will open our hearts to Him. What He gives us will be infinitely blessed.

WONDERFUL IN HIS PROMISED RETURN

He is wonderful in His coming again. You know, after reading and studying this Book for a generation, after preaching through the Apocalypse for two years, after preaching sermons on the return of our Lord without number, I still have difficulty realizing that this stolid earth will one day see the heavens rolled back and the Lord descending on the shekinah clouds of glory. Could it be? It is too wonderful. My eyes shall see Him — the King in His beauty. We shall be raised if we die before He comes, we shall be translated and glorified if we are alive in that day. Whether resurrected or raptured, we shall see Him when He comes in glory.

WONDERFUL SAVIOR NOW

"His name shall be called Wonderful." He is a wonderful Savior now. In addition to all the wonder of the ages past and the glory of the ages to come, He is a wonderful Savior right now. "I stand at the door, and knock," He said. "If any man hear my voice, and open the door, I will come in and will sup with him, and he with me." He is standing at the door of our hearts now.

"His name shall be called Wonderful." What a blessed God, not that *some day* He is our Lord or *some day* He is our Savior or *some day* He is our God. He is not just a God of tomorrow, not just a God of heaven, not just a God of a day that is yet to come, but He is the God of now, the God of our home and family, the God of our hearts and souls. He is the God who can see us through now. I do not know anything finer than for a man to announce to his employees: "From now on we have a new partner in the company. I have made God my partner."

12

The Kingdom Is Coming

Behold, the Lord, the LORD of hosts, shall lop the bough with terror: and the high ones of stature shall be hewn down, and the haughty shall be humbled.

And he shall cut down the thickets of the forest with iron, and Lebanon shall fall by a mighty one.

And there shall come forth a rod out of the stem of Jesse, and a Branch shall grow out of his roots:

And the spirit of the LORD shall rest upon him, the spirit of wisdom and understanding, the spirit of counsel and might, the spirit of knowledge and of the fear of the LORD;

And shall make him of quick understanding in the fear of the LORD: and he shall not judge after the sight of his eyes, neither reprove after the hearing of his ears:

But with righteousness shall he judge the poor, and reprove with equity for the meek of the earth: and he shall smite the earth with the rod of his mouth, and with the breath of his lips shall he slay the wicked.

And righteousness shall be the girdle of his loins, and faithfulness the girdle of his reins.

The wolf also shall dwell with the lamb, and the leopard shall lie down with the kid; and the calf and the young lion and the fatling together; and a little child shall lead them.

And the cow and the bear shall feed; their young ones shall lie down together: and the lion shall eat straw like the ox.

And the sucking child shall play on the hole of the asp, and the weaned child shall put his hand on the cockatrice's den.

They shall not hurt nor destroy in all my holy mountain: for the earth shall be full of the knowledge of the LORD, as the waters cover the sea. (Isa. 10:33–11:9)

I cannot imagine a more glorious and optimistic prophecy than the one presented in our text of the King and the coming kingdom. All of it arose out of the exigency, tragic and sorrowful, of the day in which Isaiah lived. From horizon to horizon of the civilized world the merciless and cruel empire of Assyria held the earth in an iron grip. It was when Assyria invaded Palestine that she destroyed forever the northern kingdom with its capital at Samaria. Four times in the life of Isaiah Assyria ravaged and overran Judah. Had it not been for an intervention of God in answer to the prayer of the good king Hezekiah, Assyria would have destroyed little Judah. This text with its prophecy begins and concludes with a violent and distinct contrast.

First, the prophecy concerning Assyria states that God will lop off its boughs. The mighty hand of the Lord will cut it down like a cedar in Lebanon; it will be felled. Then contrasting the destruction of Assyria Isaiah speaks of the resurrection of Israel. "And there shall come forth a rod out of the stem of Jesse, and a Branch shall grow out of his roots." The contrast here is between a cedar and an oak. When a cedar is cut down, belonging as it does to the pine family, there are no shoots or outgrowths. The stump then rots and decays in the ground. The prophet Isaiah says that the vast, merciless empire of Assyria will be like that. God Himself will fell the giant cedar and when it is cut down it will be destroyed forever. So completely did the Assyrian empire vanish from the earth, that centuries later the army of Alexander the Great marched over its capital city of Nineveh unaware that a mighty empire and an extensive civilization lay buried beneath its feet. God said Assyria would be destroyed like a mighty cedar that is cut down in which there would be no shoots and no rod that would come out of the stump that remained.

Then the prophet by inspiration contrastingly speaks of Israel as an oak tree. When an oak is cut down rods and shoots still spring up. It still has life in its roots and in the stem. Out of the destruction of Israel and out of the final, ultimate captivity of Judah there will yet be God's life remaining. Then Isaiah presents the marvelous prophecy: out of the stump there will grow a branch. Matthew refers to this shoot as "a Nazarene" who will be the Lord God our Savior. The New Testament mentions that verse often.

In Revelation 22 the Lord speaks of Himself as the root and the offspring of David. Out of the root of David the Messiah shall rise. Then Isaiah presents the description of the incomparably glorious, triumphant kingdom. Let us contrast it with Greek culture and life that so pervaded the world and still does.

Without exception the Greeks have always looked back to their golden days. Their heroes lived a long time ago. Even Plato spoke of the Utopian continent named Atlantis that once existed beyond the pillars of Hercules, beyond the Gates of Gibraltar, out in the vast ocean, now submerged and forever gone. The golden day to Plato was a yesterday forever destroyed. All the poets and dramatists of the ancient cultured world looked back to the primeval time for the day of bliss, joy, and innocence.

The Hebrew prophets and the New Testament apostles in the Bible are just the opposite. They are always looking forward: the messianic kingdom is on its way, yet to be consummated, yet to be realized. That spirit of hope and optimism, no matter how full of despair the present might be, is always written large on the pages of the sacred Book.

When Joseph died in Egypt he called his brethren and made them sware before God that they would take up his bones and carry them back to the Promised Land. We read in Genesis:

> And Joseph said unto his brethren, I die: and God will surely visit you, and bring you out of this land unto the land which he sware to Abraham, to Isaac, and to Jacob. (50:24)

When Moses faced an ultimate death he called his brethren and said:

The LORD thy God will raise up unto thee a Prophet from the
midst of thee, of thy brethren, like unto me; unto him ye shall
hearken;
I will raise them up a Prophet from among their brethren, like
unto thee, and will put my words in his mouth; and he shall speak
unto them all that I shall command him. (Deut. 18:15,18)

When the children of Judah were carried into captivity in
Babylon the prophet Jeremiah said:

For thus saith the LORD, That after seventy years be accomplished
at Babylon I will visit you, and perform my good word toward you,
in causing you to return to this place. (Jer. 29:10)

In A.D. 70 Titus destroyed the earthly Jerusalem, but in the
Revelation the seer sees a New Jerusalem coming down from God
out of heaven prepared as a bride adorned for her husband. That
spirit of hope and optimism, however dark the present hour may
be, ever characterizes the godwardness of these who are able to see
by eyes of faith the purpose of God for the human race. It is that
kingdom that is coming in time and history.

THE KINGDOM IS TWOFOLD IN ITS COMING

First, the kingdom is coming in time and in history slowly, but
surely. A truth that is difficult for us to realize is God's hand in
history. He never withdraws His omnipotent hand from His
created universe. What to us seems like blackness, despair, and
death has in it an ultimate purpose of almighty God, for the
kingdom is coming and it comes in God's way and in God's
will.

The first verse of the Bible says, "God created the heaven and
the earth," but the second verse is a dark verse: "And the earth was
without form, and void; and darkness was upon the face of the
deep." I think when Lucifer fell the whole universe fell with him.
Enormous stars collided and burst into destruction. The whole
creation of God was destroyed. Sin always destroys. Then what?
Does God leave it chaotic and dark? No, for the verse continues,
"And the Spirit of God moved upon the face of the waters." He
brought order and beauty out of chaos. So it is with God's hand in

modern history. It is as dark in some places of this world as it can be. But the hand of God is in China, in Russia, in the nations of Africa as in the islands of the sea. Though America seems bound to a dissolution and disintegration, the hand of God is on America. The kingdom is coming slowly, secretly. The Lord Himself said:

> And when he was demanded of the Pharisees, when the kingdom of God should come, he answered them and said, The kingdom of God cometh not with observation:
> Neither shall they say, Lo here! or, lo there! for, behold, the kingdom of God is within you. (Luke 17:20,21)

One cannot see the kingdom for only God can see and understand.

In Mark 4 Jesus said the kingdom of God is like a man who plants a seed in the earth and goes to sleep, and while he sleeps a mystery develops: out of the dust of the ground the seed sprouts. Out comes a little blade, a stalk, a bloom, a fruit. The growth is beyond comprehension. So is God's secret way of controlling the destiny of His created universe. So the kingdom comes, but it comes slowly, without observation. We may not see or understand, but the Lord has promised the kingdom to His people. Our Lord said, "Fear not, little flock; for it is your Father's good pleasure to give you the kingdom" (Luke 12:32).

Not only is the kingdom in time and history coming slowly, but it also is coming suddenly, triumphantly, personally. Three times in Revelation 22, the Lord says: "Behold, I come quickly." When the time of consummation comes the kingdom will come. We shall see our Lord and His reign will be established in the earth. He said it is to be as lightning cometh out of the east, and shineth even unto the west (Matt. 24:27). Openly and publicly we shall see Him. It will be glorious and triumphant day for the people of God!

In Romans 11 Paul uses the Greek word *pleroma* which means "full number" in the passage, "Until the fulness [*pleroma*] of the Gentiles be come in" (v. 25b). When the full number of the Gentiles is in, then it is time for the consummation of the age and the establishment of the kingdom. When the last man whose name is written in the Lamb's Book of Life walks down an aisle, then the consummation shall come. The Lord shall appear and establish His kingdom in the earth.

The Kingdom Is Twofold in Its Consummation

Not only is the kingdom coming twofold, gradually and without observation, openly, and triumphantly, but it is also twofold in its component constituent parts.

First, the kingdom is spiritual. The Lord said to Pilate, "My kingdom is not of this world" (John 18:36). That is, it is not like Rome, Athens, Nineveh, or Babylon. It is not like Washington, London, Paris, or Moscow. The kingdom of the Lord is of a different order and nature. Paul by inspiration wrote, "Brethren . . . flesh and blood cannot inherit the kingdom of God; neither doth corruption inherit incorruption" (1 Cor. 15:50). It is of a different order. It is a spiritual kingdom.

But the kingdom of God is also spatial. It is in time and history as real as anything we know that is real. There will be a new heaven, but it will be an actual heaven. There will be a new city, but it will be a real city. There will be a new earth, but it will be a real earth, this earth which will be renovated. We will have a new body which will be real. I cannot understand the contradiction inherent in what the Bible calls a "spiritual body." Those two words are contradictory. One might as well say "sweet sour" as to say a "spiritual body." But God says it. In time, this body will be resurrected and glorified. It will be an actual body and this is the cardinal doctrine of the Christian faith. Paul states in 2 Corinthians:

> For we know that if our earthly house of this tabernacle were dissolved, we have a building of God, an house not made with hands, eternal in the heavens.
> For in this we groan, earnestly desiring to be clothed upon with our house which is from heaven:
> If so be that being clothed we shall not be found naked.
> For we that are in this tabernacle do groan, being burdened: not for that we would be unclothed, but clothed upon, that mortality might be swallowed up of life. (5:1-4)

When the scribes and Pharisees came to the Lord and asked

Him to give them a sign that He was the Son of God, He said: "For as Jonas was three days and three nights in the whale's belly; so shall the Son of man be three days and three nights in the heart of the earth" (Matt. 12:40). On another occasion when they asked for a sign He said, "Destroy this temple, and in three days I will raise it up." John writes by inspiration, "But he spake of the temple of his body" (John 2:19,21). The resurrection of our Lord is the great sign, the living proof that He is the Son of God, the Savior of the world.

When the Lord presented Himself to His disciples He appeared in His own resurrected flesh. It is the real Jesus who gives authenticity to the Christian faith, not a philosophy or speculation, but an actuality. When the disciples saw Him coming into the room with the doors closed they were afraid thinking that they were seeing a spirit. We read in Luke:

> And he said unto them, Why are ye troubled? and why do thoughts arise in your hearts?
> Behold my hands and my feet, that it is I myself: handle me, and see; for a spirit hath not flesh and bones, as ye see me have.
> And when he had thus spoken, he shewed them his hands and his feet.
> And while they yet believed not for joy, and wondered, he said unto them, Have ye here any meat?
> And they gave him a piece of a broiled fish, and of an honeycomb.
> And he took it, and did eat before them. (24:38-43)

The kingdom of God is spiritual but it is also spatial. God invented matter and He invented eating. In the kingdom we shall sit down at the banquet feast with Abraham, Isaac, and Jacob, and shall break bread with the Lord. We shall be party to the marriage supper of the Lamb. The whole kingdom is as real in its actuality as any part of human life that we know today, only in heaven our human life will be immortalized and glorified.

The great cardinal doctrine of the Christian faith is the actual resurrection from the dead. All other religions believe in some kind of immortality, but the only faith and religion that believes in the resurrection of this body from the dead is the Christian faith. It is a cardinal doctrine because it is based upon the triumphant resurrection of our Lord over death, sin, and the grave. Because He lives, we shall live also. As He has a glorified and risen body, so we shall have a raised and glorified body. That is what God says the Christian faith is.

There is a familiar saying in physics: "Nature abhors a vacuum." That is, wherever there might be a vacuum in the earth, the forces of the universe will rush to fill it. That is why there are whirlwinds, tornadoes, and cyclones in this earth. There is a rushing in order to fill a place that has somehow become under-pressurized. "Nature abhors a vacuum" is an axiom in physics. There is an axiom equally factual and equally true: The Christian faith abhors disembodiment. The Christian faith abhors a spirit without a body. "For we that are in this tabernacle do groan, being burdened: not for that we would be unclothed, but clothed upon, that mortality might be swallowed up of life." God has promised those who trust in Him that He will raise them from the dead. This body shall be raised from the dust. We cannot understand the power of God because mystery is His signature. If God does it, all we do is observe it. So it is in the resurrection from the dead. God takes the atoms and molecules and raises them from the dead. Our bodies will be immortalized like the glorious body of our Savior when He was raised that Easter morning from among the dead. This is the kingdom that is coming.

In the First Baptist Church of Dallas there is a chapel that is dedicated to our "silent friends," those who cannot hear. For many years they had a pastor named Brother Landen. One of the members of his deaf congregation became ill and lay dying. So Pastor Landen took me to see the deaf man. When we went into the room we found him in his bed, facing that final and inevitable hour all of us some day must face. Gathered around him were the members of his family. Brother Landen and I took our places by the side of the members of the family looking down on his face. While we were there the deaf man pointed to one family member after another until he had pointed to each one of them. Then he pointed to Brother Landen and to me. After he had pointed to each one he pointed to himself and then he pointed upward. Brother Landen said to me, "What he means to tell you is, 'You my sweet family, and you my pastor, I will met you in heaven!'"

Do you believe that? If you do, you are a Christian. That is the heart and cardinal doctrine of the Christian faith, that in Christ we will see one another again.

> I will sing you a song of that beautiful land,
> The faraway home of the soul,
> Where no storms ever beat on the glittering strand,
> While the years of eternity roll.
>
> Oh, how sweet it will be in that beautiful land,
> So free from all sorrow and pain,
> With songs on our lips and with harps in our hands,
> To meet one another again.

He is an actual Savior and He will reign over an actual kingdom in an actual city in an actual home living in a real and resurrected body. Paul calls it "the blessed hope."

13

The Little Child

The wolf also shall dwell with the lamb, and the leopard shall lie down with the kid; and the calf and the young lion and the fatling together; and a little child shall lead them.

And the cow and the bear shall feed; their young ones shall lie down together: and the lion shall eat straw like the ox.

And the sucking child shall play on the hole of the asp, and the weaned child shall put his hand on the cockatrice's den.

They shall not hurt nor destroy in all my holy mountain: for the earth shall be full of the knowledge of the LORD, as the waters cover the sea. (Isa. 11:6-9)

Our text is a description of the golden age that is yet to come. A wolf devouring a lamb and a leopard stalking a kid are actions of natural enemies, but Isaiah presents the change that will come when God descends and the heavenly millennial reign covers the earth. What a remarkable change God will bring to pass in this harsh, cruel, and bloodthirsty fallen creation!

God never made animals to eat each other. He never created the tooth, the fang, and the claw for harm. A ravenous, carnivorous beast is the result of the fall — an outcome of sin. In that new age God will take all the bloodthirstiness and carnivorousness out of creation itself. In its stead there will be light, glory, beauty, peace, tranquility; and even the voracious lion will eat straw like an ox.

In the midst of this beautiful and dramatic portrayal of the coming kingdom, the prophet by inspiration of God presented a picture of it: "And a little child shall lead them." Three times in the passage that little child is mentioned. One can see the panorama, with God standing in a great grandstand and His creation passing in review before Him. Who leads the procession? The prophet says that it will be a little child. Had the prophet by inspiration written, "And the king shall lead them," one would not have been surprised. Had he written, "The high priest shall lead them," one would not have been astonished. But what an amazing revelation that the head of that great procession passing in the presence of God is a little child leading the way!

A deduction now follows that if this is God and if this is the way God has arranged for His millennial golden age, then it is true in all times, eternity, and Scripture. The principles are as eternal as God Himself.

ETERNAL PRINCIPLES REFLECT GOD'S CHARACTER

For example, morality and righteousness are a reflection of the character of God. Morality is never what a man says it is or what a court describes. Righteousness and morality are grounded in the character of almighty God. God does not change, nor do the great principles that reflect the being of God change. What was right yesterday is right today and is right forever. There is no such thing as situation ethics or a changing morality. These truths are eternal. If one reads this in the millennium then he has a persuasion that these principles of God follow after. If this is God and the heart of God, then he finds it everywhere: 'And a little child shall lead them." Is that true? Let us see.

First, it is true in history. Everyone who studies history is aware of the vast length, breadth, and force of the Roman Empire. It was the greatest, most absolute empire the world has ever known. Even the Germans called their leader a *kaiser*, their word for Caesar, and the Russians called their leader a *czar*, the Russian word for Caesar. Thus the impression the Roman Empire made upon civilization was indelible. What kind of an empire was it?

The Roman Empire could be likened to Hitler winning the war and dominating the world. The Roman Caesar held the entire civilized world in a mailed fist. The Roman legionnaire was universal and almost invincible. The whole world had been conquered by Rome. It was a world of slavery. Had one walked down the streets of Ephesus when Paul was there, three men out of five he would meet would be slaves. Had one walked down the streets of Antioch, Thessalonica, Corinth, or Rome, out of all the population, three out of every five people would be slaves. The Roman Empire had a population of about 100,000,000; 60,000,000 of whom were slaves. It is impossible for us in our enlightened age to enter into what that meant in human life. The slave had no standing. He had no rights and was treated like an animal.

Not only that, it was a world of the exposure of children. When I was studying Greek in school, I once had an assignment to examine a papyrus dug up out of the hermetically sealed sands of Egypt. The papyrus was from a husband writing to his wife telling her to expose their child that had just been born. The new baby was a girl and the father did not want her. By law, throughout the Roman Empire, if a man did not want a child, and especially a baby girl, he took the baby and set it out on a highway or wilderness for the jackals to eat, for the wolves to devour, or for someone to pick up, break its limbs, disfigure it, and set it on a city street to beg for alms. This is just a small insight as to the cruelty and darkness of the Roman Empire.

How did God answer the cries of the agony of the people so many centuries ago? You would think He would take the artillery of heaven and train it on so vile and merciless a civilization. Surely God would take His clenched fists and pound into the dust of the ground these who were so cruel. How did God answer?

He took one of His stars in the heavens and put it over a little place called Bethlehem and there He made its light fall upon the cheeks of a newborn babe. That was God's answer to the cruelty and darkness of the world: a child lying softly on its mother's breasts. "And a little child shall lead them." God said so. It is true in history.

Second, it is true in the Scriptures. God bowed His ear to hear

His people cry. As slaves they groaned under their tasks. They were forced to make brick without straw. Under the cruel whip of a taskmaster they cried to God and the Lord raised up a deliverer. Who was he? He was the son of Pharaoh's daughter. He was the heir apparent to the throne. He had been brought up in all of the knowledge, science, and culture of the Egyptians. He was prepared to be Pharaoh over the ancient kingdom of Egypt. One day when he heard the misery and agony of the people of God, he renounced his throne and left the luxury and power of Pharaoh's kingdom that he might suffer with the people of God. How did he even know them, much less identify himself with them?

There is another cry — a baby on the bosom of the Nile. Pharaoh's daughter fetched the little ark when she heard the baby crying. The baby's sister, Miriam, was standing close by, and offering to find a nurse for the child, she brought the baby's own mother. In the passing of the years as the mother nursed the child and brought up the little lad, she told him about God, about Abraham, Isaac, Jacob, and the people of the Lord. When the time came and the great decision was made, the child, taught by his mother the true name of the Lord God, cast life and lot with the people of God. "And a little child shall lead them."

During the days of apostasy in Israel in the holy tabernacle in Shiloh the priests turned the house of God into a harlot's house. The Philistines came, conquered Israel, overran the land, and captured the people. In those days in the stillness of the night a voice came to a little boy, "Samuel, Samuel." He arose and ran to old Eli and said: "Here I am. You called me?" Eli said: "I didn't call you. Lie down again." Three times this happened, and on the third time Eli perceived that God had called the child. We read in 1 Samuel:

> And he said, It is the LORD: let him do what seemeth him good.
> And Samuel grew, and the LORD was with him, and did let none of his words fall to the ground.
> And all Israel from Dan even to Beersheba knew that Samuel was established to be a prophet of the LORD. (3:18b-20)

"And a little child shall lead them."

The little maid in Naaman's household was captured and carried into a strange and foreign land. Would she not hate her captors? The little child said, "Oh, that Naaman could be healed of his leprosy and were he in the land of Israel, there is a prophet there who would heal him." Naaman was healed because of a little maid who returned good for evil. "And a little child shall lead them."

Third, eternal principles reflect God's character doctrinally. Let us read from our Lord's own words:

> At the same time came the disciples unto Jesus, saying, Who is greatest in the kingdom of heaven?
> And Jesus called a little child unto him, and set him in the midst of them,
> And said, Verily I say unto you, Except ye be converted, and become as little children, ye shall not enter into the kingdom of heaven.
> Whosoever therefore shall humble himself as this little child, the same is greatest in the kingdom of heaven.
> And whoso shall receive one such little child in my name receiveth me. (Matt. 8:1-5)

When Jesus spoke these words of humility to the disciples, one of them, full of envy and jealousy, pushed another for first place and said, "It is on His right hand I ask to stand." "I desire to sit on His left hand," said another. In the midst of that envy and contention the Lord took a little child and said, "The greatest in the kingdom is the one most like this little child." "And a little child shall lead them."

If it be true in God's character, if it is true eternally, in the Holy Scriptures, and in doctrine, then fourth, it also is true in human life and experience.

God's Eternal Principles Are Reflected in Human Life and Experience

One time after Dr. Huber Drumwright had delivered the morning sermon in our church he said to me: "Let me tell you something that you do not know. There is a professor who loves you with all his heart. He and his wife had a little boy in their home who had been born sickly and weak. As the years passed he became quite frail and in his last months was kept in the home and watched over by a loving mother. One day as the little lad neared his eighth birthday, he and his mother were listening to you preach on television. When the service was over the little lad turned to his mother and said: 'I want to be saved just like that. I want Jesus to come into my heart.' The mother picked up the frail little lad in her arms and told him how God had spoken to his heart. She carefully went over the plan of salvation and the little lad gave his heart in repentance and trust to Jesus. The little fellow died in his mother's arms and in the arms of Jesus."

> Safe in the arms of Jesus,
> Safe on His gentle breast,
> There by His love o'ershadowed,
> Sweetly my soul shall rest.

Dr. Drumwright added, "You see now why the professor and his wife so deeply love you." "And a little child shall lead them."

If you love a little child, you will love Jesus. If you minister to a child, you minister to the Lord. If you are kind to a little child, you are kind to the Savior. Somehow our hearts are bound up in the life of a little child. That is God, and that is the inspiration of His word: "And a little child shall lead them."

This is the coming kingdom. This is the millennial age God will bring to us.

14

The Book of Burdens

The burden . . . which Isaiah the son of Amoz did see. (Isa. 13:1)

In the Book of Isaiah there are three sections: a book of woes, a book of comfort, and a book of burdens. It is this book of burdens we wish to discuss in this chapter.

Isaiah 13:1 begins, "The burden of Babylon."
Isaiah 15:1 begins, "The burden of Moab."
Isaiah 17:1 begins, "The burden of Damascus."
Isaiah 19:1 begins, "The burden of Egypt."
Isaiah 21:1 begins, "The burden of the desert of the sea."
Isaiah 21:11 begins, "The burden of Dumah."
Isaiah 21:13 begins, "The burden upon Arabia."
Isaiah 22:1 begins, "The burden of the valley of vision."
Isaiah 23:1 begins, "The burden of Tyre."

Just a look at the Scripture causes us immediately to be sensitive to the revelation of God that He is the Lord of all the nations of the world. Because the Bible came through Israel, we are inclined to think that the heart and grace of God were centered in Jerusalem and in Judah alone. Not so, for the Lord God who guided the destiny and judged the future of Israel is the same Lord God who judges and guides the nations of the world. This is the lesson from Jonah which was difficult for Israel to learn. God was interested in Jerusalem. His heart went out to Samaria. But He was no less interested in Nineveh, the capital of the great empire of Assyria. The purpose of God for Israel is that they might be a teacher of, and a missionary to, all the families and peoples of the earth.

In Exodus 20 we find a list of the oracles and the covenant of God called the Ten Commandments. This is a disclosure of God's character. The two tables of the law of God were placed in the ark of the covenant, but the Ten Commandments and the covenant blessing in keeping them were meant for all the nations of the world.

In Exodus 19 God said to Israel: "Ye shall be unto me a kingdom of priests, and an holy nation" (v. 6). A priest brings a man to God. The purpose of the calling of Israel and of the delivery of the oracles of God to Israel was that Israel might be the great missionary-teacher of the covenant relationship of God to the whole world.

The Meaning of the Word "Burden"

We notice in this book of burdens that the address of God is to all the nations of the earth. Notice the reiterated use of that word "burden." "The burden of Tyre," "the burden of Egypt," "the burden of Arabia," and "the burden of Jerusalem." What is meant by the word "burden"? There is a good definition of it in Isaiah 22:

> In that day, saith the LORD of hosts, shall the nail that is fastened in the sure place be removed, and be cut down, and fall; and the burden that was upon it shall be cut off: for the LORD hath spoken it. (v. 25)

The word "burden" used here is the same word that is used to refer to the oracle of God delivered to each one of these nations.

The Hebrew word *nasa* means "to lift up a heavy load." Out of that Hebrew verb came a noun, *nasa*. *Nasa* means "a load that is lifted up." From that imagery came the idea that the delivery of the message of God was judgmental, weighty, and heavy. It is a

"burden" which you see in the message of God to the nations, a
message of terrible visitation.

For example, the burden of Babylon:

> And Babylon, the glory of kingdoms, the beauty of the Chaldees'
> excellency, shall be as when God overthrew Sodom and Gomorrah.
> It shall never be inhabited, neither shall it be dwelt in . . . wild
> beasts of the desert shall lie there. (Isa. 13:19-21)

Have you ever flown over Babylon? It is as desolate and barren as
the most wasted desert on the earth.

Consider the burden of Moab:

> In their streets they shall gird themselves with sackcloth: on the
> tops of their houses, and in their streets, every one shall howl,
> weeping abundantly. (Isa. 15:3)

Look at the burden of Damascus:

> Because thou hast forgotten the God of thy salvation, and hast not
> been mindful of the rock of thy strength, therefore shalt thou
> plant . . . thou shalt make the plant to grow . . . but the harvest
> shall be a heap in the day of grief and of desperate sorrow. (Isa.
> 17:10,11)

See the burden of Egypt:

> And the Egyptians will I give over into the hand of a cruel lord;
> and a fierce king shall rule over them, saith the Lord, the LORD of
> hosts. (Isa. 19:4)

Look at the burden of the desert of the sea:

> A grievous vision is declared unto me . . .
> Therefore are my loins filled with pain: pangs have taken hold
> upon me, as the pangs of a woman that travaileth: I was bowed down
> at the hearing of it; I was dismayed at the seeing of it.
> My heart panted, fearfulness affrighted me: the night of my
> pleasure hath he turned into fear unto me. (Isa. 21:2-4)

See the burden of Tyre:

> Howl, ye ships of Tarshish. . . . Is this your joyous city, whose
> antiquity is of ancient days? her own feet shall carry her afar off to
> sojourn. (Isa. 23:1a,7)

It is easy to see why the oracle of God should be termed "the burden of Babylon," "the burden of Arabia," "the burden of Tyre," "the burden of Egypt."

The word also describes the heavy heart of the messenger of God as he delivered his message. Jeremiah cried aloud under the message God gave him saying:

> Oh that my head were waters, and mine eyes a fountain of tears, that I might weep day and night for the slain of the daughter of my people! (Jer. 9:1)

> Then I said, I will not make mention of him, nor speak any more in his name. But his word was in mine heart as a burning fire shut up in my bones, and I was weary with forbearing, and I could not stay. (Jer. 20:9)

The word of the prophet was one that burned and seared. It was a burden from the Lord.

The same experience is found in the life of the prophet of Ezekiel. God said to Ezekiel:

> Moreover he said unto me, Son of man, eat that thou findest; eat this roll, and go speak unto the house of Israel.
> So I opened my mouth, and he caused me to eat that roll.
> And he said unto me, Son of man, cause thy belly to eat, and fill thy bowels with this roll that I give thee. Then did I eat it; and it was in my mouth as honey for sweetness. (Ezek. 3:1-3)

The words of God were sweet like honey, but the delivery of the message was bitter like gall.

In Revelation 10 a mighty angel descends from heaven with a book in his hand. He plants one foot on the land and the other foot on the sea, raises his hand toward almighty God, and swears by Him who lives forever that time shall be no longer; that is, these great prophetic events will now happen quickly. When the great consummation of the age arrives, everything will happen fast and furious — one event after another. God may delay for a long time, but when the great hour comes, it will happen swiftly. As the angel held up his hand swearing that these things would come quickly, the apostle took the book from the hand of the great angel and ate it:

And I went unto the angel, and said unto him, Give me the little
book. And he said unto me, Take it, and eat it up; and it shall make
thy belly bitter, but it shall be in thy mouth sweet as honey.

And I took the little book out of the angel's hand, and ate it up;
and it was in my mouth sweet as honey: and as soon as I had eaten it,
my belly was bitter.

And he said unto me, Thou must prophesy again before many
peoples, and nations, and tongues, and kings. (Rev. 10:9,11)

This is the burden of the prophecy, the oracle of God that is
weighty and judgmental.

God's Terrible Truths Are Not Glossed Over

The terrible truth in the Lord's message is never covered but is
always revealed and unhidden. "The word of God is quick, and
powerful, and sharper than any two-edged sword, piercing even to
the dividing asunder of soul and spirit, and of the joint and
marrow, and is a discerner of the thoughts and intents of the heart"
(Heb. 4:12). The Word of God is a burden.

In the beginning God said to our first parents: "In the day that
thou eatest thereof thou shalt surely die" (Gen. 2:17). We see the
terrible truth of the judgmental commandments of almighty God.
In following the Scriptures and coming to the Revelation it is no
less the same. God says to the seven last churches that represent the
course of Christendom: "Except thou repent, I will remove thy
candlestick out of his place" (Rev. 2:5). This is the burden of the
Word of the Lord.

One could not define it better than did the apostle Paul in
Romans 11. He explains the elective purpose of God in the
destruction of Jerusalem, the holy temple, and the state of Israel, and the scattering of the people through the earth. Then Paul
says:

Behold therefore the goodness and severity of God: on them
which fell, severity; but toward thee, goodness, if thou continue in
his goodness: otherwise thou also shalt be cut off. (Rom. 11:22)

There is a play on two words, "severity" and "be cut off," which are
translations of the noun form and the verbal form of the same
Greek word, *apotomia*, which means "cut off." This is the revela-

tion of the character and being of almighty God. He is terribly severe. This "cutting off" severity can be seen in the words of our Lord to the people of Judah in Luke:

> And when ye shall see Jerusalem compassed with armies, then know that the desolation thereof is nigh. . .
> But woe unto them that are with child, and to them that give suck, in those days! for there shall be great distress in the land, and wrath upon this people. (21:20,23)

There was a time in the severity of God when in the tragedy of the judgments of the Almighty the entire race was destroyed except for one family. This severity extended to Israel when Samaria was destroyed forever. Nineveh was destroyed forever. The Syrian empire was destroyed forever. The Lord is severe. There is no sensitive student of the story of Christendom who does not see that God always has sent His chastening forces — even against the church. I cannot but tremble in reading the Book of Hebrews. Listen as the author says:

> It is a fearful thing to fall into the hands of the living God. (10:31)

> For our God is a consuming fire. (12:29)

JUDGMENTAL LAWS ARE UNIVERSAL

Nor are these judgmental interventions of the Almighty unique or limited. They are universal and applicable everywhere. There is no section, people, time, age, or place in which one escapes. We are all under the great judgmental commandments and visitations of the Almighty in heaven. All that God does is universal.

For example, gravity is a reflection of the hand of the Almighty. One finds gravity here in the earth, in the smallest things and in the greatest things in the creation. It is in the stars, spheres, and planets, as well as on the moon. It is universal because God is universal. Fire is also universal, whether it be in the heat of the sun or in the earth or in the farthest star. All of God's character is revealed to us like that. Sowing and reaping are universal. As Paul wrote it, "Be not deceived; God is not mocked: for whatsoever a man soweth, that shall he also reap" (Gal. 6:7). There is no escape.

The judgment of God pursues a man's wrong. There is no hiding from it.

I pastored in a small town that had only one store. This was during the days of prohibition. The druggist, while selling his medicines, also sold boot-leg whiskey under the counter. As the days passed he became very affluent. He was not a Christian. I stood by his side and watched his twenty-four year old son die of cirrhosis of the liver caused by the liquor his father sold under the counter. Be not deceived; God's judgmental power is universal. God is not mocked.

One time I received a letter from a young woman who had taken her own life. The end of the letter asked me to bury her. Syphilis had begun to attack the soft tissues of her eyes and she was going blind. The promiscuous often shake their fists at God and say, "Ha." Be not deceived, God is not mocked. What you sow, that you also reap.

Were it not for the grace and mercy of God, we would be of all God's creations most miserable. Listen to Psalm 130:3,

> If thou, LORD, shouldest mark iniquities, O LORD, who shall stand?

No person can point an accusing finger at another and lift himself up in pride for his own sinlessness. We should be grateful God does not judge us by our iniquities. Who then could stand?

Does the vicious cycle of sin and death ever stop? Does it continue forever? God came to intervene and break that tragic cycle. Paul wrote in 1 Timothy:

> This is a faithful saying, and worthy of all acceptation, that Christ Jesus came into the world to save sinners; of whom I am chief. (1:15)

The great Redeemer came to break that awesome judgment of the fire and fury of God against our sins that we might have hope in God.

15

Lucifer

How art thou fallen from heaven, O Lucifer, son of the morning! how art thou cut down to the ground, which didst weaken the nations!

For thou hast said in thine heart, I will ascend into heaven, I will exalt my throne above the stars of God: I will sit also upon the mount of the congregation, in the sides of the north:

I will ascend above the heights of the clouds; I will be like the most High.

Yet thou shalt be brought down to hell, to the sides of the pit. (Isa. 14:12-15)

There is conflict and a presence of evil in the earth. I see it in my own heart, but thinking that it might be unique to me, I look around and I see conflict and the presence of evil in all the world. We study the pages of human history and find the same conflict and the same presence of evil through all of human history. Finally we go back to the Garden of Eden and find the Fall, disintegration, and conflict and evil, but outside the gates of the Garden of Eden there is a sinister and unusual creature. Who is he and where did he come from? In his able brilliance he encompassed the fall of our first parents and the destruction of the human

race. Who is that one so able, so brilliant, so gifted outside the gate
of the Garden of Eden?

Who Lives in the Third Heaven?

For our introduction to this unusual and sinister creature we
must rise to heaven, to the third heaven where God is and where
all the celestial angels of God abide. Who is there? First of all, we
find God, the one almighty God; God who in His essence and
being is revealed to us as the mighty Father; the one God who in
His creation and redemptive work is revealed to us as the *Logos*;
the one God who in His omnipresence in the earth and in our
hearts is revealed to us as the Holy Spirit.

Who else is in heaven besides God? There is also the mighty
host of celestial creations. There are the seraphim who lead in the
praise of the holiness of God, crying, "Holy, Holy, Holy." In
heaven there are also the cherubim who are the messengers and
representatives of the mercy of the Almighty. There are myriads of
angels — *angels* refers to "messengers." These are the messengers
of God who do His bidding in the earth. For example, Gabriel is
an angel who was sent to announce to Zacharias that he and aged
Elizabeth should bear a son whom they would name John. The
same Gabriel six months later was sent on a mission to Nazareth to
announce to a Jewish maiden named Mary that she was to be the
mother of a foretold messianic child. Two of the angels of God
went to Sodom and Gomorrah as instruments of destruction. An
angel destroyed Israel by pestilence because of the sin of David.
Just one angel went through the camp of Sennacherib and left
behind 185,000 of the army dead. When I think of the power
invested in those messengers of the Almighty I remember what
Jesus meant when He said:

> Thinkest thou that I cannot now pray to my Father, and he
> shall presently give me more than twelve legions of angels? (Matt.
> 26:53)

The Lord in the New Testament is called Lord of hosts, that is,
Lord of the angelic hosts in glory. There is also one archangel in
heaven. In the New Testament he is called chief angel. His name

is Michael and he represents the presence and power of God. His name means "Who is like God." He stands for the people of the Lord. He wars for the redeemed of the Almighty.

Lucifer, "The Shining One"

But there was one other angel in heaven. Over all the creation of God and over all the celestial hosts of our Lord, God created a being whom He named Lucifer. Seraphim means "the burning ones." Lucifer means "the brilliant one" or "the lighted one." To his care God assigned the over-lordship of all His creation in earth and in heaven. He is described in his glory and beauty in Ezekiel 28 as:

> . . . Thou sealest up the sum, full of wisdom, and perfect in beauty.
>
> Thou hast been in Eden the garden of God; every precious stone was thy covering, the sardius, topaz, and the diamond, the beryl, the onyx and the jasper, the sapphire, the emerald, and the carbuncle, and gold: the workmanship of thy tabrets and of thy pipes was prepared in thee in the day that thou wast created.
>
> Thou art the anointed cherub that covereth; and I have set thee so: thou wast upon the holy mountain of God; thou hast walked up and down in the midst of the stones of fire.
>
> Thou wast perfect in thy ways from the day that thou wast created, till iniquity was found in thee . . . .
>
> Thou hast sinned: therefore I will cast thee as profane out of the mountain of God: and I will destroy thee, O covering cherub, from the midst of the stones of fire.
>
> Thine heart was lifted up because of thy beauty, thou hast corrupted thy wisdom by reason of thy brightness. (vv. 12-17a)

There are five "I wills" against God. The origin of conflict and the origin of evil lies in the proud heart of Lucifer, the son of the morning, the shining one, the great light-bearer whom God set over all His creation.

The Fall of Lucifer Results in Unspeakable Catastrophe

There are four repercussions from the fall of Lucifer. The first repercussion is found in Lucifer himself. He changed and became something else. His name originally was Lucifer, the son of the morning. He became *Satan*, the Hebrew word, and he became

Diabolis, the New Testament Greek word. Both words mean "slanderer," "enemy," "opposer." He rebelled in his heart against God. His beauty and power convinced him that he had the ability to take the throne of God himself and he reached out his hand to seize it. Fallen, he is still the same; he is beautiful. In 2 Corinthians 4 Paul refers to him as "the god of this world." In 2 Corinthians 11 he refers to him as "the angel of light." Despite the fact that he is now fallen, Lucifer is still the same beautiful, glorious, incomparable person God created him in the beginning. He still rules over God's created universe. But he is no longer Lucifer the son of the morning, he is Diabolis, the adversary of God and man.

The second repercussion is found in the angels who cast their lot with him. In Revelation 12 we learn that one-third of the angels of heaven defected from God in order to follow the leadership of their great angel Lucifer. One may wonder how someone could leave God in order to follow Satan? Then why do you do it? Why does the world do it? We turn aside from the holiness and purity of God in order to be a disciple of Lucifer. Why? Because the devil is full of promises, excitement, and allurement. One-third of the angels of heaven chose to follow Lucifer when he rebelled against God.

The third repercussion is found in the destruction of God's handiwork, the creation above and around us. In Job 30 we are told that when God made the world and the universe, the stars sang together and all the sons of God rejoiced. "Stars" and "sons of God" refer to the angels. When they saw the creation of God's hands, the beauty of the whole universe, they sang and rejoiced. It was a world of beauty and harmony. But when Satan fell, he destroyed that universe. Wherever sin enters it destroys, it ruins, it corrupts, and it did so in God's beautiful universe. In Genesis 1 we read the result of his fall:

> And the earth was without form, and void; and darkness was upon the face of the deep. (v. 2a)

The fourth repercussion is the conflict that has raged throughout the ages between Satan and the hosts of the angels of God. A

part of that conflict we can see in the earth. In Genesis 3 God
predicted the course of that conflict.

> And I will put enmity between thee and the woman, and between
> thy seed and her seed; it shall bruise thy head, and thou shalt bruise
> his heel. (v. 15)

That conflict has been witnessed from the beginning. One sees
only a small example of it in the story of the temptation of our
Lord.

Driven into the wilderness, our Lord was tried by Satan. We get
the idea from the translation in the King James version that Satan
said to the Lord Jesus, "*If* you are the Son of God, turn these stones
into bread." Jesus and Satan knew each other from the beginning
of Lucifer's creation and they had confronted each other from the
outset. What Lucifer actually said was an avowal: "*Since* you are
the Son of God, turn the stones into bread." He wanted our Lord
to undo the whole redemptive purpose of His incarnation, the
reason He assumed flesh and form in the world.

THE CONFLICT IS IN HEAVEN AS IN EARTH

The conflict has continued through the centuries. We observe
this in the earth. But by revelation we are introduced to that
conflict in heaven. In the heavens Satan stands to accuse us. He is
the adversary and accuser of the brethren. Day and night he lays
our sins in castigation before God. In Job we read that he goes in
and out when the angels appear before the Father (1:6). Satan is in
heaven and is the mightiest of all God's creations. To show you
how mighty he is, let us compare him with Michael, the one
archangel of God

In Daniel 10 and 12, when Lucifer intervened, it took the angels
and Michael standing by their side to get a message through to the
weeping, fasting, and praying Daniel. We read in Daniel 10:

> But the prince of the kingdom of Persia withstood me one and
> twenty days: but, low, Michael, one of the chief princes, came to
> help me; and I remained there with the kings of Persia. (v. 13)

A far greater demonstration of the superior might of Lucifer is
found in Jude 9:

> Yet Michael the archangel, when contending with the devil he disputed about the body of Moses, durst not bring against him a railing accusation, but said, The Lord rebuke thee.

What did the devil want with the body of Moses? For 700 years the brazen serpent that Moses lifted up in the midst of the camp was an idolatrous snare to the people of God. When good King Hezekiah came to the throne, he broke it to pieces. Can you imagine what a snare to idolatry it would have been had Satan been able to seize the body of Moses and preserve it there for the people to see?

How strange people are. The Russians say they do not believe in God but everyone seems to have to worship something. One day I stood in line to walk by and look on the pale face of Nikolai Lenin. Since 1924 thousands of people gather every day to pay obeisance to the dead form of Lenin. Can you imagine what a snare it would have been to idolatry had Satan been able to seize the body of Moses and bring it before the people and let them bow before the great lawgiver? Michael the archangel, when contending with Satan, dared not accuse him but said: "The Lord rebuke thee." Satan is by far the mightier.

THE FINAL CONFRONTATION

But let us look at the final confrontation between Michael and Satan in heaven. For the Scriptures say by inspiration in 1 Thessalonians:

> For the Lord himself shall descend from heaven with a shout, with the voice of the archangel, and with the trump of God: and the dead in Christ shall rise first:
> Then we which are alive and remain shall be caught up together with them in the clouds, to meet the Lord in the air: and so shall we ever be with the Lord. (4:16,17)

By inspiration it is revealed to the apostle Paul that the end of the age will be announced by the voice of the archangel. At the sound of Michael's voice all the dead in Christ will rise and the living will be raptured, glorified in the twinkling of an eye. The voice of Michael the archangel will introduce Christ as He descends from heaven and welcomes His saints who are raised from the dead and transfigured in a moment.

However, Satan has gathered together his angels to confront almighty God and Michael, saying, "These bodies are mine." Satan thus challenges Michael. Michael gathers the angels of God together and confronts Satan for one final time. The Bible records the battle in Revelation 12:

> And there was war in heaven: Michael and his angels fought against the dragon; and the dragon fought and his angels,
>
> And prevailed not; neither was their place found any more in heaven.
>
> And the great dragon was cast out, that old serpent, called the Devil, and Satan, which deceiveth the whole world: he was cast out into the earth, and his angels were cast out with him.
>
> And I heard a loud voice saying in heaven, Now is come salvation, and strength, and the kingdom of our God, and the power of his Christ: for the accuser of our brethren is cast down, which accused them before our God day and night. . .
>
> Therefore rejoice, ye heavens, and ye that dwell in them. Woe to the inhabiters of the earth and of the sea! for the devil is come down unto you, having great wrath, because he knoweth that he hath but a short time. (vv. 7-10,12)

When God flings Satan forever out of heaven and he is cast down to the earth, woe to the earth and its inhabitants. How can any of us escape if Michael cringes before him?

In the Book of Revelation we read that the saved ones have been sealed by the seal of God. They are saved by the blood of the crucified One. That means our great defender Michael is standing by our side and the guardian angels of heaven have given themselves to present us some day to the living Lord.

What a hope we have in God. God makes us strong and able over our adversary. He is victory and triumph forever. Praise His name!

16

Peace Between Jew and Arab

In that day shall five cities in the land of Egypt speak the language
of Canaan, and swear to the LORD of hosts; one shall be called, The
city of destruction.

In that day shall there be an altar to the LORD in the midst of the
land of Egypt, and a pillar at the border thereof to the LORD.

And it shall be for a sign and for a witness unto the LORD of hosts
in the land of Egypt: for they shall cry unto the LORD because of the
oppressors, and he shall send them a saviour, and a great one, and
he shall deliver them.

And the LORD shall be known to Egypt, and the Egyptians shall
know the LORD in that day, and shall do sacrifice and oblation; yea,
they shall vow a vow unto the LORD, and perform it.

And the LORD shall smite Egypt: and he shall smite and heal it:
and they shall return even to the LORD, and he shall be entreated of
them, and shall heal them.

In that day shall there be a highway out of Egypt to Assyria, and
the Assyrian shall come into Egypt, and the Egyptian into Assyria,
and the Egyptians shall serve with the Assyrians.

In that day shall Israel be the third with Egypt and with Assyria,
even a blessing in the midst of the land:

Whom the LORD of hosts shall bless, saying, Blessed be Egypt my
people, and Assyria the work of my hands, and Israel mine inheritance. (Isa. 19:18-25)

We look first at the nations that are named in this golden

prophecy. Had the prophecy been read a few years ago a critic could have said: "Such events are impossible of realization for there is no state of Israel nor has there been for centuries." But God says the people will return to the land and there will be a nation in Palestine called Israel. In our lifetime we have seen that prophecy of God come to pass, and the prophecy in our text concerns the state of Israel and their enemies.

The prophecy also concerns Egypt and Assyria. Today we do not know Assyria by that name because the great empire has been broken up. Today we would say Syria, Jordan, and Saudi Arabia, or, as the newspapers lump them together, the Arab world.

The prophecy concerns the bitter enemies of Israel. Far to the north of the state of Israel was Assyria, and to the south was Egypt. Between those two great empires in ancient days, Israel was a common battlefield. She was invaded, ravaged, and taken captive by first one and then the other. The story of the ancient empires of the world is a story of the merciless and ruthless ravaging of the people of God. From Egypt on the south there were those who slew good King Josiah. From Assyria on the north there was Tiglath-pileser and others who laid the foundation for the Maccabean revolt. The ancient story has been nothing other than the cruel and merciless ravaging of the state of Israel — nor has the modern prophecy of the state been any different. Our Lord said, "Behold, your house is left unto you desolate."

ISRAEL TODAY IS ALSO SURROUNDED BY OPPRESSIVE ENEMIES

The modern story of Israel has been the same record of tears, agony, and torment. Ever since Israel became a state they have either faced the prospect of war or were in conflict. In 1948 and 1949 the War of Independence took place. In 1956 it was the Sinai War. In 1967 it was the Six-Day War. In 1970 they were involved in the War of Attrition, and in 1973 it was the Yom Kippur War. Israel's history has been one of bloodshed, misery, agony, and torment. Israel is surrounded by fifty million hostile Arabs and they are a tiny country of less than three million Jews.

THE GOLDEN MILLENNIAL FUTURE

Can you imagine, therefore, that such a prophecy as found in our text should ever come to pass? The prophet lifts up his eyes to the day of the millennial kingdom of our Savior, and sees that the land of Egypt will speak the language of Canaan, that is, the language of Zion, the language of the people of God. They will swear to the Lord of hosts. They will pledge allegiance to the great God of the universe. In that day there will be an altar and a pillar to the Lord in the land of Egypt, and it will be for a sign and witness to the Lord of hosts in the land of Egypt. It will be erected at the border between Egypt to the south and Israel to the north and will be a witness that both nations worship the great God Jehovah. Egypt will cry to the Lord because of their oppressors and God will send them a Savior, even the Lord Christ, and He will deliver them. The Lord will be known to Egypt, and the Egyptians will vow a vow to the Lord and perform it. The Lord will smite Egypt whom He loves, and Egypt will be smitten because of her transgressions. But God will also heal Egypt. They will return to the Lord. In that day a highway will come out of Egypt to Assyria and the Assyrians will come into Egypt and the Egyptians will go into Assyria. The Egyptians will serve God with the Assyrians and in that day Israel will be the third nation with Egypt and with Assyria, a blessing in the midst of the world.

Israel belongs particularly to God as the leader of the people of the world. Can you imagine that a time would ever come when there would be peace and communion between Israel and her bitter enemies who seek the destruction of her state and life? Yet, this is what God is promising to the Arab world.

We have a tendency to feel that God forgets His covenants, for the years pass and some of His promises are not fulfilled. Remember what Peter said in 2 Peter 3:

> Knowing this first, that there shall come in the last days scoffers, walking after their own lusts,
> And saying, Where is the promise of his coming? for since the fathers fell asleep, all things continue as they were from the beginning of the creation. (vv. 3,4)

We have not seen all these events come to pass, but God never forgets. This prophecy concerns a covenant that God made with Abraham for his son Ishmael.

GOD'S REMEMBRANCE OF ISHMAEL

All of the Arab world looks to Ishmael as their father. The followers of Mohammed look upon themselves as the descendants of Isaac and Israel. In the Scriptures the Arab is looked upon and is referred to as a descendant of Ishmael. What is this covenant and holy promise that God made with the Arab world? We read about it in Genesis 16. Sarah, who was barren, suggested to her husband Abraham that he father a child by Hagar, her maid. Abraham listened to the voice of his wife and became the father of Hagar's son, Ishmael. When Hagar saw that she had conceived, she looked haughtily upon her mistress, and Sarah was envious of her. So Abraham and Sarah sent Hagar away. As she wandered in the south of the desert an angel of the Lord spake to her:

> And the angel of the LORD said unto her, Return to thy mistress, and submit thyself under her hands.
> And the angel of the LORD said unto her, I will multiply thy seed exceedingly, that it shall not be numbered for multitude.
> And the angel of the LORD said unto her, Behold, thou art with child, and shall bear a son, and shall call his name Ishmael; because the LORD hath heard thy affliction. (Gen. 16:9-11)

We read in Genesis 17 that Ishmael is thirteen years of age when God makes a covenant with Abraham. God says that Sarah, though she is ninety years of age and barren, will give birth to a child, and from his seed the great Messiah will be born. But Abraham asked the Lord to make His covenant with Ishmael. God told him no, it would be a child from Sarah's womb. "As for Ishmael, I have heard thee: Behold, I have blessed him and will make him fruitful, and will multiply him exceedingly; twelve princes shall he beget, and I will make him a great nation."

In the same chapter, Genesis 17, we read of Isaac's birth. Abraham was one hundred years old and Sarah ninety years old at the time and they had laughed when God told them they would have a child. Thus they called the boy *Isaac*, meaning "laughter."

In Genesis 21 we read that Ishmael ridiculed and made fun of Isaac, and his mother, Sarah, was unhappy. We read:

> And Sarah saw the son of Hagar the Egyptian, which she had born unto Abraham, mocking.
>
> Wherefore she said unto Abraham, Cast out this bondwoman and her son: for the son of this bondwoman shall not be heir with my son, even with Isaac. (vv. 9,10)

So a second time Hagar was cast out, this time with a son thirteen years of age. Wandering in the desert of the south she laid the boy under the shade of a desert plant and hid her face so she might not see the boy die. While Hagar wept and cried before the Lord, God visited her once again. He repeated the covenant He made with Abraham regarding Ishmael:

> And she went, and sat her down over against him a good way off, as it were a bowshot: for she said, Let me not see the death of the child. And she sat over against him, and lift up her voice, and wept.
>
> And God heard the voice of the lad; and the angel of God called to Hagar out of heaven, and said unto her, What aileth thee, Hagar? fear not; for God hath heard the voice of the lad where he is.
>
> Arise, lift up the lad, and hold him in thine hand; for I will make him a great nation. (Gen. 21:16-18)

In Genesis 25 we read that Ishmael and Isaac have come together to bury their father, Abraham. In that chapter the greatness of Ishmael is recounted. He is the father of twelve sons as Jacob, Israel, was the father of the twelve patriarchs. He is the foundation of the great Arab community as we know it today. God is remembering His covenant promise to Ishmael. God says he also will be greatly blessed and we are beginning to see the blessing of God upon the descendants and children of Ishmael.

I remember once, while flying along the coast of the Persian Gulf, I looked out the window, and to my right was the most wasted desert land I had seen. I asked the steward what country that was and he replied, "That is Saudi Arabia." I saw the same thing later in a jet following the coast of the Red Sea. Twice I have flown across the Sahara from one side to the other, and I have never seen a land more desolate. The second richest nation in the world, next to the might of industrial United States of America, is Saudi Arabia. A wasted and desert land is the home of the children of Ishmael.

Who put that oil there — billions of barrels of it? The Lord placed it there. It is a part of the covenant God made with the children of Ishmael. "That they also shall be greatly blessed."

<h3 align="center">The Jew and Egyptian Will Be Saved</h3>

Will the Jew and Arab always hate each other, war against each other, and seek the destruction of each other? Is that the way it is to be for all of time? The prophet lifts up his voice and prophesies of the glorious millennial kingdom of our Savior. Who will be in it?

The Jew will be in it. He will lead the nation as the priests of God in the spiritual service of almighty God. We read about the conversion of the Jew in Zechariah 12 – 14. The prophet says that a time is coming when the Messiah will appear to the nation of Israel. He sees them back in their land, gathered from the east and west. They will ask the Messiah, "Where did you get those scars in your hands and in your feet?" He will reply, "From my own people. I came to my own and my own did not receive me." The prophet says that seeing Him whom they have pierced, they will wail because of Him. They will cry in repentance and there will be a great mourning. All Israel will cry before God and repent of their sins and receive the Lord Jesus as Savior. Then shall come to pass one of the strangest verses in the Bible:

And so all Israel shall be saved. (Rom. 11:26)

Think of it! A whole nation born in a day when the covenant of God with the children of Isaac is faithfully remembered, and the people come in trust and belief before Christ. God never forgets His promise, and He has made a promise to the Jew. The Jew will be saved and he will be the leader of the spiritual worship of the nations of the earth in that great day.

There are others also who are saved. "For [Egypt] shall cry unto the Lord because of the oppressors, and he shall send them a saviour, and a great one, and he shall deliver them." What a glorious prophecy! Christ will include in His millennial kingdom the children of Ishmael, the Arab world. They will repent and will trust in the Lord and be saved. They will bow down to the Lord and pledge allegiance to the great King.

> For the love of God is broader
> Than the measure of man's mind,
> And the heart of the Eternal
> Is most wonderfully kind.

God has a purpose and program for the Arab as well as for the Jew. In time He will bring to a consummation that glorious tomorrow.

We Also Can Be Saved

But what of us? I am not a child of Ishmael. I am not an Arab. I am not a child of Isaac or of Israel. What about us who are Gentiles?

Christ extends His hands in the name of the Lord to the Gentiles. We read in 2 Corinthians:

> For he saith, I have heard thee in a time accepted, and in the day of salvation have I succoured thee: behold, now is the accepted time; behold, now is the day of salvation. (6:2)

To us who are Gentiles the covenant of the Lord is opened wide. We also can be saved. We can belong to the covenant children of God by faith in the great Redeemer Christ Jesus.

A eunuch stood in the presence of Philip and asked: "I am a dry and dead branch. Can I be saved?" Philip answered and said, "If you believe with all your heart, you may." And he was baptized into the family of God.

The centurion said to the apostle Peter: "I am the leader of an occupation army, hated and despised. Can I be saved?" Peter replied, "Whosoever believes in His name will receive remission of sins." And the household of Cornelius was added to the kingdom of God.

The cruel Philippian jailer fell down before Paul and Silas and cried, saying, "Is it possible I could be saved?" They replied, "Believe on the Lord Jesus Christ and thou shalt be saved."

Lydia, the merchant woman, bowing before the apostles of Christ says, "Could it be that a woman could be saved?" The apostle replied, "This day is salvation come to the household of Lydia, the merchant woman."

Oh, the golden tomorrows that God has reserved for those who trust in Him. That is the spirit of the Book: always there is a greater day coming. The kingdom is coming! He taught us to pray:

> Our Father which art in heaven,
> Hallowed be thy name,
> Thy kingdom come. Thy will be done
> In earth, as it is in heaven.

The Assyrian will join hands with the Egyptian and the two will join hands with the Jew. It will be a glorious and triumphant day God has in store for the nations of the earth.

17
Watchman, What of the Night?

The burden of Dumah. He calleth to me out of Seir, Watchman, what of the night? Watchman, what of the night?

The watchman said, The morning cometh, and also the night: if ye will inquire, inquire ye: return, come. (Isa. 21:11,12)

A casual reading of the passage can leave us with a feeling of riddle or lack of understanding, but by studying the text, and especially its Hebrew words, it unfolds before us a solemn and sober message.

Mt. Seir was Esau's home. His name also is Edom, meaning "red." The Edomites lived in Mt. Seir. Their ancient capital was discovered in recent archaeological finds. The capital is Petra, one of the most unusual capitals in the world, for it was carved out of solid rock. The country was located in the rugged desert terrain south of the Dead Sea. It was in the Edomite land where the descendants of Esau cried out in their agony and desperation.

The intensity of the cry of Edom is emphatically expressed in the Hebrew text. It is a present tense. The repetitive question emphasizes the urgency of his anxiety, "Watchman, what of the night?" It is identical to the cry of a man who is desperately hurting or is sick. In the agony of the interminable hours of the night he

129

calls: "How much of the night is past?" That is the Hebrew meaning of the text. The watchman replied, "The morning cometh, and also the night." Then in the text there is a hint of a word of hope. "If you will come back converted, I will have for you a message of hope. If there is no change, there is no hope but only the remaining of a people enveloped in the continuing night."

In the text the address is to the prophet. Were there no diviners in Edom to whom the nation could address their queries? Were there no astrologers there? Why do they come to this prophet in Jerusalem with their agonizing cries?

Astrologers, diviners, and soothsayers are sufficient for a temporal time when things for the most part are going well. But in the hour of agony and death, who wants a diviner? Who wants worldly wisdom? Who finds answers in culture or in silence or in tradition? What the heart cries for and the soul longs for is the question: Does God speak? What does God say?

One of the most poignant stories in the Old Testament comes from the life of Ahab when he was preparing to go to Ramoth-gilead, and he asked Jehoshaphat to join forces with him against the heathen bastion. Ahab gathered around him all his diviners and sorcerers who said, "Victory and triumph." Jehoshaphat, as he listened to the cry of the sorcerers, turned to Ahab and said, "Is there yet in Israel a man of God of whom we might inquire?" Ahab replied, "Yes, his name is Michaiah, but I hate him." Jehosaphat asked that he be brought to him, whereupon Michaiah delivered God's message, "You will come back from this battle slain." In the battle a man drew back his bow without aiming, and it found a joint in the harness of Ahab, pierced his heart, and his blood poured out into the chariot. When they brought the chariot back to Jezreel they washed it out and the dogs licked up the blood according to the saying of the man of God. Diviners have interesting things to say in good times, but in the day of agony and darkness, people look for a man of God.

WHO HAS A NIGHT?

The nations of the world have a night. We sometimes are

inclined to think that the ancient days were peculiar to that which we read in the Scriptures. But they are exactly like our days. In Isaiah's days he had a message for Egypt, Syria, Moab, Lebanon, Tyre, Babylon, and Assyria. The same Lord God has a message today for all the nations of the world.

In 1914 the Foreign Minister of the British Empire was a godly man named Lord Gray. In a session of the cabinet that lasted through the night, it was decided to go to war against Germany. In the early hours of the morning, just as it began to dawn, Lord Gray walked out of the foreign office with one of his cabinet officers. When he stood on the steps he saw down the street the lamplighter putting out the gas lights. Lord Gray, seeing that, turned to his companion and said, "See, the lights are going out over all of Europe."

The Allied Powers were triumphant in the war against Germany between 1914 and 1918. "The morning cometh, and also the night." For a period after the war there was infinite optimism and rejoicing in the earth. I grew up in that wonderful era of golden optimism. I also lived to see the rise of Hitler and to see the great armies of the Allied powers drawn against the bastions of continental Europe. I lived in the days when Hitler was destroyed, but we really only traded Hitler for Stalin. We traded fascism for communism. We traded the freedom of that golden vision of the latter 1920s for the despair that grips millions of people of the earth today. There are something like two billion people who are under the iron hand of communism today.

A recent article which appeared in a Foreign Mission Board news digest states: "Johannesburg, South Africa: Southern Baptist Missionaries to Mozambique have withdrawn to South Africa. The overall political climate makes it impossible to continue our missionary work." This is the darkness that is settling over the face of the earth.

The nations of the earth have a night. There are some nations that have no future and no destiny. Edom was one of those nations. We read in Psalm 137:

> By the rivers of Babylon, there we sat down, yea, we wept, when we remembered Zion.

> We hanged our harps upon the willows in the midst thereof.
> Remember, O LORD, the children of Edom in the day of Jeru-
> salem; who said, Rase it, rase it, even to the foundation thereof.
> (vv. 1,2,7)

They rejoiced over the destruction of Solomon's temple and the destruction of the nation of Judah. Continuing in this passage we read:

> O daughter of Babylon, who art to be destroyed; happy shall he
> be, that rewardeth thee as thou hast served us.
> Happy shall he be, that taketh and dasheth thy little ones against
> the stones. (vv. 8,9)

There are nations such as Edom that have no destiny and no future. Russia is another nation with no future but whose destiny is one of absolute annihilation.

The notorious French scientist, Blaise Pascal, cried, "The silence of the universe frightens me." How much more when God turns His face and refuses to answer, and a nation and a people die.

THE LOST

Do you suppose America will live? I do not know. The psalmist said, "The wicked shall be turned into hell, and all the nations that forget God" (Ps. 9:17). As fast as we can forget and as rapidly as we can reject God's Holy Word, America is turning away from God. Who has a night?

Sin has a night. The fruits and results of sin work in every man's soul and life. One does not have to go around condemning and judging. Sin has its own night. Paul says:

> Be not deceived; God is not mocked: for whatsoever a man
> soweth, that shall he also reap. (Gal. 6:7)

In Hebrews we read:

> . . . Vengeance belongeth unto me, I will recompense, saith the
> Lord. And again, The Lord shall judge his people
> It is a fearful thing to fall into the hands of the living God.
> For our God is a consuming fire. (10:30,31; 12:29)

Do you remember when Jesus took the sop and gave it to Judas Iscariot? Having received the sop, Judas went out immediately —

"and it was night." Why was that observation added to the record? Sin has a night.

There was a night in the life of Edom and Esau. How poignantly the Book of Hebrews describes it when the author says:

> . . . Esau, who for one morsel of meat sold his birthright.
> For ye know that afterward, when he would have inherited the
> blessing, he was rejected: for he found no place of repentance,
> though he sought it carefully with tears. (12:16b,17)

This was Esau's night.

Adam had a night. God told him if he ate of the fruit he would surely die. I wonder if he and Eve remembered that when they stood over the silent form of their son Abel.

Jerusalem had a night. "Behold," said our Lord, "your house is left unto you desolate." The great Christian world has a night. I was in Istanbul in 1950 when they were building enormous monuments, one of which was a wide boulevard many miles long. The Turks were getting ready for the five-hundredth anniversary of the destruction of the Christian faith in that country and the rising of the star of Mohammed. When one looks at the greatest church in Christendom, St. Sophia, he sees the crescent of Islam instead of the cross. As I looked upon it I remembered the words of the Lord, "Except you repent, I will remove your lampstand out of its place." Sin has a night.

Death has a night. "I will pull down my barns, and build greater" (Luke 12:18). When the rich man finished it he looked over the work and the prosperity of his hands and said: "Soul, thou hast much goods laid up for many years: take thine ease, eat, drink, and be merry" (Luke 12:19). That night the Lord said: "Thou fool, this night thy soul shall be required of thee: then whose shall those things be which thou has provided? So is he that layeth up treasure for himself, and is not rich toward God" (Luke 12:20,21). Death has a night.

The judgment has a night. "Depart from me, I never knew you." With no Savior we are alone in the presence of our sins and rejections.

Hell has a night. "And they shall be cast out into outer dark-

ness." Never be persuaded by those who describe hell as being a
boon companion and convocation of all who are going to eat,
drink, and be merry in damnation. The Bible says you are by
yourself, weeping and wailing, tormented day and night —
forever.

THE BURDEN OF DUMAH

How does the prophet react to this judgment of Edom? It begins
with "The burden of Edom." I have heard men preach on hell,
judgment, and damnation as though with triumph and victory.
What is the biblical attitude toward the revelation of that awesome
doctrine?

The Bible speaks of it as a burden. Isaiah did not rejoice to see
his people sink into gloom and silence and into the grave. It was a
burden to his heart. Any time a man preaches on hell and damnation, he should do it with tears and a broken heart. To see a family
and people destroyed should be a subject of weeping and lamenta-
tion.

I well remember the first drunkard I buried in my first pastorate.
He was run over by a car. He was a vile and evil man. When I held
his funeral service, people came from all around to see what the
preacher would say about that man. I said to them: "All of us know
the life he has lived and how he died. What I would like to know is,
was there anyone here who wept over him? Was there anyone here
who went to his home and prayed with him? Is there anyone here
who tried to win him to Jesus?" The service was one of self-
condemnation.

This is our assignment: not to condemn, not to judge, no matter
what the person does. Our assignment is to pray, love, weep, visit,
and bring the person to God. "Vengeance is mine; I will repay,
saith the Lord." The Lord will judge His people.

18

To Whom God Teaches His Doctrine

> Whom shall he teach knowledge? and whom shall he make to understand doctrine? them that are weaned from the milk, and drawn from the breasts.
>
> For precept must be upon precept, precept upon precept; line upon line, line upon line; here a little, and there a little. (Isa. 28:9,10)

There are two approaches to this passage in Isaiah. By far the majority of Hebrew scholars will say that the prophet repeats here the critics who scornfully mocked and ridiculed his message. The chapter begins with the prophet addressing the drunkards of Ephraim. Then he turns to Jerusalem in verse 14: ". . . ye scornful men, that rule this people which is in Jerusalem." These so-called wise and gifted rulers of the people who themselves were antithetic to the Word of God, scoffed and ridiculed the message of the prophet Isaiah.

If I could phrase this passage in my own words it would go like this. The scoffers and those who were ridiculing Isaiah say: "What does he think we are? Does he think that we are babes, just weaned from the breast, that we are little ones who need to be taught in monotonous syllables? For that is the way Isaiah speaks to us. He is repetitious. He deals in trifles. He says it and says it — a line here, a line there, a precept here, a precept there, til we are weary of it." Practically all Hebrew scholars will say that is the meaning of the text.

In 2 Corinthians 10 Paul refers to something similar. Those who ridiculed the apostle Paul said:

> For his letters, say they, are weighty and powerful; but his bodily presence is weak, and his speech contemptible. (10:10)

That is an unusual thing to say about a mighty apostle like Paul, but that is what they said about him. Also in Acts 17 we see the Athenian philosopher's reaction to Paul. He was called a *spermalogos*, a "seed-picker," one who deals in repetition. That was said about Isaiah, too, and he is quoting here what his enemies said as they ridiculed and scoffed at him.

There are also some scholars who will say that the prophet is only describing the simplicity of his message, that when he delivers the message from God, he does it in a way so simple that a child who cannot read or write but who knows only by listening, could not miss its meaning. It is plain and simple. Isaiah delivered the message of God in simplistic words and fashion.

However one would interpret the verse, the ultimate meaning is the same. The message of God truly delivered is always plain. It is simple. Even a child can understand it. Those who refuse the message of God do not do so because they do not understand it, but because they are obdurate and incorrigible.

So the prophet begins: "Whom shall he teach knowledge?" *Daah*, "good knowledge," is the same word he used in the eleventh chapter when he said, "The earth shall be full of the [*daah*] knowledge of the LORD, as the waters cover the sea" (v. 9). "And whom shall he make to understand doctrine?" *Shemuah*, "doctrine," is that which is heard, that which God says. What is that *shemuah* and *daah*, that knowledge and doctrine?

What Doctrine Is

First, doctrine is not that narrow trick by which debating denominationalists beat one another over the head. That is not the knowledge and doctrine of God. The knowledge and doctrine of

God is the summation of God's self-revelation to us. This is what He is like and those great truths are encased in the holy pages of the Bible; and we call them the doctrines of faith.

For example, when the Lord finished the Sermon on the Mount He so amazed the people who listened to Him as He spoke of His heavenly Father, that the Scriptures say they were astonished at His *didoxe*. Again, in the Book of Acts, the Sanhedrin called in the apostles whom they interdicted speaking in the name of Jesus and said to them: "You have filled all Jerusalem with your *didoxe*."

What is that *didoxe*? Let us look at it in two languages. *Didasko* is the Greek word for "teach." *Didaskolos* is a "teacher" and *didoxe* is "what is taught." In Latin *docere* means "to teach." *Doctor* is a "teacher," and *doctrina* is "the teaching." So the King James Version rightly translates the word, "And they were astonished at his *didoxe*, doctrine." The teaching and truth of almighty God is doctrine. Every department of God's Word has its *didoxe*, its teaching, or truth.

Music has its truths and teaching, as does astronomy, biology, chemistry, and physics. It is true in all of God's creation, but this is the work of God. When one studies doctrine, he is studying God Himself. To know the truth is to know the Lord Himself. We read in John 17:3, "And this is life eternal, that they might know thee the only true God and Jesus Christ, whom thou hast sent."

Doctrine is also the essence and the substance of the strength of the Christian faith. Without it the Christian system is nothing but a sentimental, formless mass of moralistic cliches. We need the great revelation and truths of God in order that we might have a foundation upon which to stand and in order that we might stand ourselves.

One of the great systematic theologies of all time was written by A. H. Strong, a mighty Baptist theologian. In that systematic theology he wrote this sentence: "A man need not carry his backbone in front of him, but he needs to have one, and a straight one, or else he will be a flexible and hump-backed Christian." Every man needs a backbone, that is, a great stack of truths around which his life is built. Without it he is a sentimentalist or a moralist.

Peter Marshall once prayed, "Lord, help us to stand for something, for if we do not stand for something, we will fall for anything." We need a great doctrinal basis upon which to build our lives, our hopes, and our faith. That truth is revealed to us in the powerful doctrines, *didoxe*, of the Bible.

I would also point out that these doctrines are the decisive and fundamental characterizations of all of life. They are more real than a stone or a mountain. A stone or a mountain is dead, but an idea, a doctrine is explosive.

WE ARE COMMANDED TO TEACH THE TRUTHS OF CHRIST

God has given to us a body of truth. The self-revelation of God in the Scriptures, incarnate in Jesus Christ, is our heavenly mandate. In Matthew 28:19 the Lord says, "Go ye therefore and *mathetuo* all the world." *Mathetuo* is the Greek word for "teaching," "making disciples," "making learners." Why did the Lord not say *euaggelizo*, "evangelize"? We do have that mandate. We are to do the work of an evangelist, but when God gave the Great Commission He chose the word *mathetuo*. The word "mathematics" comes from this word. What God is saying to us is this: there is more to discipleship, more to church membership, and more to the salvation of our soul than just an evangelistic meeting and people coming down the aisle. There is a lifetime of learning connected with it. There is a dedicated study of God's Word and God's will.

The church is called the pillar and the ground of the truth. That is, as the dipper will hold and shape water, so the church must hold and shape its people in the truth of God. We are to meet, pray, study, be taught, listen, and preach. The assignment of the church is to make learners of these who seek the truth.

This is also the great mandate of the pastor and preacher. He is to inculcate in his people the heavenly doctrines of the faith. Paul wrote to his son in the ministry and said, "Till I come, give attendance to reading, to exhortation, to doctrine . . . Take heed unto thyself, and unto the doctrine; continue in them: for in doing this thou shalt both save thyself, and them that hear thee" (1 Tim. 4:13,16). When a man stands in the pulpit he has an assignment from heaven. He is to take the truths of almighty God and is to expound them to the people, for in doing it he saves himself and those who listen to him.

Look at 2 Timothy:

> All scripture is given by inspiration of God. . .
> I charge thee therefore before God, and the Lord Jesus Christ, who shall judge the quick and the dead at his appearing and his kingdom;
> Preach the word; be instant in season, out of season; reprove, rebuke, exhort with all longsuffering and doctrine. (3:16; 4:1,2)

There is to be meat and foundation in the message a man preaches. "All scripture is given by inspiration of God, and is profitable for doctrine, for reproof, for correction, for instruction in righteousness." This is the great basis upon which the minister is to stand Sunday by Sunday and day by day as God gives him the heart and the ears of the people, expounding to them the truth of God.

It is astonishing to me that these are truths and doctrines for which martyrs laid down their lives, and yet we either ignore them or take them for granted. We become involved in some light thing or personal consideration, all the while forgetting that the man of God is supposed to stand in the pulpit and open God's Word to the people.

The congregation also has its assignment. The Lord said in Matthew 13:

> But other fell into good ground, and brought forth fruit, some an hundredfold, some sixtyfold, some thirtyfold. (v. 8)

There is no fruit without a root. There must be sowing before there is reaping. When we seek to gather Christian fruit without the roots we are obviating the command and program of God. The Lord never made the world that way. If I do not have the Christian tree, I cannot gather Christian fruit. If there is not in us a great commitment to the truths of God, we cannot have the fruit of the Christian life.

How do we learn the doctrines and truths of God? We learn them exactly as Isaiah describes it to us in our text: "Whom shall he teach knowledge? and whom shall he make to understand doctrine? them that are weaned from the milk, and drawn from the breasts. For precept must be upon precept, precept upon precept; line upon line, line upon line, here a little, and there a little."

Every once in awhile little children come to me and want to be saved. I have written a book just for them telling what it means to be saved, what it means to be baptized, what it means to take the Lord's Supper, and what it means to be a good church member. This is line upon line, here a little, there a little, precept upon precept. That is the way God teaches us His knowledge and doctrine.

Actually, this is the way we learn everything. A musician learns slowly, here a little, there a little. You were taught to speak that way. If you had not been taught to walk erectly you would ramble on all fours like an ape. We are challenged to teach people a little at a time bringing them up in the knowledge, teaching, and doctrines of the Lord.

I delivered the stewardship address to the First Baptist Church of Amarillo, Texas, whose goal was $1,500,000 for the new year. After the address was over the pastor said to me, "When Dr. Howard Williams came to be pastor of this church the whole of the giving of the church was $36,000." I could not conceive of that. When Dr. Williams went to the church in Amarillo he taught the people little by little about stewardship, tithing, and giving to the Lord; and the church began to grow. Then the people grew. When God added it all up it became a tremendously alive lighthouse for the Lord. It is a mighty congregation because of the teaching of a godly man working slowly, here a little and there a little.

When I was in Baylor University as a young preacher I took a course in trigonometry, all because of Professor Harrell who was a born philosopher. Here is one of the things he said: "I saw a great building being erected and a tremendous stone was to be split in half and placed above the enormous door through which the people would enter the big building. When I saw that big stone to be split, I imagined how the workman would split it. He would take a wedge made of heavy steel, cut a slit in the middle of the stone, and then take a forty-pound sledge hammer and beat on the wedge until the stone would split right down the middle. Do you know what he did? He took a tiny piece of steel and drilled tiny holes and placed tiny steel pegs in those holes. This he did through the entire length of the stone. Then he took a little hammer and went back and forth — tap, tap, tap, until one day I saw the stone split right in the middle, beautifully done according to the grain and the strength of the stone. I watched them elevate it above the door and thousands of people go through that door into the building even to this day."

When I heard Professor Harrell tell the story I thought of this text: "Precept must be upon precept, precept upon precept; line upon line, line upon line; here a little, and there a little."

Let us listen to the word of the almighty God and let us ask Him to bless us as we grow in the knowledge of the Lord and in the doctrine of the faith.

19

Walking in the Way of the Lord

And therefore will the LORD wait, that he may be gracious unto you, and therefore will he be exalted, that he may have mercy upon you: for the LORD is a God of judgment: blessed are all they that wait for him.

For the people shall dwell in Zion at Jerusalem: thou shall weep no more: he will be very gracious unto thee at the voice of thy cry; when he shall hear it, he will answer thee.

And though the Lord give you the bread of adversity, and the water of affliction, yet shall not thy teachers be removed into a corner any more, but thine eyes shall see thy teachers.

And thine ears shall hear a word behind thee, saying, This is the way, walk ye in it, when ye turn to the right hand, and when ye turn to the left. (Isa. 30:18-21)

The fulfillment of the prophecy lies in the day of the millennium, at the consummation of the age when the Lord Himself shall be seen by us. There are numerous translations of this prophecy that capitalize on the word "teacher." Our Lord will go before as a shepherd leads his flock, we shall see Him, and His voice will guide us when we would err to the right or to the left. Ultimately the fulfillment of the prophecy lies at the consummation of the age, but now it is as pertinent for us as it was for Isaiah and the people of his time.

The prophecy says, "The Lord gave you the bread of adversity, and the water of affliction, yet shall not thy teachers be removed . . . thine ears shall hear a word behind thee, saying, This is the way; walk ye in it, when ye turn to the right hand, and when ye turn to the left."

The passage has in it a double reference to voice. First, we see the voice of the teacher — the godly parent, the earnest pastor, the voice of the servant of God who pleads with us. It also has a reference to the voice of the Lord who speaks to our hearts. Second, the Lord speaks through the teacher and pleads with us personally. Third, the voice speaks to the assembly of the saints, the gathering of God's children in the church.

The teacher, the godly parent, and the earnest pastor plead: "Turn from the way you are going, for here is the way. Walk in it." The wanderer has his back to God, and when the Lord speaks, He speaks from behind him pleading with him to turn. Sometimes the wanderer will go right, sometimes he will turn left, but never does he turn to face God. He has given himself to a rejection of the overtures of God's mercy and grace. So the Lord speaks to him from behind. When we are tempted to turn to the right, there are right-handed sins. There are sins of respectability. A man would be aghast at the thought that he would bathe his hands in human blood, that he would be a murderer. Cultural and acceptable sins are right-handed sins.

There are also left-handed sins, which are sins of the flesh: sex, passion, and lust. Whether it be the sin of the right which is respectable or sin of the left in lust and darkness, behind them is always that voice expressed in a godly father or mother, in an earnest, faithful pastor, in a godly teacher or shepherd, entreating us to turn and come back. The pleading pathos of the voice increases as the wanderer goes farther and farther away from God.

THE INNER VOICE OF GOD

The prophecy says not only is it the voice of the teacher, parent, or faithful pastor, but it is also the inner voice of God that pleads with us. You see, God can speak to a man's heart. A man can speak only to someone's ears. It is a wonderful thing that God can talk to our hearts. His voice is heard in our souls. We see this experienced when Elijah stood in front of the cave on Mount Sinai, after he ran away from his prophetic post in Israel because he was afraid of the king and queen. As he stood in the cave a mighty storm came up. Lightning flashed, thunder roared, and the mountain was shaken, but God was not in the storm. Then there was an earthquake that rent the mountain in two, but God was not in the earthquake. Following was a furious fire, but God was not in the fire. Then there was a stillness, and Elijah heard a small voice. He covered his face with his mantle and bowed in the presence of the great God with his face to the earth. God was in the still, small voice. He speaks to us like that. His presence and voice are universal.

If you visit Florida in the winter you will be surrounded by thousands of square miles of orange orchards, all of them in full bloom. The area is filled with the fragrance of those thousands of trees and blossoms. The aroma is everywhere, outside and inside, and it even incorporates itself in your hair and clothes. Thus it is with the voice of God that speaks to us in our hearts.

I remember listening to our choir as they sang a song which I lived through again and again. The melody began so plaintively, with such pathos. The lyric said: "This melody does not exist; I will change the tune, I will seize it, and kill it, and nail it to a tree. That is that!" But as the listener walked away he heard it all over again. The psalmist says:

> Whither shall I go from thy spirit? or whither shall I flee from thy presence?
> If I ascend up into heaven, thou art there: if I make my bed in hell, behold, thou art there.
> If I take the wings of the morning, and dwell in the uttermost parts of the sea;
> Even there shall thy hand lead me, and thy right hand shall hold me.
> If I say, Surely the darkness shall cover me; even the night shall be light about me. (Ps. 139:7-11)

Always there is that voice in my heart.

Second, the voice is addressed to us individually. Proverbs tells us: "There is a way that seemeth right unto a man, but the end thereof are the ways of death" (Prov. 14:12). He likes it and it is pleasurable to him, so he follows it. Or, consider a man who is determined to give himself to a self-chosen life of damnation as though it were something to be prized rather than a doom to be dreaded. While he is walking down this pathway, his chosen life, the Lord speaks to him. How infinitely precious that the Lord would speak to him, encouraging him in the right way!

Oh, the mercy and goodness of God to us! He not only gives us something to hear, but He also gives us ears to hear it. He not only spreads for us the feast, He also gives us appetites to enjoy it. He not only furnishes the garments, but He also gives us a sense of nakedness. He not only tells us to walk in the way, but also He gives us feet to follow after.

God's Instructions Are Plain

Have you noticed how specific and how plain God is when He speaks to us? Is it possible that God has an assignment He has chosen for us? Yes, there is a way God has chosen for us. There is an assignment for each one of us. There is a heavenly plan which you will hear in your heart and soul. This is God telling you His will for your life. There is no fullness of life so rewarding and so glorious as when we listen to the voice of the Lord and follow in His will and way.

Uncounted numbers of young people have come to me and said, "How can I know the will of God?" I always reply in the same way: "God can speak to you as plainly as I speak to you. If God cannot talk to you, there is no God and it makes no difference. But if you will listen, there will be a voice of the Lord inside your heart showing you the way." If there is in us a marvelous willingness to respond, every step of the pilgrimage is sweeter than the one before.

Third, the voice is addressed also to the assembly of the saints, to the people of God, to the church of the Lord Jesus Christ. What a wonder that God shows His will for us. Sometimes, while in the pulpit, I have felt the Spirit of God in our congregation so deeply that I have bowed my head and wept. I used to wonder at that.

When we bring the Spirit of God in our hearts, we are surrounded by a little circle of love, prayer, and intercession. When we bring the Spirit of God with us, there is an aura of heaven, a feeling of interest and intercession around us. Sometimes it is so overpowering that my heart overflows.

Christians together make a wonderful church and their praying together is the kingdom of God in the hearts of men. The preaching is the faith, the practice is the walk, and the praying is the sweet blessedness of the presence of God in our midst.

20

The Highway to Heaven

The wilderness and the solitary place shall be glad for them; and the desert shall rejoice, and blossom as the rose.

It shall blossom abundantly, and rejoice even with joy and singing: the glory of Lebanon shall be given unto it, the excellency of Carmel and Sharon, they shall see the glory of the LORD, and the excellency of our God.

Strengthen ye the weak hands, and confirm the feeble knees.

Say to them that are of a fearful heart, Be strong, fear not: behold, your God will come with vengeance, even God with a recompence; he will come and save you.

Then the eyes of the blind shall be opened, and the ears of the deaf shall be unstopped.

Then shall the lame man leap as an hart, and the tongue of the dumb sing: for in the wilderness shall waters break out, and streams in the desert.

And the parched ground shall become a pool, and the thirsty land springs of water: in the habitation of dragons, where each lay, shall be grass with reeds and rushes.

And an highway shall be there, and a way, and it shall be called The way of holiness; the unclean shall not pass over it; but it shall be for those: the wayfaring men, though fools, shall not err therein.

No lion shall be there, nor any ravenous beast shall go up

thereon, it shall not be found there; but the redeemed shall walk there:

And the ransomed of the LORD shall return, and come to Zion with songs and everlasting joy upon their heads: they shall obtain joy and gladness, and sorrow and sighing shall flee away. (Isa. 35:1-10)

This is the climactic chapter of the first part of the glorious prophecy of Isaiah. Its background makes it all the more pertinent, meaningful, and poignant. When Isaiah uttered the prophecy the northern kingdom had already been destroyed and led into captivity by the bitter Assyrians. In prospect the prophet had already predicted that Judah would be carried into captivity by the ruthless and merciless Babylonians. In sight there lay before him the barren and wasted land. The people were carried into slavery in Babylon and were scattered over the earth, weeping in repentance and contrition before God.

Had the prophecy ended there it would have been sad. But God opened the eyes of the man of God, so as he lifted up his face to heaven he saw another vision. This time it was a vision of the glory of the presenece of the Lord as He remembered His repentant and contrite people. In the vision he saw the land — a desert blossoming as a rose.

I remember going through the Mandelbaum Gate when Jerusalem was so sadly divided. I went from the Arab side to the Jewish side and when I went through the gate we, as tourists, received a warm welcome. Against the wall was a large medallion, and on it was the emblem of the Israeli government with these words around it: "And the desert shall blossom as the rose." This is the prophecy of Isaiah. However, there was more, because the prophet saw a large, raised causeway, and on that road, high and lifted up, there were pilgrims and exiles returning home. They were singing because joy and gladness overwhelmed them. As they returned to their home from exile and slavery, sorrow and sighing had now flown away; nothing but the glory and goodness of God was before them.

The prophecy was partly fulfilled when the chosen family of the Lord returned home. Wherever a child of God, who has wandered away, comes back to the fold, this is a part of the fulfillment of this prophecy. Part of it has come to pass in our day as the Lord's chosen seed of Abraham, Isaac, and Jacob face homeward, and the desert of Israel blossoms like a rose. The land is green, forests are flourishing, crops are abundant, and the land is fruitful again. This is a near-term fulfillment of the glorious prophecy. But the ultimate and final fulfillment lies when the Lord's redeemed all face heavenward and upward. It is when we turn to the day of our new Jerusalem, our final and eternal home.

A Plain Way

The prophet describes that final consummation by saying that it is a plain and simple way to heaven. He says, "Wayfaring men, though fools, shall not err therein." Even a stranger, unacquainted with the way, shall be able to understand. A little child, untaught, can walk in that way. Revelation 22 says:

> And the Spirit and the bride say, Come. And let him that heareth say, Come. And let him that is athirst come. And whosoever will, let him take the water of life freely. (v. 17)

The Spirit of God pleads with man to come to Jesus. The bride of Christ (the church) pleads with man to come to Jesus. Let those who hear repeat the gracious invitation, "Come, come to Jesus." Any and all can come.

A Crimson Way

The way to heaven is a way of blood. "The redeemed shall walk there: and the ransomed of the LORD." That is, the way goes by the cross, it goes by the way of Calvary. It is a way of blood atonement, washed in the blood of the Lamb.

We read in 1 John:

> But if we walk in the light, as he is in the light, we have fellowship one with another, and the blood of Jesus Christ his Son cleanseth us from all sin. (1:7)

> > Saved by the blood of the Crucified One.
> > All hail to the Father, all hail to the Son,
> > All hail to the Spirit, the great Three in One.
> > Saved by the blood of the Crucified One.

I once preached to the faculty and students of the Southern Baptist Theological Seminary in Louisville, Kentucky. A group of students asked me to come and talk with them, and the days spent there were deeply spiritual and blessed my heart more than I could say. In the group one of the young men asked me, "What is the greatest preaching experience you ever had in your life?"

I said, "Give me a moment to think." I thought of the time some years ago when I brought the closing address at the Southern Baptist Convention in San Francisco. When I concluded the address I gave an invitation, and hundreds of people responded.

Then I thought of that day when I preached to the pastors of California. One of them came to the front and began to weep before the Lord. Many joined him one by one, and the sound of those men sobbing before the Lord was something I could never forget.

I thought of a service at the Cain Road Baptist Church in Hong Kong years ago. While I was preaching people began to stand in front of me in Chinese style with their hands clasped and heads bowed. I asked the interpreter what they were doing. He told me they could not wait until I was finished with my sermon and they were standing there in simple faith, giving their hearts to Jesus.

What is the greatest preaching experience I have ever had in my life? I could name many others, but I finally answered: "Young man, the greatest preaching experience I ever had in my life was on a Sunday night some years ago. It happened that that Sunday night fell on New Year's Eve. Some of my deacons had facetiously come to me and said, 'Now, pastor, you are everlastingly complaining that you do not have time to finish your sermon. We notice that New Year's Eve falls on Sunday night. Why not start preaching at 7:30 and preach until past midnight, and see if you can finish your sermon!' They said that to me in jest. You know, I went home and started thinking about that. So we announced that on New Year's Eve I was to preach into the next year. When I stood in the pulpit the place was jammed and the people were standing around the walls downstairs and upstairs. I thought after I had preached several hours that most of the congregation would be gone. When I finished past midnight, they were still jammed in the auditorium and standing around the walls. It was the greatest single preaching experience I ever had in my life. The subject was 'The Scarlet Thread Through the Bible.' It was the crimson story of the cross from the beginning in Genesis when the Lord slew an innocent animal to cover the nakedness and sin of our first parents, through the Old Testament sacrificial system and then the blood of John the Baptist, the blood of our Lord in Gethsemane, in the institution of the Lord's Supper, the Lord's crucifixion, the sacrifice of Stephen and James and all the martyrs through the centuries, and I ended in Revelation."

> Have you been to Jesus for the cleansing power?
> Are you washed in the blood of the Lamb?
> Are you fully trusting in His grace this hour?
> Are you washed in the blood of the Lamb?

The highway is crimson. It is a way of blood and it goes by the way of the cross.

A Humble Way

It is a penitential way, a way of confession and contrition: "And sorrow and sighing shall flee away." Those who walk that pilgrim road to glory are those who have sorrowed and wept.

Any man who ever really faces the presence of our Lord will feel unworthy and unclean. No man follows the pilgrim way to glory in pride and self-righteousness. He bows in humble confession before the presence of the great, high God. This is the road down which David trod:

> Wash me thoroughly from mine iniquity, and cleanse me from my sin.
> For I acknowledge my transgressions: and my sin is ever before me.
> Purge me with hyssop, and I shall be clean: wash me, and I shall be whiter than snow.
> Restore unto me the joy of thy salvation; and uphold me with thy free spirit.
> For thou desirest not sacrifice; else would I give it: thou delightest not in burnt offering.

> The sacrifices of God are a broken spirit: a broken and contrite
> heart, O God, thou wilt not despise. (Ps. 51:2-3,7,12,16-17)

It is a way of confession.

When the Lord looked upon Peter he went out and wept
bitterly. The publican in the house of the Lord would not so much
as lift up his face to heaven but bowed his head and beat upon his
breast and said, "Lord, be merciful to me, a sinner."

A Happy Way

The prophet says that it is a way of joy and singing: "The
ransomed of the LORD shall return, and come to Zion with songs
and everlasting joy upon their heads: they shall obtain joy and
gladness." It is unusual that we should feel contrition and confession, and at the same time a rejoicing in the Lord our Savior. But
that is what it is to be a child of God. You will have both of those
emotions in your heart at the same time. Our religion is not to
make us despairing as though God had forsaken us and life was
dark and meaningless. Our faith is not to make us miserable but is
to wipe the tears from our eyes. Our vision and dream is not of
devils descending a dreary staircase to hell, but of a ladder and the
angels ascending with the top of the ladder leaning against the
throne of God Himself. "A highway shall be there, and they shall
return to Zion with songs and everlasting joy upon their heads."

An Open, Public Way

It is a way of open and public avowal. Those who walk on this
highway are the redeemed and ransomed of God. As they gather to
the holy city it is with songs and everlasting joy upon their heads,
and sorrow and sighing shall flee away.

A highway refers to a raised road, a great causeway. One can see
it plainly, openly. God has always been like that. Moses stood in
the camp and said, "All of you who are on the Lord's side, let them
come and stand by me." Paul even defined our salvation in the
terms of open and public committal. Romans 10 says:

> If thou shalt confess with thy mouth the Lord Jesus, and shalt

believe in thine heart that God hath raised him from the dead, thou shalt be saved.

For with the heart man believeth unto righteousness; and with the mouth confession is made unto salvation. (vv. 9,10)

We read in Matthew 10:

Whosoever therefore shall confess me before men, him will I confess also before my Father which is in heaven.

But whosoever shall deny me before men, him will I also deny before my Father which is in heaven. (vv. 32,33)

That is the way God has chosen for us to walk into His kingdom and into His holy city — openly, where everyone can see it.

21

The God Who Delivers by Prayer

Now it came to pass in the fourteenth year of king Hezekiah, that Sennacherib king of Assyria came up against all the defenced cities of Judah, and took them.

And the king of Assyria sent Rabshakeh from Lachish to Jerusalem unto king Hezekiah with a great army. And he stood by the conduit of the upper pool in the highway of the fuller's field. . . .

Neither let Hezekiah make you trust in the LORD, saying, The LORD will surely deliver us: this city shall not be delivered into the hand of the king of Assyria. . . .

Until I come and take you away to a land like your own land, a land of corn and wine, a land of bread and vineyards.

Beware lest Hezekiah persuade you, saying, The LORD will deliver us. Hath any of the gods of the nations delivered his land out of the hand of the king of Assyria?

Where are the gods of Hamath and Arphad? where are the gods of Sepharvaim? and have they delivered Samaria out of my hand?

Who are they among all the gods of these lands, that have delivered their land out of my hand, that the Lord should deliver Jerusalem out of my hand?

But they held their peace, and answered him not a word: for the king's commandment was, saying, Answer him not.

Then came Eliakim, the son of Hilkiah, that was over the household, and Shebna the scribe, and Joah, the son of Asaph, the recorder, to Hezekiah with their clothes rent, and told him the words of Rabshakeh.

And it came to pass, when king Hezekiah heard it, that he rent his clothes, and covered himself with sackcloth, and went into the house of the LORD.

And he sent Eliakim, who was over the household, and Shebna the scribe, and the elders of the priests covered with sackcloth, unto Isaiah the prophet the son of Amoz.

And they said unto him, Thus saith Hezekiah, This day is a day of trouble, and of rebuke, and of blasphemy: for the children are come to the birth, and there is not strength to bring forth.

It may be the LORD thy God will hear the words of Rabshakeh, whom the king of Assyria his master hath sent to reproach the living God, and will reprove the words which the LORD thy God hath heard: wherefore lift up thy prayer for the remnant that is left.

So the servants of king Hezekiah came to Isaiah. . . .

And Hezekiah received the letter from the hand of the messengers, and read it: and Hezekiah went up unto the house of the LORD, and spread it before the LORD.

And Hezekiah prayed unto the LORD, saying,

O LORD of hosts, God of Israel, that dwellest between the cherubims, thou art the God, even thou alone, of all the kingdoms of the earth: thou hast made heaven and earth.

Incline thine ear, O LORD, and hear; open thine eyes, O LORD, and see: and hear all the words of Sennacherib, which hath sent to reproach the living God.

Of a truth, LORD, the kings of Assyria have laid waste all the nations, and their countries,

And have cast their gods into the fire: for they were no gods, but the work of men's hands, wood and stone: therefore they have destroyed them.

Now therefore, O LORD our God, save us from his hand, that all the kingdoms of the earth may know that thou art the LORD, even thou only.

Then Isaiah the son of Amoz sent unto Hezekiah, saying, Thus saith the LORD God of Israel, Whereas thou hast prayed to me against Sennacherib king of Assyria:

This is the word which the LORD has spoken concerning him; The virgin, the daughter of Zion, hath despised thee, and laughed thee to scorn; the daughter of Jerusalem hath shaken her head at thee.

Whom hast thou reproached and blasphemed? and against whom hast thou exalted thy voice, and lifted up thine eyes on high? even against the Holy One of Israel. . . .

> Therefore thus saith the Lord concerning the king of Assyria, He shall not come into this city, nor shoot an arrow there, nor come before it with shields, nor cast a bank against it.
> By the way that he came, by the same shall he return, and shall not come into this city, saith the Lord.
> For I will defend this city to save it for mine own sake, and for my servant David's sake,
> Then the angel of the Lord went forth, and smote in the camp of the Assyrians a hundred and fourscore and five thousand: and when they arose early in the morning, behold, they were all dead corpses.
> So Sennacherib king of Assyria departed, and went and returned, and dwelt at Nineveh.
> And it came to pass, as he was worshipping in the house of Nisroch his god, that Adrammelech and Sharezer his sons smote him with the sword; and they escaped into the land of Armenia: and Esarhaddon his son reigned in his stead. (Isa. 36:1-2,15,17-22; 37:1-5,14-23,33-38)

What a remarkable contrast between Hezekiah, a man of prayer, and his father Ahaz, who was a man of reproach and rejection! For in a time of like trouble Ahaz connived with Tiglath-pileser, becoming an accomplice with the Assyrians. The Assyrians came down with Shalmanezer, and when Shalmanezer died, Sargon completed the conquest, thereby destroying the northern kingdom forever and carrying away Samaria into captivity and slavery. The successor of Sargon, Sennacherib, besieged Judah and held Jerusalem like a man would hold a vise in his hand. Isaiah said to Hezekiah:

> For thus saith the Lord God, the Holy One of Israel; In returning and rest shall ye be saved; in quietness and in confidence shall be your strength. (Isa. 30:15)

Hezekiah, listening to the voice of the prophet of God, took his case to the Lord and waited upon Him who reigned in heaven. The Lord God looked down from heaven and saw Hezekiah clothed in sackcloth, covered with ashes, bowing before his great and mighty name in the house of the Lord. The Lord said, "It is against me that the king has blasphemed, even this Sennacherib." That night the Lord sent just one angel over the camp of the Assyrians. The next morning when the commander-in-chief blew the trumpet to storm the city, there was silence. One hundred eighty-five thousand dead soldiers did not rise, did not reply.

One of the famous poems of all English literature is this one written by Lord Byron, entitled, "The Destruction of Sennacherib."

> The Assyrian came down like the wolf on the fold,
> And his cohorts were gleaming in purple and gold;
> And the sheen of their spears was like stars on the sea,
> When the blue wave rolls nightly on deep Galilee.
>
> Like the leaves of the forest when summer is green,
> That host with their banners at sunset were seen:
> Like the leaves of the forest when autumn hath blown,
> That host on the morrow laid withered and strown.
>
> For the Angel of Death spread his wings on the blast,
> And breathed in the face of the foe as he passed;
> And the eyes of the sleepers waxed deadly and chill,
> And their hearts but once heaved, and forever grew still.
>
> And there lay the steed with his nostril all wide,
> But through it there rolled not the breath of his pride:
> And the foam of his gasping lay white on the turf,
> And cold as the spray of the rock-beating surf.
>
> And there lay the rider distorted and pale,
> With the dew on his brow and the rust on his mail;
> And the tents were all silent, the banners alone,
> The lances unlifted, the trumpet unblown.
>
> And the widows of Ashur are loud in their wail,
> And the idols are broke in the temple of Baal;
> And the might of the Gentile, unsmote by the sword,
> Hath melted like snow in the glance of the Lord!

What of Sennacherib, the blaspheming king who shook his fist in the face of almighty God and who dared to reproach and taunt the people of the Lord? Would he escape unharmed, uncondemned, and unjudged?

The eyes of the Lord followed him as he made his way back to the capital city and to the palace at Nineveh. The finger of the Lord pointed at him every mile of the way. The Lord God said, "Not in a foreign land, but at home in the house of his god, among his own sons will I judge him." Then one day when Sennacherib was in the house of his god, his own sons assassinated him and he lay dead in his own blood. Thus we see the hand of almighty God.

THE DUALITY IN GOD

In heaven sits a great and mighty God, the King of glory, the Creator of all heaven and earth, and He has a duality in His self-revelation. There is a two-sidedness to God in everything that we know about Him and in everything by which He has disclosed Himself to us. There is in God damnation and deliverance. There is in God blessing, battering, and blasting. Wherever there is any disclosure of Him, there are always those two character traits in God.

One finds the duality of God in Exodus 20 when the Lord God, giving the Ten Commandments said:

> Thou shalt have no other gods before me.
> Thou shalt not make unto thee any graven image.
> . . . for I the LORD thy God am a jealous God, visiting the iniquity of the fathers upon the children unto the third and fourth generation of them that hate me;
> And shewing mercy unto thousands of them that love me, and keep my commandments. (vv. 3-6)

One sees the duality in the lives of the prophets: "The soul that sinneth, it shall die," said Ezekiel. Then he also says, "As I live, saith the Lord GOD, I have no pleasure in the death of the wicked; but that the wicked turn from his way and live: turn ye, turn ye from your evil ways; for why will ye die, O house of Israel?" (Ezek. 18:4,11).

One sees that same duality of God in the gospel of Christ:

> He that believeth on the Son hath everlasting life: and he that believeth not the Son shall not see life; but the wrath of God abideth on him. (John 3:36)

The apostles preached:

> Be not deceived; God is not mocked: for whatsoever a man soweth, that shall he also reap. (Gal. 6:7)

It is a terrible thing to fall into the hands of the living God. (Heb. 10:31)

For our God is a consuming fire. (Heb. 12:29)

WE HAVE DELIVERANCE IN PRAYER

In our world it is true that God is a God of judgment, for what a man sows, that does he reap. But He is also, as in Hezekiah's case, a God of deliverance, a God who answers prayer, a God who bares His mighty arm to help, work with, stand by, and bless His people. Jehoshaphat said to the Lord,

O our God, wilt thou not judge them? for we have no might against this great company that cometh against us; neither know we what to do: but our eyes are upon thee. (2 Chron. 20:12)

Then the Scriptures say that Judah stood before the Lord with her priests, soldiers, fathers, mothers, and families. Even the little ones were standing there looking up to heaven. God delivered them with a mighty arm.

On the wall of the second floor of our chapel in the First Baptist Church of Dallas, are found two pictures of Daniel in the lion's den. He stands in quietness and confidence with his hands folded behind him, looking up to the Lord who is able to answer prayer and to deliver. The king asked, "Daniel, is thy God able to deliver thee from the lions?" Daniel replied, "My God hath sent His angel to close the mouths of the lions." He walked in perfect peace and confidence among those ravenous beasts. The prophet Isaiah says, "Thou wilt keep him in perfect peace, whose mind is stayed on thee" (Isa. 26:3).

But someone could say: "That is a long time ago. God does not answer prayer like that today. The events in Isaiah 36 and 37 happened seven hundred years before Christ. Daniel's experience took place five hundred fifty years before Christ. These events occurred long ago, but God is not that kind of a God today. He does not answer His people today." Nay, but He is the same yesterday, today, and forever. He answers prayer today, He delivers today, and He blesses today as miraculously and as triumphantly as He did in the years gone by.

22

Prayer and the Will of God

In those days was Hezekiah sick unto death. And Isaiah the prophet the son of Amoz came unto him, and said unto him, Thus saith the LORD, Set thine house in order: for thou shalt die, and not live.

Then Hezekiah turned his face toward the wall, and prayed unto the LORD,

And said, Remember now, O LORD, I beseech thee, how I have walked before thee in truth and with a perfect heart, and have done that which is good in thy sight. And Hezekiah wept sore.

Then came the word of the LORD to Isaiah, saying,

Go, and say to Hezekiah, Thus saith the LORD, the God of David thy father, I have heard thy prayer, I have seen thy tears: behold, I will add unto thy days fifteen years.

And I will deliver thee and this city out of the hand of the king of Assyria: and I will defend this city.

And this shall be a sign unto thee from the LORD, that the LORD will do this thing that he hath spoken;

Behold, I will bring again the shadow of the degrees, which is gone down in the sun dial of Ahaz, ten degrees backward. So the sun returned ten degrees, by which degrees it was gone down.

At that time Merodach-baladan, the son of Baladan, king of Babylon, sent letters and a present to Hezekiah: for he had heard that he had been sick, and was recovered.

And Hezekiah was glad of them, and shewed them the house of his precious things, the silver, and the gold, and the spices, and the precious ointment, and all the house of his armour, and all that was found in his treasures: there was nothing in his house, nor in all his dominion, that Hezekiah shewed them not.

Then came Isaiah the prophet unto king Hezekiah, and said unto him, What said these men? and from whence came they unto thee? And Hezekiah said, They are come from a far country unto me, even from Babylon.

Then said he, What have they seen in thine house? And Hezekiah answered, All that is in mine house have they seen: there is nothing among my treasures that I have not shewed them.

Then said Isaiah to Hezekiah, Hear the word of the LORD of hosts:

Behold, the days come, that all that is in thine house, and that which thy fathers have laid up in store until this day, shall be carried to Babylon: nothing shall be left, saith the LORD.

And of thy sons that shall issue from thee, which thou shalt beget, shall they take away; and they shall be eunuchs in the palace of the king of Babylon. (Isa. 38:1-8; 39:1-7)

Hearing the sentence of death from Jehovah in heaven, Hezekiah prayed and wept, and out of deference to the prayer of the good king, God added fifteen years to his life. When we read of this event in the Book of Isaiah we first think how marvelous of God to answer the prayer of Hezekiah, and add fifteen years to his life. But instead of praying, "Not my will, thine be done," Hezekiah prayed that he might live, and we will see that during those added fifteen years two things happened.

RESULTS OF THE FIFTEEN YEARS

First, during that time his son Manasseh was born. Many times God says in His Word that because of the sins and the wickedness of Manasseh, the son of Hezekiah, He would destroy an entire people. He would lay waste their land and send them into slavery and captivity.

In 2 Kings 21 Manasseh was twelve years old when he began to reign. That is, he was born in the third year of the fifteen years. He reigned fifty-five years in Jerusalem and his reign was one of evil in the sight of the Lord. He built altars to all the gods of the heathen in the temple of the Lord. He made his sons pass through fire. He offered his own sons as a burning sacrifice to the heathen god Molech. We read of these wicked acts of Manasseh in 2 Kings:

> . . . Manasseh seduced them to do more evil than did the nations whom the LORD destroyed before the children of Israel.
>
> And the LORD spake by his servants the prophets, saying,
>
> Because Manasseh king of Judah hath done these abominations, and hath done wickedly above all that the Amorites did, which were before him, and hath made Judah also to sin with his idols:
>
> Therefore thus saith the LORD God of Israel, Behold, I am bringing such evil upon Jerusalem and Judah, that whosoever heareth of it, both his ears shall tingle . . . .
>
> Moreover Manasseh shed innocent blood very much, till he had filled Jerusalem from one end to another; beside his sin wherewith he made Judah to sin, in doing that which was evil in the sight of the LORD. (21:9-11,16)

In 2 Kings 22 we read about good king Josiah, the grandson of Manasseh. There was none like him, says the Bible. No king before him had turned to the Lord with all his heart and soul and might according to the law of Moses. Neither was any king after him like him. Josiah was a wonderful king.

Notwithstanding, the Lord did not turn from the fierceness of His great wrath against Judah because of all the provocations of Manasseh. The Lord said He would remove Judah out of His sight.

As though that were not enough, the Bible picks the story up again in 2 Kings 24:

> In his days Nebuchadnezzar king of Babylon came up. . . .
>
> And the LORD sent him against him bands of the Chaldees . . . and sent them against Judah to destroy it, according to the word of the LORD, which he spake by his servants the prophets.
>
> Surely at the commandment of the LORD came this upon Judah, to remove them out of his sight, for the sins of Manasseh, according to all that he did;
>
> And also for the innocent blood that he shed: for he filled Jerusalem with innocent blood; which the LORD would not pardon. (24:1-4)

Then we read in Jeremiah 15:

> Then said the LORD unto me, Though Moses and Samuel stood

before me, yet my mind could not be toward this people: cast them out of my sight, and let them go forth.

And it shall come to pass, if they say unto thee, Whither shall we go forth? then thou shalt tell them, Thus saith the LORD; Such as are for death, to death; and such as are for the sword, to the sword; and such as are for the famine, to the famine; and such as are for the captivity, to the captivity.

And I will appoint over them four kinds, saith the LORD: the sword to slay, and the dogs to tear, and the fowls of the heaven, and the beasts of the earth, to devour and destroy.

And I will cause them to be removed into all kingdoms of the earth, because of Manasseh the son of Hezekiah king of Judah, for that which he did in Jerusalem. (vv. 1-4)

All of these horrible acts occurred because of an answered prayer. Had fifteen years not been added to Hezekiah's life, Manasseh would never have been born. But out of the answered prayer came this son for whose iniquity God would not pardon Jerusalem, but sent the people out into judgment and slavery.

The second result of those added fifteen years given to Hezekiah is that Merodach-baladan, the son of Baladan, became king of Babylon. The crown prince was sent by the king of Babylon to Hezekiah with flattery. Assyria was the great empire with its capital at Nineveh, and south was the province of Babylonia with its capital on the Euphrates River. A king prince in Babylon decided to overthrow the king of Assyria and to build a great world empire himself. When he heard about Hezekiah's illness and recovery he sent his son, the future king of Babylon, to see Hezekiah and to flatter him, thus to gain his support in his conspiracy against the king of Assyria.

Hezekiah, because of the favor of God upon him, was proud and haughty. Full of pride because God had given him fifteen years and many other blessings besides, Hezekiah boastfully showed the prince when he came to visit him, everything that God had done for him. It was then that Isaiah the prophet of God came to Hezekiah with the word that the day would come when everything in his storehouse would be carried into Babylon. Not only that, but the people and Hezekiah's own descendants would be taken away, emasculated, and made slaves in the palace of the king of Babylon.

In all the circumstances of life our prayer ought always to be: "Lord, if it is better for me to die, let me die. If it furthers Thy kingdom in the earth, then God let it be. Not I, but Thee, O Lord."

To any man and to any family, death is a horrible ghost. So, when the judgment of death was delivered to Hezekiah by the prophet, he cried to God, "O Lord, deliver me from this sentence of death."

The Child of God and Death

What about our attitude toward the sentence of death? First, let us look at the children of God in the Bible who faced death. The Lord said to David, "This child also that is born unto thee shall surely die." Hearing the word from the Lord, David sat down in an ash heap dressed in sackcloth, and in tears cried to God, but the child died despite the intercessions of David:

> And he said, While the child was yet alive, I fasted and wept: for I said, Who can tell whether GOD will be gracious to me, that the child may live?
> But now he is dead, wherefore should I fast? can I bring him back again? I shall go to him, but he shall not return to me. (2 Sam. 12:22,23)

Death to the believer is being brought to God's people in glory. The Old Testament often speaks of death using the words, "He was gathered to his people." The Lord Jesus used that as the great doctrinal basis for the resurrection of the dead. The Lord said: "I am the God of Abraham, and the God of Isaac, and the God of Jacob. God is not the God of the dead, but of the living" (Matt. 22:32). On the basis of our resurrection from the dead, we are numbered with the redeemed.

The Lord said of His own death;

> . . . It is expedient for you that I go away: for if I go not away, the Comforter will not come unto you; but if I depart, I will send him unto you. (John 16:7)

We have a God who is not just on a throne in Jerusalem, but He is in our hearts, our homes. He is wherever we are. We can come before Him and lay before Him any cause, any decision. We can talk to Him and He can talk to us. The Comforter is come because Jesus died.

When Paul was in the dungeon in Rome facing execution he wrote to Philippi, saying:

> For I am in a strait betwixt two, having a desire to depart, and to be with Christ; which is far better:
> Nevertheless to abide in the flesh is more needful for you. . .
> For to me to live is Christ, and to die is gain (Phil. 1.23,24,21)

The only reason Paul would choose to live is that he might be a servant to help and encourage others, but to depart and be with Christ would be far better. This is the attitude of the children of God in the Bible.

What should be our attitude toward death? Is it something that we cringe before, something we pray against, something we dread, a terrible and awesome sentence in our lives? Is this to be our attitude toward dying? God says to those of us who look in faith to Him that it is better over there than it is here. God says that we will have a new body, a new home, a new resurrected and glorified body in that world beyond the gates of death. There will be no more blind eyes or crippled bodies. There will be no graves on the hillsides of glory. There will be no processions down the streets paved of gold behind which follow those who weep and cry. God has prepared something better for us. Not only that, but we will be with these who have been redeemed from all the ages. We will sit down with Abraham, Isaac, and Jacob, with the apostles and prophets, with the children of God through all the centuries. Best of all, we will break bread at the table of our Lord.

Why do we dread death and the sentence of the grave? I am afraid it is because we do not believe. Our lack of faith blinds our eyes, hardens our hearts, and fills us with dread, foreboding, and fear. Instead of anticipating those gates by which we enter into the glories of the world to come, we are fearful of them, and dare not even speak about them.

When I was a youth an old pastor said to me: "Son, so often

when older people want to talk to young people about heaven and about the land that is yet to come, they will turn aside as though it would be something not appropriate. You see, older people have faced a long journey and want to talk about death, heaven, the grave, and the resurrection. Do not turn them away. If you were going on a long journey, would you not be interested in talking to someone who has been there? If they talk to you about heaven, talk to them, listen to them, read to them, say things to them that God has revealed in His sacred book and it will comfort and strengthen their hearts as they face that great and final hour." Death has for us the glories of the blessedness of the life God has promised to us who have looked in faith to Him.

So much in human experience denies that faith. How often have you seen someone whose life is lived, the time has come to enter into the joy of the Lord, and instead of their being allowed to die and to be with Jesus, all kinds of gadgets and instruments are brought to their bedside by the latest achievements of science.

When I was a young man a great scientist and doctor, by the name of Alexis Carrell, kept a chicken heart alive for twenty-seven years. The only reason he stopped the experiment after that time was that he found he could keep it alive forever by feeding it and taking away the waste. Science can do the same with the protoplasm in our bodies. To give vent to such an artificial method of extending life has an inherent overtone that it is terrible to die. We keep protoplasm alive as long as we can because death is horrible. Can you believe that God has so forgotten us and heaven is so blotted out against us that with our last breath we must strive to breathe one more time? God says that "Eye hath not seen, nor ear heard, neither have entered into the heart of man, the things which God hath prepared for them that love him" (1 Cor. 2:9). If there is work I can do and a task that I might be able to offer to God, then may God give me health, strength, wisdom, and length of days to do it. But when my task is finished and my work is done, then, Lord, let me rest in Thee.

To the Christian, death is not a horrible thing. "O death, where is thy sting? O grave, where is thy victory?" (1 Cor. 15:55). Thanks be to God who has given us every treasure, every assurance, and every hope in Christ Jesus our Lord!

DEATH TO A CHRISTIAN

What is death to the Christian? First, death is a falling asleep in Jesus. The entire New Testament presents the death of the Christian in those terms, a falling asleep in Jesus. In Acts we read of Stephen's death:

> And he kneeled down, and cried with a loud voice, Lord, lay not this sin to their charge. And when he had said this, he fell asleep. (7:60)

That is the New Testament description of what happens to our mortal frame.

The Greek word *koimao* means "to fall asleep." From that Greek word is derived another form of the word, *koimeterion*, "a sleeping place. The early Christians took that Greek word and applied it to the place where they laid aside their beloved dead. Spelled out in English *koimeterion* becomes "cemetery." The world never heard or used the word until Christians applied it to the laying away of their dead.

Have you heard of the catacombs in Rome? We are told there are miles of subterranean passages where the Christians hid when they were persecuted by the Roman Caesar. Actually, the catacombs were dug out of the rock on which the eternal city of Rome is built so that the Christians could have a place to lay away their beloved dead. Burning the body was the heathen way of putting aside the body in which the soul had lived. The Christians felt that it was not appropriate to take the house that God would raise from the dead and burn it.

In India I have watched people bury their dead by the scores. They place the bodies on platforms, surround the bodies with wood, and set them on fire. Because the Christians refused to burn their dead, they dug subterranean caverns and lovingly laid their dead away.

William Cullen Bryant, when he was but eighteen years of age, wrote his first great poem on American soil, called *Thanatopsis.* Listen to the closing verses:

> So live, that when thy summons comes to join
> The innumerable caravan which moves
> To that mysterious realm, where each shall take
> His chamber in the silent halls of death,
> Thou go not, like the quarry-slave at night,
> Scourged to his dungeon, but, sustained and soothed
> By an unfaltering trust, approach thy grave
> Like one that wraps the drapery of his couch
> About him, and lies down to pleasant dreams.

Our rewards are not here, but there. Our eternal home is not here, but there. If you live long enough, the day will come when you will live alone in this earth. Every member of your family will be gone, and every friend will be gone.

I remember conducting the funeral of a saint in one of my churches who died when he was 103 years of age. He had one request and that was to be buried by his wife who had died so many years before. When time came to lay him to rest, there was no one living who could remember where his wife was buried. He had outlived them all, and the place of her burying had been forgotten. So they went to the side of the fence and buried him there alone. I would think that the old man, having loved his wife, wanted to be by her side in the great resurrection day.

"For me to live is Christ, and to die is gain."

> Safe in the arms of Jesus,
> Safe on His gentle breast;
> There by His love o'ershaded,
> Sweetly my soul shall rest.

Jesus came to destroy the power of death. Death now to the Christian is just his entrance into glory.

23

The Meaning of Miracle

Comfort ye, comfort ye my people, saith your God. (Isa. 40:1)

In recent years we have seen a large increase in the number of theologians who have denied that Isaiah wrote chapters 40-66 of his book. They say that Isaiah spoke of King Cyrus who would live 200 years after the time of Isaiah. They say the same thing about Daniel and Moses — they couldn't have written the books ascribed to them because the events they refer to happened after they were supposed to have written their books. But they forget that God is the author and He can reveal any message to His writers He desires.

In God's library of books, without exception, the signature is "Miracle," supernatural wonder. That is the signature of almighty God, whether it be of one book or another.

THE WORLD AROUND US

First, we shall look at the world around us, the world in which we live, for the signature of God. Our world is a world of miracle and wonder because God created it. There is a universal law of physics which proclaims that heat expands, and the hotter an object becomes the more it expands. Cold has the opposite effect; it contracts. That universal law continues until God intervenes. For example, water will contract as it gets colder, but when the temperature falls to 32° F., it expands. Why? Because had water continued to contract when it got colder, freezing ice would have, by its weight, fallen to the floor of the ocean. The ocean would have been solid ice at both poles from the bottom to the top. The great currents that ameliorate the temperatures of the world would have been impossible. A person could not live near the poles because he would freeze to death. He could not live near the center of the earth because the torrid heat would burn him up. Such is a miracle of God, and such is the world around us.

In the field of biology there is a law that states that in human life all the cells in living creatures have a certain number of chromosomes. Every species has its own set. Let us say there are forty-eight chromosomes in every cell of the human body. In the miraculous process of mitosis, every cell will split down the middle and there will be forty-eight in one and forty-eight in the other. This happens, except, in the miracle of God, in the female ovum where there are twenty-four and in the male spermatozoon where there are twenty-four. When the male spermatozoon fertilizes the female ovum, the twenty-four chromosomes form the man and the twenty-four chromosomes from the woman combine, and the child, therefore, has forty-eight chromosomes in all of the cells of his body. The child will inherit characteristics from the mother and also from the father. This recreation of life is a miracle of God. There is no way in the world that one could explain the miracle of birth except in the intervention of almighty God.

THE WORLD BENEATH US

Look at the world beneath us. There is a law in medicine and in biology which states that germs multiply, expand, and produce more germs. This sounds awesome because germs are contagious. A dead body is buried in the earth and one would think that for thousands, and maybe millions of years, there has been untold accumulation of a germ-laden mass of dead animals and dead human beings which have been buried in the earth. The entire earth would be filled with infectious and deadly diseases. If all the germs continued to grow, what disease would one contract merely by touching the earth?

The Lord planted in the moist soil a miraculous creation of His divine hand. He created it in the beginning and only in recent years has man discovered God's creation, penicillin, which kills germs, and now the earth is sweet, fertile, and pure. We can walk on it and live on it in perfect health. This also is the miraculous intervention of almighty God.

THE WORLD WITHIN US

Now let us look at the world within us. There is a law in psychology that states that we are the products of our environment. Psychologists teach us that whatever we are is due largely to our environment. They say a man is a criminal because he was brought up poor. They say it is not his fault. So society strays more and more away from the persuasion that what a man does is because of his choice.

Some years ago West Dallas became famous because Bonnie Parker, Clyde Barrow, and Raymond and Floyd Hamilton, notorious robbers and outlaws, grew up there. One day Hattie Rankin Moore, living in Dallas, began to listen to our broadcast, and sometime later she and her sister accepted the Lord and were baptized. She became deeply interested in West Dallas and gave us money to build our George W. Truett Chapel there. She also was interested in the families of West Dallas. When Raymond Hamilton was electrocuted in the penitentiary at Huntsville, Texas, she stayed up all night with the mother of that prodigal boy. Raymond Hamilton had a brother, Floyd, in whom Hattie Rankin Moore was also deeply interested. He was sentenced to a life term in Alcatraz. One day, when she learned that I was going to visit San Francisco, she asked me to visit Floyd Hamilton. She and the prisoner had been corresponding while he was in Alcatraz.

Upon arriving in San Francisco I called the warden who said that I would be most welcome to visit. After crossing the bay and going through extensive security investigation, I was locked up in an iron cubicle with Floyd Hamilton, whom I met for the first time. We talked for more than an hour and at the end of the hour we knelt together on the steel floor of the prison. When I stretched forth my hand, he clasped it warmly in return, giving his heart in trust to the Lord Jesus. He said, "If God ever lets me out, the first thing I will do is come to Dallas and walk down the aisle in the church and I will be baptized in confession of my faith in the Lord Jesus." As the years passed, Hattie Rankin Moore died. Floyd Hamilton was pardoned, and he came down the aisle of this church and was baptized. From that day until this he has gone from city to city, church to church, and boys' club to boys' club witnessing to the grace, love, and forgiveness of God in Christ Jesus. That is a miracle of intervention, a miracle of grace. We live in that kind of a world.

THE WORLD ABOVE US

The world above us is miraculous also. On a powerful throne sits the Creator of this universe who holds the destiny of the world in His omnipotent hands. Look at His intervention, and we use the history of the Jews as an example. There were times when they were highly moral and committed and God blessed them. Then they became affluent, and as a result decay set in. They became corrupt on the inside, lost their moral dedication, and finally reverted to slavery. All the nations of the world, including America, have gone through the cycle of accumulated affluence followed by decay of the people from within. In America we are beginning to lose our great spiritual and moral commitment. Americans are increasingly dependent upon a handout from the government, and I'm afraid bankruptcy and slavery will soon follow. This law of history is to be found in the story of the ancient Assyrians, the Sumerians, the Akkadians, and the Babylonians as well, and is a recurring cycle through all of history and life.

But look at an intervention of God. He said to Ezekiel the prophet in Ezekiel 37, "What do you see?" Ezekiel said, "I see a great valley of dry bones." The Lord said, "Preach to them." Ezekiel said: "What? Preach to dry bones?" The Lord answered,

"Yes." God told him to call the Spirit to breathe upon the bones. Ezekiel did and a great people, a great nation, stood before him. The Lord said, "That is Israel My people, buried among the tongues and languages of the earth. I will raise them up and speak life to them, and they will live on the face of the earth and in My sight."

The miracle of the resurrection of Israel is written large on the pages of the history of the world and in the headlines of the newspapers today. God said to Jeremiah:

> Thus saith the LORD, which giveth the sun for a light by day, and the ordinances of the moon and of the stars for a light by night, which divideth the sea when the waves thereof roar; The LORD of hosts is his name:
> If those ordinances depart from before me, saith the LORD, then the seed of Israel also shall cease from being a nation before me for ever.
> Thus saith the LORD; If heaven above can be measured, and the foundations of the earth searched out beneath, I will also cast off all the seed of Israel for all that they have done, saith the LORD. (Jer. 31:35-37)

Matthew says, ". . . upon this rock I will build my church; and the gates of hell shall not prevail against it" (Matt. 16:18b). The church of the Lord shall rise forever to live in the presence of God We live in that kind of a miraculous world. So it is in all of God's books, in all the library of the law. His signature is miracle, supernatural, wonder. There is no area of the earth in all God's creation but that we see the wonder working of the mighty God in the world above us, around us, and within us.

When we read Isaiah 44 and 45, where God calls Cyrus by name two hundred years before he lived, we should say that that is a small thing for God to do when we look around us and see the astonishing miracles and the might of God on every hand, every day and every hour of our lives.

24

Comfort My People

Comfort ye, comfort ye my people, saith your God.

Speak ye comfortably to Jerusalem, and cry unto her, that her warfare is accomplished, that her iniquity is pardoned: for she hath received of the LORD's hand double for all her sins.

The voice of him that crieth in the wilderness, Prepare ye the way of the LORD, make straight in the desert a highway for our God.

Every valley shall be exalted, and every mountain and hill shall be made low: and the crooked shall be made straight, and the rough places plain:

And the glory of the LORD shall be revealed, and all flesh shall see it together: for the mouth of the LORD hath spoken it.

The voice said, Cry. And he said, What shall I cry? All flesh is grass, and all the goodliness thereof is as the flower of the field:

The grass withereth, the flower fadeth: because the spirit of the LORD bloweth upon it: surely the people is grass.

The grass withereth, the flower fadeth: but the word of our God shall stand for ever.

O Zion, that bringest good tidings, get thee up into the high mountain; O Jerusalem, that bringest good tidings, lift up thy voice with strength; lift it up, be not afraid; say unto the cities of Judah, Behold your God!

Behold, the Lord GOD will come with strong hand, and his arm shall rule for him; behold, his reward is with him, and his work before him.

He shall feed his flock like a shepherd: he shall gather the lambs
with his arm, and carry them in his bosom, and shall gently lead
those that are with young. (Isa. 40:1-11)

The need for a message on comfort for God's chosen seed,
Israel, is most apparent as we follow the story of the life of the
people of God. In earlier chapters in Isaiah the Lord had warned
the Hebrew nation of impending and disastrous judgment. In the
midst of these first chapters is a book called the "Book of Woe."
Isaiah 28:1 says, "Woe." Isaiah 29:1 says, "Woe." Isaiah 30:1 says,
"Woe." Then we read in Isaiah 30:

Behold, the name of the Lord cometh from far, burning with his
anger, and the burden thereof is heavy: his lips are full of indigna-
tion, and his tongue as a devouring fire:
And his breath, as an overflowing stream. . . . (v. 27)

Isaiah 31:1 says, "Woe." Isaiah 33:1 says, "Woe." Then we read of
the tragic pronouncement in Isaiah 39:

Then said Isaiah to Hezekiah, Hear the word of the Lord of hosts:
Behold, the days come, that all that is in thine house, and that
which thy fathers have laid up in store until this day, shall be carried
to Babylon: nothing shall be left, saith the Lord.
And of thy sons that shall issue from thee, which thou shalt beget,
shall they take away; and they shall be eunuchs in the palace of the
king of Babylon. (v. 5-7)

That awesome prophecy in the vision of Isaiah has now come to
pass. The nation has been destroyed. The temple lies in ruins. The
people have been carried away into captivity and they sit in despair
and in slavery in a far away and foreign land. In their despair they
cry the cry of Isaiah 40:27. God says to them, "Why sayest thou, O
Jacob, and speakest, O Israel, My way is hid from the Lord, and
my judgment is passed over from my God?" They feel the Lord has
forgotten them and is indifferent to their need.

What God did with His chosen family of Israel is what He
always does with a nation, a people, a home, a soul. The soul that
sins shall die and all nations who forget God shall be turned into
hell. Sin always carries with it judgment. Judgment fell upon the
people of the Lord. They lost their vision. They lost their holy city.

They lost their beautiful sanctuary. They lost their freedom. The judgment of sin sent them into slavery and they sat by the banks of the rivers of Babylon and wept, so full of despair. To those people who are so cast down and so deeply judged, the prophet lifts up his voice and cries his word of comfort and assurance: God has not forgotten and the Lord is not indifferent. He still cares for His own.

All of Us Need a Message of Assurance and Comfort

We all need this message of assurance and comfort of Isaiah 40:1: "Comfort ye, comfort ye my people, saith your God. Speak ye comfortably to Jerusalem, and cry unto her, that her warfare is accomplished, that her iniquity is pardoned: for she hath received of the Lord's hand double for all of her sins." This is the message the whole world needs.

The world is not made up of strong people who need to be skinned alive. The world is made up of weak people who need to be forgiven, saved, and redeemed. We are among them.

One day a man in a big, new Buick passed me at a high speed on a highway when I was driving to my little country church. I turned off the highway to the little road that led up to my church. The next turn off the road, about a mile further, took an immediate 90° angle where the road builders had cut out the soil making an embankment. When I reached that turn in the road, I saw that the man in the speeding car evidently had not been able to negotiate the angle and had driven his beautiful new Buick right into the heart of that embankment. Nearby, up the hill, was the home of a farmer family in our church. By the time I reached the wrecked car, the injured driver was being helped by the old farmer and his wife. The driver was covered with blood. That old farmer and his dear wife were slowly helping the wounded man up to their house to care for him. One could have taken time to lecture the man, "Do not drive recklessly like that, for it is dangerous." But at that time the poor victim did not need a lecture. He needed someone to help him up and to care for him like the farmer and his wife did.

The whole world is like that, crying for direction, for help, forgiveness, and comfort. We can find such an appeal poignantly stated in some of the songs our people sing which come out of their souls. Oh, how we need God! I think of a song that comes out of the heart of Africa, "Kum Ba Yah." It means "O Lord, come by me."

Kum ba yah, my Lord,
Kum ba yah.
Kum ba yah, my Lord,
Kum ba yah.
Kum ba yah, my Lord,
Kum ba yah.
O Lord, kum ba yah.

Someone's crying, Lord,
Kum ba yah.
Someone's crying, Lord,
Kum ba yah.
Someone's crying, Lord,
Kum ba yah.
O Lord, kum ba yah.

Someone's praying, Lord,
Kum ba yah.
Someone's praying, Lord,
Kum ba yah.
Someone's praying, Lord,
Kum ba yah.
O Lord, kum ba yah.

Not only in the heart of Africa where the tribal people sang, but out of the life of America comes a sweet song of pathos and appeal to God. The words are, "Lord, stand by me."

When the storms of life are raging stand by me,
When the storms of life are raging stand by me;
When the world is tossing me like a ship upon the sea,
Thou who rulest wind and water, stand by me.

In the midst of tribulations stand by me,
In the midst of tribulations stand by me;
When the hosts of hell assail, and my strength begins to fail,
O thou mighty God of battles, stand by me.

> In the midst of faults and failures stand by me,
> In the midst of faults and failures stand by me;
> When I do the best I can, and my friends misunderstand,
> Thou who knowest all about me, stand by me.
>
> When I'm growing old and feeble stand by me,
> When I'm growing old and feeble stand by me;
> When mine eyes grow dim in death and I draw my latest breath,
> O thou God of all the ages, stand by me.

We are not strong but weak. We need to be comforted, not denounced. We need to be forgiven and strengthened. So the message of the prophet to the people in slavery and despair was, "Comfort ye, comfort ye my people."

When we study our text we notice that the prophet speaks throughout the passage in triads, a presentation in threes.

First, his triad of imperatives is: "Comfort ye, comfort ye my people, saith your God." The word "saith" is in the imperfect tense and means that God repeats His words over and over again lest we forget. The second and third imperatives are, "Speak ye comfortably to Jerusalem" (translated literally, "Speak ye to the heart of Jerusalem"), "and cry unto her."

This is followed by a triad of concluding objective clauses. What does he cry? First, "That her warfare is accomplished." The word "warfare" refers to toil and burden; in other words, that Jerusalem's toil in slavery is finished. God has forgiven. The second of the triads of objective clauses is that her "iniquity is pardoned," and the third, that she has "received from the LORD's hand double for all her sins." God announces that Israel's slavery is finished, that her iniquity is pardoned, and that her chastisement is more than commensurate with her assigned punishment.

Next, we see a triad of strophes and voices. We do not see the speaker but listen to the message that is delivered. The first triad is found in verses 3-5. "The voice of him that crieth in the wilderness, Prepare ye the way of the LORD, make straight in the desert a highway for our God. Every valley shall be exalted, and every mountain and hill shall be made low: and the crooked shall be made straight, and the rough places plain: And the glory of the LORD shall be revealed, and all flesh shall see it together: for the mouth of the LORD hath spoken it." A celestial voice in heaven cries to his fellow angelic messengers saying, "Let us build the great causeway for our God." The imagery of this comes from the ancient king who, when he came into a city, was welcomed by the people who prepared for him a great road as we would roll out the red carpet. Isaiah is saying that there is to be a triumphant, decisive event in history when God will come down and the glory of the Lord will be revealed, and we will look upon it and rejoice in it together.

All of us know of the decisive event in history when the angels announced in melodious song and all of the heavenly choirs joined in the singing of its glory. John the Baptist says that he is a part of the fulfillment of that prophecy:

> He said, I am the voice of one crying in the wilderness, Make straight the way of the Lord, as said the prophet Esaias. (John 1:23)

This is a prophecy of the birth of King Jesus.

The second triad is seen in verses 6-8 and refers to a doubt that such a thing could ever be. "The voice said, Cry. And he said, What shall I cry? All flesh is grass, and all the goodliness thereof is as the flower of the field: The grass withereth, the flower fadeth; because the spirit of the LORD bloweth upon it: surely the people is grass." How could such a mighty thing ever come to pass? All things, whether human or earthly, are like grass. "The grass withereth, the flower fadeth: but the word of our God shall stand for ever." The second triad is an avowal that the prophecy is true and that it certainly will come to pass.

The third triad is seen in verses 9-11, "O Zion, that bringest good tidings, get thee up into the high mountain; O Jerusalem, that bringest good tidings, lift up thy voice with strength; lift it up, be not afraid; say unto the cities of Judah, Behold your God!" (v. 9). Look upon Him: born in a manger; preaching the gospel to the people; dying for our sins; laid in the tomb; raised from the dead; ascending into heaven; coming again in power and glory.

Look at the triad of "Beholds." First, "Behold your God!" The second one is, "Behold, the Lord GOD will come with strong hand." The third is, "Behold, his reward is with him, and his work before him." In Revelation we read:

> And, behold, I come quickly; and my reward is with me, to give every man according as his work shall be. (22:12)

He comes not only as a conqueror or a great and mighty King, but He comes also as a gentle Shepherd. He shall feed His flock like a Shepherd. He shall gather the lambs with His arms. He is our great and mighty King!

25

My Favorite Text

The grass withereth, the flower fadeth, but the word of our God
shall stand for ever. (Isa. 40:8)

In our study of Isaiah we now find the people of God in
captivity. Their nation has been destroyed, their holy city has been
set on fire, their holy temple has been cast down and lies in ruins,
and the people in despair sit on the banks of the rivers of Babylon.
The Lord God gave the prophet Isaiah a message for the desperate
children of Israel with the word, "Comfort ye, comfort ye my
people." Then there follows a marvelous, unbelievable prophecy
that God will come, that a great highway will be built for Him in
the desert and every valley will be exalted and every mountain will
be made low, the crooked made straight and the rough places
plain, and the glory of the Lord will be revealed, and all flesh shall
see it together. A prophecy that is beyond imagination: God
Himself is coming down to earth in human flesh and His glory
will be seen by all the earth "for the mouth of the LORD hath spoken
it."

The passage that follows is my favorite text: "The grass withereth, the flower fadeth, but the word of our God shall stand for

181

ever." How could such a thing be, for everything we see in this earth is temporal and transient? We live in a dissolving culture. We even live in a dissolving family circle. The voice said, "Cry this prophecy." Another said, "How shall I cry a prophecy such as that?" All flesh is grass.

The reason that Isaiah 40:8 is my favorite verse is because it includes the entire revelation of God. We would not know God without the Book. We would not know Jesus Christ without the Book. We would have no assurance of salvation or of heaven without the Book. Our eternal hope lies in the promise, assurance, and revelation of the Lord God written in His Book.

We shall look at this text in three ways.

God's Word Was Preexistent

First, the Word of God is founded, fixed, and established forever in heaven before the foundation of the world was made. The Word was in heaven before Jesus was born. God looks upon His holy Word, and what I have in my Bible is but a copy of the everlasting Word of God that was fixed and founded in heaven.

Psalm 119:89 says, "For ever, O LORD, thy word is settled in heaven." The word "settled" could also be translated "fixed," "established." The Word of God has been forever in heaven. For example, the psalmist writes in Psalm 119:152: "Concerning thy testimonies, I have know of old that thou has founded them for ever." Then again we read in verse 160, "Thy word is true from the beginning: and every one of thy righteous judgments endureth for ever." "For ever, O LORD, thy word is settled (fixed, established, founded) in heaven."

In Washington, D.C. we find the National Bureau of Standards, the central measurement laboratory of the United States, which develops standards and methods for accurate measurement and disseminates precise data on the properties of matter. There is a perfect weight, a perfect inch, foot, gallon, pint, ounce, and yard. All of the other measurements in the United States must conform to that standard. If a man sells meat on a scale that does not match a pound weight in Washington, he can be fined and imprisoned. All of the weights and measurements in the United

States follow after the pattern of the Bureau of Standards in Washington.

In the Naval Observatory, also in Washington, D.C. there is a clock which is set every day at high noon by the concourse of the stars in God's firmament. Thereafter every clock in America is set by that one standard of measurement in Washington. The Lord God told Moses to see that he made everything in the tabernacle according to the pattern shown him on the mount. There is a tabernacle of God in heaven. God gave the pattern of it to Moses and had him make every part according to the pattern He showed him from heaven. So it is with the Word of God. "For ever, O Lord, thy word is settled." His Word is fixed and lies before God. The original pattern of God's Word is in glory, and that which we have the Lord wrote out before the foundation of the world was laid.

Thousands of years ago there were thirty-nine books in the Old Testament. There are thirty-nine books in the Old Testament today. In the first Christian centuries there were twenty-seven books in the New Testament. There are twenty-seven books in the New Testament today. They do not change. They are forever settled. They are fixed in heaven.

The Dead Sea Scrolls have an enormous significance for us who are assured of the transmission of the Word of God. For you see, the oldest manuscripts we had for the Old Testament were the Masoretic Texts which were written about A.D. 900 to 1,000. But the Dead Sea Scrolls are scrolls that were written before Christ. A Shrine of the Book is found on the campus of the Hebrew University in which some of the Dead Sea Scrolls are beautifully exhibited, one of which is the Book of Isaiah. That Book of Isaiah was written about one hundred fifty years before Christ. The text is exactly like the texts of the Masoretes. The significance of the Dead Sea Scrolls is that: the transmission of the Word of God has been faithful and true according to the careful preservation of the edict and mandate of God in heaven. It is fixed by almighty God.

GOD'S WORD IN THE LIVING PRESENT

Second, in our generation the Word of God abides incorruptible and imperishable. Let us look at what Peter says:

> Being born again, not of corruptible seed, but of incorruptible, by
> the word of God, which liveth and abideth forever.
> For all flesh is as grass, and all the glory of man as the flower of
> grass. The grass withereth, and the flower thereof falleth away:
> But the word of the Lord endureth for ever. And this is the word
> which by the gospel is preached unto you. (1 Peter 1:23-25)

He adds the word *phthartos*, which means "perishing," "corrupt-
ing." Now a denial to it is *aphthartos*, "incorruptible," "imperishable." The Word of God cannot possibly be corrupted.

The Lord God preserved the life of the incarnate Word, Jesus
Christ, from the sword of Herod when He was born in Bethlehem.
The Lord God preserved the body, the incarnate Word of Jesus
from corruption when He died and was laid in Joseph's tomb. The
same Lord God preserves His true believers so that they some day
will appear in heaven, justified and redeemed. It is the same Lord
God who preserves His Word incorruptible through the present
and continuing generations. The Holy Spirit wrote and keeps the
Word incorruptible.

How does God do that? How does He keep out corruption
and error from the Word of God? The way God accomplished
that was by the multiplying of the text. Printing was not invented
until fifteen hundred years after Christ and all the Bible was in
manuscript form. Men wrote down God's holy Word. There are
4,105 ancient Greek texts of the New Testament. There are almost
30,000 ancient Latin versions of the New Testament. There are
more than 1,000 other versions besides the papyri and the quota-
tions from the Fathers. Let us examine what a miracle that is.

Fifteen hundred years after Herodotus there was only one manuscript copy of his history in the whole world. Twelve hundred
years after Plato there was only one manuscript copy of his great
classics. In the world today there is just one manuscript of the
annals of Tacitus, and there are few more than that of Sophocles,
Euripides, Thucydides, Virgil, and Cicero. But of the Bible there
are thousands and thousands of ancient manuscripts. The reason
that God caused so many to be written was that if a copyist made an

error, or if someone tampered with the text, we could easily see the error by comparing it with the other copies. To see where a copyist made an error in the Holy Scriptures is easily identifiable. God made provision to keep His Word infallible then, and He continues to provide for the preservation of His Word through the earth. If there is a modernist translation of the Word of God, the Lord will see to it that there are many other translations that are true and faithful to the infallible Word. God does that in every area of His spiritual life. If a preacher apostasizes, God will raise up a preacher in another pulpit who will be true to the Word of the Lord. That is true of a church. If a church turns aside from the faith, God will raise up another church that will be true to it. That is true of a denomination. If a denomination wanders from the faith, God will raise up another community of churches and another denomination which will preach the gospel in faith and power and in the unction of the Lord. That is the way God works. That is the way He keeps His Word incorruptible, *aphthartos*. God's Word cannot be corrupted nor be written with error. It cannot be continued with emendations, because God sees to it that any discrepancies in the copies are pointed out, corrected, and removed. "The grass withereth, the flower fadeth: but the word of our God shall stand for ever."

GOD'S WORD IN THE WORLD TO COME

Third, the Word of God endures through all the ages that are yet to come. *Yakum* is from the Hebrew word *kum* and means "rise." *Yakum* finally came to mean "endure," "unfailingly persevere," "remain." *Kum* actually means "to rise," "to stand." The imagery that lies back of the word is of desolation and dissolution. Everything in the earth is in a passing, temporal position. Even the heavens and earth shall pass away, but God's Word is *yakum*; that is, rising out of persecution, destruction, corruption, and decay. His Word stands and does so forever.

PAGAN ATTACK

There have been merciless attacks to destroy the Word of God. They have been pagan, ecclesiastical, and rational. Diocletian, in

A.D. 303, was the Roman emperor who saw the spreading influence of the Christians who based their faith upon a book, the Bible. He decreed that all Bibles in the world should be destroyed, and that the people who loved them and believed in them should be slain. In the awesome persecution of Diocletian, Christians died by the thousands. Every Bible that could be found was burned and destroyed. So successful and victorious was Diocletian in what he had done that he thought he had destroyed the Christian faith forever. Over a burned and destroyed Bible he erected a Roman column and placed this caption on it, *Extincto Nomine Christianorum*, "Extinct is the Name of Christian."

Constantine followed Diocletian and in A.D. took the insignia of the pagans off the shields of his Roman soldiers and placed on the shield a cross and underneath, "In This Sign, Conquer." When did this happen? It was less than ten years after Diocletian! One does not destroy the Word of God nor the Christian faith.

ECCLESIASTICAL ATTACK

One of the bitterest antagonists of the Bible was the dogmatism of the church itself seeking to substitute for the Bible the doctrines, creeds, and edicts of men. When men sought to take the Scriptures and to place them in the language of the people, such an attempt evoked bitter and awesome persecution. The Bible was taken from the hands of the people and was denied them for hundreds of years. Martin Luther was a grown man when he said, "I have never seen a Bible," and he was an ecclesiastic.

John Wycliffe translated the Bible into the language of the people. He wanted to make it possible for all to know the Word of God. Before the Inquisition could slay John Wycliffe, he died and was buried. But the inquisitors exhumed and publicly burned his body and cast the ashes upon the River Swift. If any man in England was found with a Bible, the Bible was hung around his neck and he was publicly hanged and burned. What the English inquisitors did not realize was that when they burned the body of John Wycliffe and scattered his ashes on the River Swift, the river flowed into the Avon and the Avon flowed into the Severn. The Severn flowed into the sea, and the sea lathed the shores of the continents of the world including the new land of America. Wherever the sea carried the ashes of John Wycliffe, there God scattered the truth of the Word of the living Lord. We have learned of the people in Russia who are hearing the Word of God for the first time. In the Philippines there are fifty tribes who have the Word of God. More than one hundred tribes in Old Mexico already have the Word of God in their own language.

RATIONAL ATTACKS

In our day we face the most cruel, devastating, and effective of all the onslaughts against the Word of God in the years of God's dealing with men. This is the onslaught of rationalism. Rationalism is a denial of the Word of the Lord. The Wellhausen, Bauer, Strauss, and Tubingen schools have been and are tearing the Bible apart. They are like termites, living and working at the foundations of every institution known to man. The rationalist denies the supernatural, the deity of Christ, the Resurrection, the miracles, that we will ever see God again, and the reality of conversion. He denies everything that we identify with as God present in the earth, Immanuel. So effective have they been that some of the great intellectuals of the world have been swept into their persuasion. Voltaire, the great French philosopher, who died in 1779 said, "One hundred years from now there will not be a Bible in the earth save as an antiquarian curiosity." The infidel Hume said, "I see the twilight of Christianity."

Will we finally succumb to the terrible ravages of the infidel and the rationalist? Voltaire was a brilliant philosopher who thought there would be no Bible in the next hundred years. Did you know that one hundred years to the day after Voltaire stated the Bible would become extinct, a first edition of Voltaire sold in Paris for eleven cents, and on the same day the British government paid $500,000 to the Czar of Russia for Codex Sinaiticus? By today's prices the amount would be about $2,000,000. On display today in the British Museum in London is the Codex Sinaiticus, one of the earliest manuscripts of the Bible in Greek, both the Old Testament and the New Testament. All the Voltaires in the world with their scoffing, infidel barbs of cynicism and unbelief cannot destroy the Word of God.

As for Hume, he mixed up his sunsets and sunrises. What he thought was twilight was sunrise. There has never been an age when the Bible was so circulated as it is today. The Bible continues to be a best seller year after year. Who reads a book one thousand years old? Once in awhile we will observe a student who is reading Caesar in Latin because of his school requirements, and there aren't even many students who do that.

Who reads a book of religion? Do you see anyone going around reading the *Avesta* of the Parsis, the six *Classics* of Confucius, or the *Four Vedic Hymns* of the Hindu? No, but all over the world we find men and women pouring over the Word of God.

Few books are translated from one language to another that have any sort of circulation. But the Bible is translated into hundreds of languages and dialects, and it is the same powerful Word of God in any language. The Bible is glorious in every language of the world.

"The grass withereth, the flower fadeth: but the word of our God shall stand for ever."

26

Waiting Upon the Lord

Hast thou not known? hast thou not heard? that the everlasting God, the Lord, the Creator of the ends of the earth, fainteth not, neither is weary? there is no searching of his understanding.

He giveth power to the faint; and to them that have no might he increaseth strength.

Even the youths shall faint and be weary, and the young men shall utterly fall:

But they that wait upon the Lord shall renew their strength; they shall mount up with wings as eagles; they shall run, and not be weary; and they shall walk, and not faint. (Isa. 40:28-31)

All of us in our pilgrimage to the heavenly city know troubles, sorrows, and trials. There is no pilgrim on the road but who finds it rough and difficult. As John Bunyan's Pilgrim in *Pilgrim's Progress*, we find ourselves in times of despondency, climbing up hills of difficulty, and facing giants of doubt and discouragement. So many of us fall into faintheartedness and failure. To the man who does not have God as his strength and his Savior, life is a hopeless affair. The godless man is always the hopeless man, for trial and trouble drive happiness and joy out of a man's life.

This world is either a place where there is no God anywhere, or it is the place where there is the one true God everywhere. There is

189

no middle ground between. This world is either without cause, without meaning, without purpose, without destiny, or else it is our Father's house and He keeps watch above His own.

The Hope, Strength, and Comfort of the Trusting Man

The prophet writes by divine inspiration in Isaiah 40:31, "They that wait upon the LORD shall renew their strength; they shall mount up with wings as eagles; and not faint." As I meditated upon that beautiful text, I wondered why the sequence is as it is. We would almost think that the prophet would have spoken of those who walk, then of those who run, and finally of those who soar into the blue of the sky like an eagle. But he turned it around. The thought occurred to me that the prophet possibly was speaking first to the youth in his strident strength with vision, purpose, and destiny in his soul. He soars and mounts up like an eagle into the blue of the sky. Then he spoke of the man in his sober maturity and judgment as he runs without weariness. Finally, he spoke to those of old age who walk and do not faint, being in the care of the Lord through all the days of their life. There is no time when the Lord withdraws from us strength for our failing and fainting life. If there is a cross to bear, He always carries the heavier end. If there are troubles that assail us, they are but golden chains that bind us to the heart of our sympathetic and understanding Lord.

Psalm 27:1 says, "The LORD is my light and my salvation; whom shall I fear? the LORD is the strength of my life; of whom shall I be afraid?" Wait on the Lord. Be of good courage and He will strengthen your heart.

They Who Wait on the Lord Are Given Strength for the Way

What comes to those who wait upon the Lord? First, they receive guidance and strength for their pilgrimage of life. In Isaiah 40 the prophet speaks of a highway for God's redeemed on which we sing the songs of Zion, and sorrow and sighing flee away. The Lord is to us a pillar of cloud by day and a pillar of fire by night, as He guides us through the weary years of this world.

In Isaiah 40:10 he speaks of the Lord God as coming to us with a strong hand and with a mighty arm. The Lord keeps and protects us. Then we read in Isaiah 40:11, "He shall feed his flock like a shepherd: he shall gather the lambs with his arm, and carry them in his bosom, and shall gently lead those that are with young." God looks upon us as a flock and He never overdrives His sheep. Our Lord is the great and Good Shepherd and the flock gathers around Him. Especially in a storm would you find sheep gathering together. So we, as the flock of our Lord, gather near our Shepherd and He strengthens, comforts, and feeds us.

How often we persuade ourselves that our lives are worthless, that we are nothing in the sight of God, and that we do not amount to any more than a falling leaf in the presence of the Lord in this world? Out of the thousands of people in the world, what significance is that one who stumbles and falls? We sometimes look upon ourselves as being weak, amounting to nothing, and soon completely lost in the memory of the world.

Does God look upon us like that? He says that He takes care of His little ones. He picks us up in His arms and carries us in His bosom. Our Good Shepherd especially holds dear to His heart the poor, the weak, the helpless, the sick, and the hurt.

Let us picture a mother of five children. Four of the children are well and strong but one is sick and weak. Tell me, of the five children, which one is she thinking about most? She is thinking about the child who is sick and weak. God's heart is like a mother's heart and He cares and lifts up to His bosom the young who are helpless, needy, and sometimes forgotten.

The prophet says in Isaiah 40:26, "Lift up your eyes on high, and behold who hath created these things, that bringeth out their host by number: he calleth them all by names by the greatness of his might." The mighty God who created the universe, the firmament, and all that is in it, He is the same Lord God who picks up the lambs in His arms and carries them in His bosom.

There is not a more beautiful or more poignant Psalm in the Bible than these verses of Psalm 147:

He healeth the broken in heart, and bindeth up their wounds.

He telleth the number of the stars; he calleth them all by their names. (vv. 3,4)

Could it be that the mighty God who created the stars and calls each one of them by name is the same God who binds up the broken-hearted and who heals all their wounds?

On any clear night looking up into the sky with the naked eye, we can see something like 3,000 stars. In 1600 Galileo invented a telescope and, while scanning the heavens with his new telescope, he discovered in the sweep something like 30,000 stars. Then in the years that followed men who improved upon Galileo's telescope discovered 640,000 stars. In 1800 Sir William Herschel invented a telescope that made Galileo's telescope look like a play toy. With the magnitude of that giant telescope he swept into view something like 26,000,000 stars. Then improving that telescope, Sir Robert Ball discovered there were more than 50,000,000 stars. In our lifetime at Mt. Palomar in California men have placed together a giant telescope and discovered that in the sweep of the glory of the firmament there are uncounted billions of stars. There are millions of galaxies like our Milky Way to which our sun belongs. There are sidereal spheres and creative handiworks of God beyond counting and beyond imagination. "He calleth them all by their names." Think of the billions of stars that His hands created, and He calls them all by their names! Yet He cares for the least of us.

THEY WHO WAIT UPON THE LORD
OFFER AN ACCEPTABLE SERVICE

Psalm 147:3 says, "He healeth the broken in heart, and bindeth up their wounds." Not only does God strengthen, comfort, shepherd, feed, and heal the pilgrims, but He also says that waiting is an acceptable sacrifice in His name. "They that wait upon the LORD shall renew their strength." They who wait and pray, also serve. They present an acceptable sacrifice. Could it be that a man can serve God in an acceptable way just by waiting in His presence, just by calling upon His name? I am an activist. I believe in doing things and getting on with it. God has given us a great and heavenly mandate and we must be busy doing His assignment. But also there is a ministry that is acceptable to God in prayer, quietness, and confidence.

One of the most unusual passages in the Bible is in Isaiah 30. In a time of great despair the nation was turning to Egypt for help and in Isaiah 30:1,2 the prophet speaks of those who have gone down to Egypt to find strength in Pharaoh. Then Isaiah says in Isaiah 30:15, "For thus saith the Lord GOD, the Holy One of Israel; In returning and rest shall ye be saved; in quietness and in confidence shall be your strength."

John Milton was a great Puritan poet who wrote literature as no man has ever written outside the Word of God. He lost his sight in the cause of liberty and righteousness, standing by Oliver Cromwell and the Puritan commonwealth. In his blindness he wrote *Paradise Lost*. He also wrote a sonnet on his blindness. The last verse says, "They also serve who only stand and wait." God gives to us who wait on the Lord His finest gifts, and that may seem strange to us. Somehow God may take from us earthly things that He might bestow upon us heavenly things. Sometimes God will take away from us human strength that He might bestow upon us heaven's strength. John Milton's eyesight was taken away in order that he might see the celestial cities of God. John Bunyan was imprisoned in order that he might make a journey with Christians throughout life that leads to heaven. Alfred Tennyson was broken in heart that he might write, "Thou strong Son of God, immortal love." The chosen nation and family of God was sold into slavery and lived in foreign captivity in order that they might love the Promised Land. To this day wherever you find the Jew, you will find in him an imperishable love for his promised home. God sometimes takes away the old Jerusalem that we might lift up our eyes to the New Jerusalem. God lets this house turn back to the dust of the ground in order that He might build for us another house, one made without hands, eternal in the heavens. God bestows His best gifts upon those who look up to Him.

THOSE WHO WAIT UPON THE LORD
SHALL BE EMPOWERED

God gives power to those who will wait upon Him. He said to

the eleven apostles, "Tarry ye in the city of Jerusalem, until ye be endued with power from on high" (Luke 24:49). So they waited, praying before God. Then came the outpouring of the Holy Spirit without measure at Pentecost. How we need to learn that! The greater the assignment, the longer we need to wait upon the Lord. If He has for us a small task, maybe we can dash into it, but if our assignment is extensive, how we need to tarry in the presence of God! He gives power and strength to those who wait upon Him.

An Assured Victory Is Given to Those Who Wait

God gives to those who wait upon Him the ultimate, final, and assured victory that they cannot, they will not fail. We read in 1 Corinthians 2:9, ". . . Eye hath not seen, nor ear heard, neither have entered into the heart of man, the things which God hath prepared for them that love him." Isaiah writes in Isaiah 64:4, "For since the beginning of the world men have not heard, nor perceived by the ear, neither hath the eye seen, O God, beside thee, what he hath prepared for him that waiteth for him." For those who trust in Him, there cannot be default or failure. God gives them victory. He never fails those who trust in Him. Sometimes that seems impossible to believe, but the Lord has demonstrated it for our encouragement throughout the story of the human heart that has leaned upon Him and looked up in trust to Him.

At the entrance to Oxford University in England is located the Martyr's Monument which is dedicated to Archbishop Cranmer, to Bishop Latimer, and to Master Ridley who were burned at the stake. They were mighty preachers of the gospel, and because of their loyalty to the Lord they were burned at the stake in October, 1555. When the flames were rising Master Ridley began to cry before the leaping fire. Bishop Latimer, tied to the stake on the other side, turned and said: "Be of good cheer, Master Ridley. By God's grace we shall light a fire this day in England that shall never go out." In my reading for this message I stumbled across the bill of expense that was sent to the crown for the burning of Latimer and Ridley. It was:

One load of fire fagots:	3 shillings, 4 pence
Cartage for four loads of wood:	2 shillings
Item, one post:	1 shilling, 4 pence
Item, two chains:	3 shillings, 4 pence
Item, two staples:	6 pence
Item, four laborers:	2 shillings 8 pence

That totals twenty-five shillings and eight pence. What a cheap fire! It didn't even cost $5.00. But the martyrs trusted in God, and that day they lighted a fire in England and in the world that burns to this hour, preaching the gospel of the grace of the Son of God. We never fail trusting God.

Those who ridiculed and mocked our Lord walked up and down as He hung dying and said, "He trusted in God. Let us see if God will save Him." When our Savior bowed His head on the cross He cried saying, "Father, into thy hands I commend my spirit." His friends took a corpse down from the cross and buried it in a tomb. The sun may go out in the sky, the light of the world may turn to darkness, the tides of the sea may cease to ebb and flow, the stars may grow old and dim, and nature may rack itself on the tides of time and fortune, but that Christ should remain dead is impossible and unthinkable, for He trusted in God. All through life and even to death He will carry us, holding us next to His heart, that we might have strength to finish our pilgrimage in this life. Oh, what a wonderful Lord! He is ours.

"But they that wait upon the LORD shall renew their strength; they shall mount up with wings as eagles; they shall run, and not be weary; and they shall walk, and not faint."

27

Our God of Strength

Fear thou not; for I am with thee: be not dismayed; for I am thy God: I will strengthen thee; yea, I will help thee; yea, I will uphold thee with the right hand of my righteousness.

Behold, all they that were incensed against thee shall be ashamed and confounded: they shall be as nothing; and they that strive with thee shall perish.

Thou shalt seek them, and shalt not find them, even them that contended with thee: they that war against thee shall be as nothing, and as a thing of nought.

For I the LORD thy God will hold thy right hand, saying unto thee, Fear not; I will help thee.

Fear not, thou worm Jacob, and ye men of Israel; I will help thee, saith the LORD, and thy redeemer, the Holy One of Israel.

Behold, I will make thee a new sharp threshing instrument having teeth: thou shalt thresh the mountains, and beat them small, and shalt make the hills as chaff.

Thou shalt fan them, and the wind shall carry them away, and the whirlwind shall scatter them: and thou shalt rejoice in the LORD, and shalt glory in the Holy One of Israel.

When the poor and needy seek water, and there is none, and their tongue faileth for thirst, I the LORD will hear them, I the God of Israel will not forsake them.

I will open rivers in high places, and fountains in the midst of the

196

valleys: I will make the wilderness a pool of water, and the dry land springs of water.

I will plant in the wilderness the cedar, the shittah tree, and the myrtle, and the oil tree; I will set in the desert the fir tree, and the pine, and the box tree together:

That they may see, and know, and consider, and understand together, that the hand of the LORD hath done this, and the Holy One of Israel hath created it. (Isa. 41:10-20)

Our Lord uses some strong language when He says, "Thou worm Jacob." The humanist and the rationalist consider this an insult. They say: "I am no worm. I am a man. I can do anything. Have I not walked on the moon? My own hand will bring me salvation and my own sword will win the victory for me." Not only do we find the attitude of superiority and self-sufficiency in the world of the humanist and the rationalist, but we also find such prideful claims paraded in the world of the ecclesiastic and the theologian.

Many of our older hymnals contain the beautiful hymn of Isaac Watts:

> Alas, and did my Saviour bleed?
> And did my Sovereign die?
> Would He devote that sacred head
> For such a worm as I?

Many modern hymnals change the last phrase to, "For sinners such as I." The reproach of a worm does not fit a man who exalts human nature. But God said, "Thou worm Jacob." When we consider the helplessness of a man before God, before life, death, and the judgment, how else could God describe us but, "Thou worm Jacob."

> What is man, that thou art mindful of him? and the son of man, that thou visitest him? (Ps. 8:4)

So cried the psalmist thousands of years ago. Nor have we cause to change the thought of that verse. In the face of the ages, the life of a man is like a moth. In the morning a moth's life passes away. Before the great infinitude of God's creation our existence is like a passing atom. A man may be boastful and proud among his fellow men, and he may be proud of his accomplishments in prosperity, but what does he do in the day of sorrow, adversity, anguish, and death? How helpless a man feels before these providences that overwhelm his life!

MEN ARE HELPLESS

How does a man wash the stain of sin out of his soul? There is a black drop coursing in our veins that we inherited from those who lived before us. Man cannot help it. He is a sinner and he cannot save himself. Nor is a man any more able in the face of the pale visitor of death. What is a man's strength against the victories of death and the grave? We who bury our loved ones visit the cemetery, and we leave a part of ourselves behind. Death wastes our families, destroys our homes, and finally lays us in the dust of the ground. How can I take arms to battle against that last enemy, death?

I am even overwhelmed by the providences of life over which I have no control. Sometimes we are drowned in a sea of sorrows, sometimes we are swept away in a flood of disappointments and frustrations. How do we find ourselves equal to the providences that sweep us away in this life?

THE HEAVENLY PROMISE

Look at the promises of God: "Fear thou not; for I am with thee . . . I will stengthen thee; yea, I will help thee; yea, I will uphold thee with the right hand of my righteousness." As though one time were not enough, God repeats the promises: "For I the LORD thy God will hold thy right hand, saying unto thee . . . Fear not, thou worm Jacob, . . . I will help thee, saith the LORD." All three persons in the Godhead avow to help us. "I will help thee, saith the LORD." The word used for Lord is actually *Yahweh*, or Jehovah, and refers to God our Father. Then we read "I will help thee . . . thy redeemer." That is the Lord Jesus Christ, the second person of the Trinity. After that we read ". . . the Holy One of Israel," and that refers to the Holy Spirit of God poured out upon this world in our hearts. We are encouraged to be bold because of the help we receive. God would never send us on a task or mission for Him without first enduing us with power from on high. If God has mandated the assignment, He gives along with the assignment ability sufficient for the mission.

What a power man has when God is with him! With the jawbone of an ass Samson slew uncounted Philistines. God was in the arm of Samson. Holding just a sling in his hand, the little shepherd boy, David, brought down the giant Goliath. Simon Peter at Pentecost won thousands to the faith, some of whom had crucified our Lord.

One time I spoke to the Florida State Evangelism Conference and shared the occasion with the governor of the state, Reuben Askew. What he said made the headlines of the papers the following morning. "After my election I moved to Tallahassee, the capital city, coming early in order to choose the men who were to work with me in my commissions and to form my new government. As I began to work, the pressures and burdens of my responsibilities were so heavy upon me that I could not sleep and I could not keep down my food. I thought I was going to be the first governor in the history of the state who resigned his office even before he was inaugurated. In my desperation, I bowed in my room and said to myself, 'What am I doing wrong that I cannot sleep or eat?' The answer came to me as though it were a revelation from heaven, that I was doing the assignment in my own strength and that I should ask God to help me. I knelt down before God and asked Him to help me. When I stood up, I stood up in the power of the Lord. From that day until this, I have slept like a child every night. I am in strength and in health. People everywhere ask me: 'How is it that you are so bold to speak for Christ in the legislature and the political convocations of the state?' 'I was a Christian before I was elected governor. I shall be a Christian after I cease to be governor. I see no reason to change in between.'" "Fear not, thou worm Jacob, and ye men of Israel; I will help thee, saith the LORD, and thy redeemer, the Holy One of Israel."

Do you see in this passage what God has promised to those who look in faith and assurance to Him? In verse 13 He likens us to a man who is doing a service. He says, "For I the LORD thy God will hold thy right hand, saying unto thee, Fear not; I will help thee."

In verses 15–19 he likens his servant to a man who has gone to war and says:

> Behold, I will make thee a new sharp threshing instrument having teeth: thou shalt thresh the mountains, and beat them small, and shalt make the hills as chaff.
>
> Thou shalt fan them, and the wind shall carry them away, and the whirlwind shall scatter them: and thou shalt rejoice in the LORD, and shalt glory in the Holy One of Israel.
>
> When the poor and needy seek water, and there is none, and their tongue faileth for thirst, I the LORD will hear them, I the God of Israel will not forsake them.
>
> I will open rivers in high places, and fountains in the midst of the valleys: I will make the wilderness a pool of water, and the dry land springs of water.
>
> I will plant in the wilderness the cedar, the shittah tree, and the myrtle, and oil tree; I will set in the desert the fir tree, and the pine, and the box tree together.

The Lord delights in taking weak instruments and magnifying them in His holy power.

GOD HELPS US IN OUR PILGRIMAGE

Sometimes a new Christian will feel that the problems of life are now settled and that he will never have to fight or war again. But he soon learns that now that he is saved, the hosts of hell seem to assail him more. Oh, the temptations that overwhelm a young Christian! Many times he will feel the war is greater than he can win and the journey is farther than he can go. Sometimes he's ready to turn to the old life and to the world. But then the Lord comes to encourage and lift him up: "Fear not . . . I will help thee, saith the LORD." Even for us who are veterans in the Christian faith, it is easy to fall into a feeling of failure, inadequacy, disappointment, and frustration. But God says, "Fear not . . . I will help thee."

What can a man do with his sins? If I were to avow from this moment on, "I shall be perfect and never sin again," what about the sins of the days that are past? We sin in our childhood, in our youth, and in our adulthood. How can we ever stand before God, accepted in His sight? We know God's promise: "For I the LORD thy God will hold thy right hand . . . I will help thee." It is something God does for us.

Before coming to be undershepherd of the First Baptist Church of Dallas I was a pastor in Muskogee, Oklahoma, the seat of the five Indian tribes the government settled in eastern Oklahoma. I love to visit those Indian people, to sit down and to talk with them. One of the oldest Baptist associations in America is the Cherokee Association. When they were driven out of their homes in North Carolina and in Georgia, they carried with them their pastors, their Cherokee Bibles, and their commitment to Christ. One of those old Cherokee Indians was asked, "How is it you say God saved you?" The Indian took some dried leaves and placed them in a circle. Then he took a worm and set it in the middle of the circle. He lit a fire which ran around the circle of leaves. The little worm in the inside crawled different ways, seeking an escape, but always found the fire. It drew as far back from the fire as it could in the center of the circle and curled up to die. It was then that the old Indian took his hand and lifted the little worm up and out and placed it in safety. He said, "That is what He did for me."

28

The Faithfulness of Jesus

Behold my servant, whom I uphold; mine elect, in whom my soul delighteth; I have put my spirit upon him: he shall bring forth judgment to the Gentiles.

He shall not cry, nor lift up, nor cause his voice to be heard in the street.

A bruised reed shall he not break, and the smoking flax shall he not quench: he shall bring forth judgment unto truth.

He shall not fail nor be discouraged, till he have set judgment in the earth: and the isles shall wait for his law.

Thus saith God the LORD, he that created the heavens, and stretched them out; he that spread forth the earth, and that which cometh out of it; he that giveth breath unto the people upon it, and spirit to them that walk therein:

I the LORD have called thee in righteousness, and will hold thine hand, and will keep thee, and give thee for a covenant of the people, for a light of the Gentiles;

To open the blind eyes, to bring out the prisoners from the prison, and them that sit in darkness out of the prison house.(Isa. 42:1-7)

The glorious prophecy of Isaiah 42 was referred to by Jesus in Matthew 12:

Then the Pharisees went out, and held a council against him, how they might destroy him.

But when Jesus knew it, he withdrew himself from thence: and great multitudes followed him, and he healed them all;

And charged them that they should not make him known:

That it might be fulfilled which was spoken by Esaias the prophet, saying,

Behold my servant, whom I have chosen; my beloved, in whom my soul is well pleased: I will put my spirit upon him, and he shall shew judgment to the Gentiles.

He shall not strive, nor cry; neither shall any man hear his voice in the streets.

A bruised reed shall he not break, and smoking flax shall he not quench, till he send forth judgment unto victory.

And in his name shall the Gentiles trust. (vv. 14-21)

Look at the prophecy in Isaiah, then see how Matthew applies the fulfillment of the prophecy in the life of our Lord. In Matthew 12, as in the chapter preceding, Matthew has described the miraculous wonders of divine power resident in Jesus of Nazareth. Then he is struck by the humility and gentleness of that same mighty and wonderful Healer and Teacher of men. He applies the prophecy portraying a union of the divine power of heaven in this humble and lowly Jesus, a man of such godly ableness and yet a man free from ostentatious ambition who quietly, humbly does His work of healing and teaching the people.

THE LORD'S REACTION

So Matthew presents the story: "Then the Pharisees went out, and held a council against him, how they might destroy him. But when Jesus knew it, he withdrew himself from thence: and great multitudes followed him, and he healed them all." What a contrast between those who officially rejected and sought to destroy Him and the continuing, humble ministry of the Lord Jesus as He taught and healed the people! Who can understand the compassionate, loving ways of our Lord? The official mind had rejected Him and the leaders of the nations were plotting to destroy His life. Surely the Lord would fall into deep depression. He would become discouraged and forget the needs of the multitudes. He would quit in the face of such frustrating and confusing opposition. What does the Bible say? It tells us that when the Pharisees discussed with council how they might destroy Him, the great multitudes continued to follow Him and He healed them all. He kept on with His ministry of blessing and encouragement. The sectarian mind might hate Him, but the common mind loved Him for the Scriptures say, "And the common people heard him gladly."

Doesn't the Lord realize the council is plotting His assassination? They want Him dead. But the Master continues on in His healing and teaching ministries. He does not look at the trial or at the trouble or at all the bitter and hateful opposition, but He looks at the needs of the people and continues to teach and heal.

Would it not be wonderful if we could be like that? Not to look at the discouragement and at the trials of life, but to look at the needs of a great work done for God? We tend to think of the money, the time, the tears, and blood. I know. There is no mighty work for God ever done without sacrifice, trouble, and discouragement, but if God is in the assignment, and if it is a work for which we are called from heaven, then the time, trouble, and sacrifice are something by which God blesses us and strengthens us — and He works with us. The discouragement our Lord met in His humble and tender ministries among the people never discouraged Him. He kept on in His sweet and quiet way, ministering to the people, doing the work of God in the earth.

Jesus Did Not Retaliate

Whatever people might have said about Jesus, He continued His work. When they arrested Him, there were those who covered Him with their spittle. There were those who plucked out His beard. There were those who walked up to Him and said: "Thou Christ, prophesy. What is my name, who strikes you?" When they struck Him He didn't say a word. He was calm and quiet. When they arraigned Him before Pilate, He answered nothing in His defense, no matter how many witnesses spoke against Him. When they nailed Him to the tree, He was in their hands, yielded and without resistance. He was like a lamb led to the slaughter, and as a sheep before her shearer is dumb, so He opened not His mouth.

They walked up and down before His cross wagging their heads and saying, "Come down from the cross and we will believe in You." When I read that story I say in my heart, "Lord, come down from the cross and strike unmitigated terror in their hearts." When He did come down from the cross, His body was a limp, dead corpse. They wrapped Him in a winding sheet and placed Him in a tomb. With all of their insults and blasphemies, all He said was, "Father, forgive them; for they know not what they do." But the third day He was raised from the dead and said, "All power is given unto me in heaven and in earth." He called His disciples and said, "In My name, preach the remission of sins for all who will turn and trust in Me." He is the gentle, faithful, loving Lord Jesus, continuing His work even today.

Then there follows two analogies which are incomparably beautiful and precious. Matthew 12 says:

> A bruised reed shall he not break, and smoking flax shall he not quench, till he send forth judgment unto victory.
> And in his name shall the Gentiles trust. (vv. 20,21)

The "bruised reed" could have been a bullrush that a heavy animal crushed and broke as he made his way down to the river. Or it could have been a little succulent and tender plant ground under the iron heel of an indifferent man, and the Lord Jesus picked it up and rejoined it. Or the "bruised reed" could have been a little pipe made out of a bullrush or papyrus and had been made into a flute. Someone might have stepped on it so that it would not play anymore, so the Lord Jesus picked the reed up, mended it, and gave the song back to the flute. I think the analogy of verse 20 is something like that. When life seems so spoiled and ruined and seems to have lost its song, the Lord picks it up, tunes it beautifully, and the soul sings and praises God again.

One of the most beautiful and meaningful poems I know is entitled "The Touch of the Master's Hand." It begins with an auctioneer selling an old violin. He holds it up and says: "What am I bid for this violin? One dollar? Two dollars? Who will make it three?" Just before the old violin was sold for three dollars, from the back of the room an old, gray-haired man came forward, took the violin and the bow, and wiped off the dust. He tightened the bow and tuned the strings and began to play angelic music. When the auctioneer held it up again he said, "What am I bid for it? A thousand dollars? Two thousand dollars? Who will make it three?" The concluding stanzas of the poem read:

> The people cheered, but some of them cried,
> "We do not quite understand
> What changed its worth." Swift came the reply:
> The touch of a master's hand.
>
> And many a man with life out of tune,
> And battered and scarred with sin,
> Is auctioned off cheap to the thoughtless crowd,
> Much like the old violin.
>
> A "mess of pottage," a glass of wine;
> A game — and he travels on.
> He is "going" once, and "going" twice,
> He's "going" and almost "gone."
>
> But the Master comes and the foolish crowd
> Never can quite understand
> The worth of a soul and the change that's wrought
> By the touch of the Master's hand.
> — *Myra Brooks Welch*

Second, "And smoking flax shall he not quench." The imagery here can be illustrated by a wick in a cheap clay lamp which is almost gone, is barely aflame. The one little hope left in a man's heart is smoking to extinction. But the Master trims the wick, and He pours in oil of heaven and of the Holy Spirit. He nurtures the life back and it flames and shines again. There are many souls in whose heart the light of hope has nearly died — it barely flickers.

How often does a man come to the age of retirement, and because he has nothing to do he soon dies. There is nothing that destroys the fiber of a man's life like feeling useless and unwanted, having nothing to do, and with no purpose in life to live. Many elderly and invalid feel they have no purpose in life, but God has given to them a ministry of intercession and prayer. They can pray for their pastors and Christian workers, and name them before the throne of grace. I have never heard a sweeter word than what

Spurgeon once said to a humble disciple, "My friend, some day when you have the ear of the great King, will you call my name?" The ministry of praying and sustaining before God's throne is desperately needed. This is a ministry we can have in our midst.

The message of Jesus' care and concern is addressed to the lost who also lose hope. God alone knows the number of young men and women who find themselves enmeshed in the weaknesses of life in sin and compromise who nearly give up. The Lord takes a broken life and mends it. He forgives and lifts the person up. He strengthens and encourages. The Lord's great assignment in the earth is not to destroy men's lives but to save men's lives that we might have strength and ability in Him. There is no person whom the Lord cannot lift up and set his feet upon a rock. He puts a song in the heart and the redeemed person can go forward forgiven, strengthened in the name of the Lord.

Jesus came into the world that we might be saved. He did not come to condemn the world. He did not come to blame, but to seek and to save. When we call Him Jesus, Savior, we call Him by His name.

29

Passing Through Deep Waters

But now thus saith the LORD that created thee, O Jacob, and he that formed thee, O Israel, Fear not: for I have redeemed thee, I have called thee by thy name; thou art mine.

When thou passest through the waters, I will be with thee; and through the rivers, they shall not overflow thee: when thou walkest through the fire, thou shalt not be burned; neither shall the flame kindle upon thee. (Isa. 43:1,2)

The address of the passage is directed to Israel. "I have created thee, O Jacob . . . formed thee, O Israel." When the Lord speaks of the fire and the water through which the nation would pass, He is speaking of His preservation of that holy and chosen family. For centuries the Hebrew nation has known nothing but bitter and fierce persecution. The Jewish people have been hated and hounded to the ends of the earth. Some of the experiences through which the nation has gone are harbingers of their history. When they stood at the waters of the Red Sea and when they stood before the swollen Jordan, it was God who parted the waters that they might have deliverance and find the way through. When Moses saw the bush burning unconsumed and when the three Hebrew children, Shadrach, Meshack, and Abed-nego, were thrown into the fiery furnace heated seven times hotter, these events are figures of the trial, tribulation, and persecution of the nation. But God promised that the nation of Israel would exist forever. No matter how extensive the effort or plan or persecution of man to destroy the Jew, God will never allow the Jew to be destroyed. Not only that, but we find in Romans 11 the outline for the future conversion and glory of Israel.

This passage of assurance and promise is the possession of all God's people through the ages. Break down the children of the Lord into groups as small as you please. The promise always keeps its same form and pertinency. Whether the promise is to the people of God in Israel, or to the people of the Lord in the church, whether it is broken down into family groups, or into two or three or just one, the promise is ever the same. It is forever true. "When thou passest through the waters, I will be with thee; and through the rivers, they shall not overflow thee: when thou walkest through the fire, thou shalt not be burned; neither shall the flame kindle upon thee." This is God's promise to His children.

A Fearful But Faithful Revelation of Our Spiritual Pilgrimage

First, I see that God has revealed to us a fearful and frightful revelation. Not "*if* thou passest through the water, flood, fire, and flame" but "*when* thou passest through the water, flood, fire, and flame." In the first verse I read such heavenly benedictory words about God's people. The Lord has created us, formed us, redeemed us, called us by His name; we are His. We would suppose that those who belong to God would never know trial or suffering. They are God's. He knows them and calls them by name. He says they are His. Therefore, we would conclude that they are exempt from all the tragedies and sorrows of life. But not so, for the next verse immediately follows: "When thou passest through the waters . . . rivers . . . fire . . . flame." It must be that the nearer one gets to God, the nearer he gets to the fire. There is an apocryphal word of Jesus where the Lord is quoted as saying, "He that is near me is near the fire." In the gospel of John the Lord says,

"In the world ye shall have tribulation." Is that true of the children of God? Yes. There never was a man more tried than righteous Job.

The Lord chose Peter to be the head of the apostles. He was the chief spokesman of the opening of the door to the Gentiles. God said, "I give to thee the keys of the kingdom of heaven." He opened wide the doors to the Jews in Jerusalem, to the Samaritans in Samaria, to those who were Gentiles in Caesarea. Yet the Lord said to Peter:

> Verily, verily I say unto thee, When thou wast young, thou girdest thyself, and walkedst whither thou wouldest: but when thou shalt be old, thou shalt stretch forth thy hands, and another shall gird thee, and carry thee whither thou wouldest not.
> This spoke he, signifying by what death he should glorify God. And when he had spoken this, he saith unto him, Follow me. (John 21:18,19)

That is, Simon Peter would die with outstretched hands. He would be crucified, and in crucifixion and suffering unspeakable, he would glorify God. In Acts 9:16 the Lord says of Saul of Tarsus, "For I will shew him how great things he must suffer for my name's sake." To be an heir of heaven is to be an heir of trial and tribulation.

These trials and troubles come in many forms and fashions. We see that in our Scripture passage, "When thou passest through the waters . . . fire . . . flame." Some of the experiences inevitable in our life are chilling to the bone. But we also read, "I will be with thee. . . ." No rolling river will separate us from God and no consuming and flaming fire will destroy His presence. There are no more precious words to the soul of the saint than those in Romans 8:

> For I am persuaded, that neither death, nor life, nor angels, nor principalities, nor powers, nor things present, nor things to come,
> Nor height, nor depth, nor any other creature, shall be able to separate us from the love of God, which is in Christ Jesus our Lord. (vv. 38,39)

There are no providences however tragic; there are no trials however heartbreaking that can separate us from God. I am not the less loved of God, nor am I thrust from His presence because I am troubled, poor, sick, or needy. It is in those difficulties and trials that I most sense the presence and encouragement of God. If one never experiences a broken heart and never knows fierce trials, he will never have the experience of the real nearness of God.

In our passage the Lord uses the word "through." "When thou passest *through* the rivers . . . *through* the fire." The Christian pilgrim not only comes to the edge of the chilling tide, he not only looks into the fiery furnace, but he also is often plunged into the tide, the roaring seas, and the overflowing rivers, and he is thrown into the fiery furnace. But the word is always "through." The flood never drowns us and the fire never consumes us, for God is with us through the fire and through the flood. The comfort of Psalm 23 is this: "Yea, though I walk through the valley of the shadow of death, I will fear no evil: for thou art with me; thy rod and thy staff they comfort me" (v 4).

When the three Hebrew children were cast into the fiery furnace, the king looked and said: "Did not we cast three men bound into the midst of the fire? . . . Lo, I see four men . . . and the form of the fourth is like the Son of God." The three Hebrew children were walking free in the furnace. The fire did nothing but bring to them the living presence of the living Lord and it burned up their bonds. They were free. So it is that the trials, fires, and floods that overwhelm us in our life free us from the visible world that we might live in the invisible. Our bodies carry our souls, it is not our souls that carry our bodies. The flame and fire burn our bonds and liberate us to walk in the presence of the great and living God. This is God's way of preparing us for the victories of the kingdom. "Every one that is called by my name . . . I have created him for my glory" (Isa. 43:7). This is God's purpose for us that we might reign with Christ. If we suffer with Him, we also shall reign with Him. No man could know victory who has not first been in a battle or a conflict. If we are to wear the crown in heaven, we first must bear the cross here on earth. Shall I cower and cringe before the warfare?

Am I a soldier of the cross?
A follower of the Lamb?
And shall I fear to own His cause
Or blush to speak His name?

Must I be carried to the skies
On flow'ry beds of ease,
While others fought to win the prize
And sailed thro' bloody seas?

Are there no foes for me to face?
Must I not stem the flood?
Is this vile world a friend to grace,
To help me on to God?

Sure I must fight if I would reign —
Increase my courage, Lord!
I'll bear the toil, endure the pain,
Supported by Thy word.

THE TRIALS ARE WITHIN THE PURPOSE OF GOD

"Fear not, for I am with thee, for I am the LORD thy God, the
Holy One of Israel, thy Saviour." He has already informed us that
He has created us and formed us, for He has redeemed us. We are
twice His. With a great and awesome price He bought us to
Himself. We are not just numbers in God's sight. We are dear and
known to Him. He says, "I even count the hairs on your head." He
knows all about us. "I have called thee by thy name; thou art
mine." Do not be afraid for your trials, for your life is under the
surveillance and the elective purposes of God. The fire will not
consume you. The river will not overwhelm or overflow you.

Is there any heart discouraged
    As it journeys on its way?
Does there seem to be more darkness
    Than there is of sunny day?
Oh, it's hard to learn the lesson,
    As we pass beneath the rod,
That the sunshine and the shadow
    Serve alike the will of God;
But there comes a word of promise,
    Like the promise in the bow —
That however deep the waters
    They shall never overflow.

When the flesh is worn and weary,
  And the spirit is depressed,
And temptations sweep upon it
  Like a storm on ocean's breast,
There's a haven ever open
  For the tempest-driven bird,
There's a shelter for the tempted
  In the promise of the Word;
For the standard of the Spirit
  Shall be raised against the foe,
And however deep the waters
  They shall never overflow.

When a sorrow comes upon you
  That no other soul can share,
And the burden seems too heavy
  For the human heart to bear,
There is One whose grace can comfort
  If you'll give Him an abode;
There's a Burden-bearer ready
  If you'll trust Him with your load;
For the precious promise reaches
  To the depths of human woe,
That however deep the waters
  They shall never overflow.

When the sands of life are ebbing
  And I near the Jordon's shore,
When I see its waters rising
  And I hear its billows roar,
I will reach my hand to Jesus,
  In His bosom I shall hide,
And 'twill only be a moment
  Till I reach the other side;
It is then the fullest meaning
  Of the promise I shall know —
"When thou passest through the waters
  They shall never overflow."

— Author Unknown

30

Look and Live!

Look unto me, and be ye saved, all the ends of the earth: for I am God, and there is none else. (Isa. 45:22)

The words of our text speak of the Lord's tremendous and significant word to mankind. This is the message of the prophets and of the psalmists through the centuries. Upon man's answer to this message depends his condition, his character, his salvation, and his destiny forever. We will follow the text in a reverse order. We will take the last clause first, "for I am God, and there is none else." Next we will look at the second part, the message of God to the ends of the earth. Then we will examine the third part: "Look unto me, and be ye saved."

THE ONE TRUE AND ONLY GOD

The context of the passage is clear. The last clause is a summation of the whole Word of God. We read in Isaiah 45:

For thus saith the Lord that created the heavens; God himself that formed the earth and made it; he hath established it, he created it not in vain, he formed it to be inhabited: I am the Lord; and there is none else.

214

I have not spoken in secret, in a dark place of the earth: I said not unto the seed of Jacob, Seek ye me in vain: I the LORD speak righteousness, I declare things that are right.

Assemble yourselves and come; draw near together, ye that are escaped of the nations: they have no knowledge that set up the wood of their graven image, and pray unto a god that cannot save.

Tell ye, and bring them near; yea, let them take counsel together: who hath declared this from ancient time? who hath told it from that time? have not I the LORD? and there is no God else beside me; a just God and a Saviour; there is none beside me.

Look unto me, and be ye saved, all the ends of the earth: for I am God, and there is none else. (vv. 18-22)

The text represents the cry of the prophets — there is only one true God. When a prophet is able to lead his people into that same praise and adoration such as in the days of Elijah when he stood on Mt. Carmel, the whole Bible rings and resounds with the great revelation of the one true Lord. Where are the gods of Nineveh before whom the multitudes prostrated themselves? Ask the mounds of earth under which those false deities are buried. They lie in ruin and in departed glory. Where are the false gods of ancient Greece? Where are these deities to whom they address their adorning and adorable poetry, these gods for whom they built sanctuaries and temples that were the wonder of the world? What has been true of these gods of the ancient world shall be true also of the gods of this present world. There will come a day when Buddha will be forgotten. The false gods that America worships — power, money, prestige, fame, fortune, amusement — these also shall perish with the passing age. For there is but one true God and His name is the Lord Jehovah.

To Whom the Address Is Made

To whom does He refer when He says, "all the ends of the earth"? If I stand in Dallas, then the ends of the earth are the places which are the farthest from me. The ends of the earth are the Aborigines of central Australia, the Bantu, the Bushmen, and the Hottentot of central Africa. The Stone Age Indians in the Amazon jungles of South America are a part of the ends of the earth. Depending on where we stand, we all are considered a part of the end of the earth.

Look at the descriptive appeal of our text, "Look unto me, and be ye saved, all the ends of the earth; for I am God, and there is none else." The ancient philosophers were as brilliant men as we could ever know. I once looked through the courses offered at Oxford University in England. There were something like four hundred different courses offered in Aristotle alone. Those great thinkers of the ancient world — Socrates, Plato, and Aristotle — asked the right questions and sought the right answers, but they groped in the dark. Death, the grave, and the world to come lay beyond their grasp and comprehension. They taught, lived, and died never having known the ultimate truth. They sought after and inquired about the truth, but they never saw it. The truth came to us only when God incarnate walked the face of this earth and taught us His truth. It is Christ Jesus the incarnate God who revealed to us the full truth of the Almighty and the character of the great, invisible God, whom no man has ever seen and whose mind no man could ever comprehend. Christ brought life and immortality to light. It is He who says, "Look unto me and be ye saved, all the ends of the earth."

God Provides a Simple Plan

Notice how plain and simple the plan of deliverance and salvation is. "Look unto me." Anyone can look. It does not require an education to look. A man need not have prestige, status, or political power to look. It does not require an education to look. It does not even demand moral excellence or righteousness. The vilest and most wretched of sinners can look. How could it be that in so simple a thing as a look I could be forgiven my sins, that I could be regenerated and saved? We feel there must be something else. Surely there are deep mysterious ceremonies, rites, and rituals that are required. To look is so simple a thing. We feel like Naaman who was a mighty man with his master and the head of all the hosts of Assyria. But he was a leper. Standing before the house of Elisha, Naaman waited for the man of God that he might be cleansed. But Elisha did not even walk out the door to see him. He sent one of his servants to him and told the great general to go down to the Jordan and wash seven times in the muddy water and his flesh would again be like the flesh of a little child. Naaman was insulted. He thought the prophet would come out and call upon the name of his God and in a great dramatic gesture strike the leper and he would be clean. But just to wash, anyone could wash! So we stumble and hesitate.

Can a man be saved just by a look? If we have any tendency whatsoever to look, we look at everything and everyone except God. Some look to Moses and to the lightnings and thunderings of Sinai and they look to the righteousness of the law to be saved. There are some who look to the priests, to the ministers, and to the church in order to be saved. There are others who look to ordinances, to baptism, and the water, thinking this will wash their sins away. There are others who look to themselves and examine themselves and ask: "Did I repent just right? Did I believe just right? Did I join the church just right? Am I living just right? Is my consecration just right?" They look inwardly to themselves, while all the while the voice of the living God is the same. "Look unto me, and be ye saved, all the ends of the earth." God did not say "see" or "comprehend" or "understand." He said, "look."

When the Israelites were dying because of the terrible toxin in their system from the bite of venomous serpents, I can imagine their going blind. Because a man is blind, does that mean that God can not save him and that God can not forgive him? God never said "see." He said "look." Salvation is not in our seeing, our understanding, nor our comprehending, but it is in our turning, our looking, our expectancy, our faith and trust that we are healed, saved, and delivered.

Dr. George W. Truett, my predecessor in First Baptist Church, Dallas, in a little passage in one of his sermons which I copied, tells of his witness of his conversion: "I sat in the audience one night and listened to the preacher as he pleaded that Christ might have His own way and save a soul. I said, 'Lord Jesus, it is all dark, I cannot understand, but dark or light, live or die, come what may, I surrender right now to Christ.' He saved me then."

Spurgeon's Conversion

When the text of our discussion in Isaiah 45 was elaborated

upon by a Primitive Methodist layman, the greatest preacher we
have ever known since the days of the New Testament, Charles
Haddon Spurgeon, was won to faith in Christ. Listen to the words
of Spurgeon as he describes his own conversion:

> I had been about five years in the most fearful distress of mind, as
> a lad. If any human being felt more the terror of God's law, I can
> indeed pity and sympathize with him.
>
> I thought the sun was blotted out of the sky — that I had so sinned
> against God that there was no hope for me. I prayed — the Lord
> knoweth that I prayed — but I never had a glimpse of an answer that
> I knew of. I searched the Word of God: The promises were more
> alarming than the threatenings — I read the privileges of the people
> of God but with the fullest persuasion that they were not for me.
> The secret of my distress was this: I did not know the gospel. I was in
> a Christian land; I had Christian parents; but I did not understand
> the freeness and simplicity of the gospel.
>
> I attended all the places of worship in the town where I lived, but I
> honestly believe I did not hear the gospel fully preached. I do not
> blame the men, however. One man preached the divine
> sovereignty. I heard him with pleasure; but what was that to a poor
> sinner who wished to know what he should do to be saved? There
> was another admirable man who always preached about the law;
> but what was the use of plowing up ground that needed to be
> sown? I knew it was said, "Believe on the Lord Jesus Christ, and
> thou shalt be saved"; but I did not know what it was to believe in
> Christ.
>
> I sometimes think I might have been in darkness and despair
> now, had it not been for the goodness of God in sending a
> snowstorm one Sunday morning, when I was going to a place of
> worship. When I could go no further, I turned down a court and
> came to a little Primitive Methodist chapel. In that chapel there
> might be a dozen or fifteen people. The minister did not come that
> morning; snowed up, I suppose. A poor man, a shoemaker, a tailor,
> or something of that sort, went into the pulpit to preach.
>
> This poor man was obliged to stick to his text, for the simple
> reason that he had nothing else to say. The text was, "Look unto
> Me, and be ye saved, all the ends of the earth." He did not even
> pronounce the words rightly, but that did not matter.
>
> There was, I thought, a glimpse of hope for me in the text. He
> began thus: "My dear friends, this is a very simple text indeed. It says
> 'Look.' Now that does not take a great deal of effort. It ain't lifting
> your foot or finger; it is just 'look'. Well, a man need not go to
> college to look. You may be the biggest fool, and yet can look. A

man need not be worth a thousand a year to look. Anyone can look: a child can look. But this is what the text says. Then it says, 'Look unto me'. Many look to themselves. No use looking there. You'll never find comfort in yourself. Some look to God the Father. No; look to Him by and by. Jesus Christ says, 'Look unto me'.

Then the good man followed up his text in this way: "Look unto Me; I am sweating great drops of blood. Look unto Me; I am hanging on the cross. Look! I ascend; I am sitting at the Father's right hand. O look to Me."

When he had got about that length and managed to spin out ten minutes or so, he was at the length of his tether. Then he looked at me under the gallery, and I dare say, with so few present, he knew me to be a stranger. He then said, "Young man, you look so miserable." Well, I did; but I had not been accustomed to having remarks made on my personal appearance from the pulpit before. However, it was a good blow struck. He continued: "And you will always be miserable — miserable in life, and miserable in death — if you do not obey my text. But if you obey, now, this moment, you will be saved."

Then he shouted, "Young man, look to Jesus Christ; look now." I did look to Jesus Christ. I looked until I could have looked my eyes away; and in heaven I will look still, in joy unutterable.

There and then the cloud was gone; the darkness had rolled away, and that moment I saw the sun. I could have risen that moment and sung with the most enthusiastic of them of the precious blood of Christ, and the simple faith which looks alone to Him. Oh, that somebody had told me that before — look unto Christ and you shall be saved.

*   *   *

I've a message from the Lord, hallelujah!
The message unto you I'll give;
'Tis recorded in His Word, hallelujah!
It is only that you "look and live."
Look and live, my brother, live!
Look to Jesus now and live;
'Tis recorded in His Word, hallelujah!
It is only that you "look and live."

Come without money, come without price. It is not that we need to be educated or learned. It is not that we should be morally excellent, for all of us know how it is to fail, to be crushed with our own inabilities and thoughts. Our only need is to look. We turn our face godward, and in that turning we are saved.

31

Predestination

> Remember the former things of old: for I am God, and there is
> none else; I am God, and there is none like me,
> Declaring the end from the beginning, and from ancient times
> the things that are not yet done, saying, My counsel shall stand, and
> I will do all my pleasure:
> Calling a ravenous bird from the east, the man that executeth my
> counsel from a far country: yea, I have spoken it, I will also bring it
> to pass; I have purposed it, I will also do it. (Isa. 46:9-11)

Isaiah never hesitated to challenge the false gods before whom
the entire ancient world bowed itself in worship. The Lord challenges the false gods to foretell what is yet to come to pass. They
cannot speak, and do not know, much less could they prophesy
what is yet to come. But the Lord says, "I can tell what is yet to
come to pass, because I decree it and it is My counsel that brings it
to pass."

For example, in Isaiah 41:20-23 and 45:20-22 the Lord challenges these false deities to declare the future. Then God says in
our text in Isaiah 46 that He is the One who from ancient days
declares what is going to come to pass. "My counsel shall stand,
and I will do all my pleasure." He cites an instance of it: "Calling a

ravenous bird from the east," which is referring to Cyrus who was born one hundred fifty years after this prophecy. "The man that executeth my counsel from a far country: yea, I have spoken it, I will also bring it to pass; I have purposed it, I will also do it." He decrees the return of God's people to the Promised Land. In Isaiah 44 He calls Cyrus by name:

> That saith of Cyrus, He is my shepherd, and shall perform all my pleasure: even saying to Jerusalem, Thou shalt be built; and to the temple, Thy foundation shall be laid.
> Thus saith the LORD to his anointed, to Cyrus, whose right hand I have holden, to subdue nations before him. (44:28–45:1)

God uttered this prophecy more than one hundred years before Cyrus was born, but that is the great Lord God, and His magnitude and omnipotence are as real today. The same Lord God presides over the destiny of men and the history of nations.

There is no religion that has prophecy except the religion of Jehovah. Had Mohammed, Buddha, Confucius, or any other false gods tried to predict the future, their ridiculous inanity would have been apparent. No one knows the future but God.

THE ETERNAL PURPOSE OF GOD
WORKED OUT IN THE SCRIPTURE

God says, "I am he that purposes" and "My counsel shall stand, and I will do all my pleasure." The entire panorama of history from the beginning to the end stands before God in a perfect presence. He sees all history now before Him. The hand of God in sovereign grace guides the great movements of time, tide, and history throughout the generations and the aeons. Part of the perfection of God is that He has a plan and a purpose. As we cannot think of the sun without heat or light, so we could not think of God without a plan and a purpose. God does not act whimsically or sporadically, but He moves according to a great plan. Also, a part of the sovereignty of God is that He achieves His purpose in human history. Events in the human story that happen do not surprise Him, for they are according to His foreknowledge. As Isaiah says in chapter 14:

> This is the purpose that is purposed upon the whole earth: and
> this is the hand that is stretched out upon all the nations.
>   For the LORD of hosts hath purposed, and who shall disannul it?
> and his hand is stretched out, and who shall turn it back? (vv. 26,27)

Above the earth and its history presides a sovereign Lord who guides the events of time and tide according to His foreknowledge and His elective choice.

The Bible clearly reveals that the Lord will announce an event that is going to happen, and then through the centuries He will guide the movement of history to that prophecy's fulfillment. For example, the Lord says in Genesis that the seed of the woman would bruise Satan's head. Then hundreds of years later He says that He will direct His plan for human story through the seed of Abraham. Years later He says that history will be shaped through the seed of Israel, Jacob. Many years later He says that His plan of molding all events will be through the seed of David. Then hundreds of years after that He says that all the world will be changed by the virgin Jewish maiden, Mary, and finally it will reach a climax in the atoning death of our Christ on the cross.

Through uncounted ages the hand of God guides to the fulfillment of a marvelous prophecy. We can see the moving of God in the prophetic fulfillment in the blood sacrifices in the Old Testament. The blood of an innocent lamb is offered by Abel. Then through the years we trace that scarlet thread through the Bible: the blood of the Passover; the scarlet line behind which Rahab saved herself and her family; the blood of the daily sacrifice; and on through the centuries until the blood of the atoning Christ on the cross. We can see it in the life of our Lord. Satan tried to slay Jesus by Herod's sword when He was a babe in Bethlehem. His own townspeople sought to stone Him to death when He spoke in Nazareth. In Gethsemane Satan tried to slay our Lord before the day of the cross. But God's hand guided through the years until His great sacrifice and atoning death on Calvary. This is the hand of God in human history.

We see God's hand plainly in the preparation of the civilized world for the apostle Paul. Hundreds of years before Paul a man named Alexander taught the whole world the Greek language.

When Paul wrote his letter to the church at Rome, the Latin capital of the world, he wrote the letter in Greek. God was preparing the world for the preaching of the gospel of Jesus Christ. The Roman Empire laced the world together with a network of roads on which the apostles could walk, carrying the good news of the Son of God. He provided that these roads be built so that the emissaries of the gospel of the grace of the Son of God might have free access everywhere. The old covenant preceded the gospel wherever it was preached, and God had scattered the Jew in preparation for the feet of those who would preach the grace of the Son of God. This is the Lord's sovereign hand through all history.

BEHOLDING THE EVIDENCES OF GOD'S SOVEREIGN PURPOSES AROUND US

We can see God's hand when we read the headlines today. He is the same God today that He was yesterday. He holds the whole world in His hands. He guides the destiny of all the nations of the earth. In Acts 16 the apostle Paul is prohibited from turning east. The Holy Spirit turns him westward and finally to the evangelization of the English nation. In God's good providence, He chose the English nation to evangelize the world, and thousands of missionaries have gone out. The English-speaking world still sustains in every corner of this earth men and women who mediate the mind of God that was in Christ Jesus.

When the Pilgrim fathers came to this country, they not only came to have their own church, their school, and their Christian homes, but they also came for the evangelization of the new world. William Bradford, the governor of Plymouth Colony, in his story of Plymouth Plantation, gave the reason why the Pilgrim fathers left England and finally left Holland to come to the new world:

> Lastly and which was not least, a great hope and inward zeal we had of laying some good foundation or at least to make some way thereunto for the propagating and advancing the Gospel of the Kingdom of Christ in those remote parts of the world.

One of their purposes when they came to the new world was to evangelize the people who lived in the new land. This has been

God's hand in the history of the English-speaking nations; of England, America, Canada, Australia, and New Zealand, making English a universal language in the multi-faceted life of the nations of the world today.

The same sovereign hand of God can be seen today in the dispersing of the Jewish people. God says they will be a nation before Him as long as the sun shines during the day and the moon at night. He also says they will face homeward; He will gather them together, and they will have their own state, nation, government, and rulers. We can see that coming to pass before our eyes.

The same Lord also writes much about Russia in prophecy. Without exception, the Lord God says that one day Russia will be annihilated. We can see as we read the headlines of the newspapers today God's hand in judgment upon atheistic, Communist Russia. Built into the Communist ideology is its own seeds of annihilation. One of the maxims of Marxism is that communism cannot succeed in one nation until it succeeds in all the nations of the world. There cannot be revolution in just one country, but revolution must occur in all the countries of the world. So, basically, one of the ideologies of the Communist world is that they must exploit revolution. By watching world events we can see the hand of God working for the ultimate destruction of the Russian nation.

For a thousand miles Russia is bordered by the giant, China. For many years China has been docile and quiet. They had a great religious leader named Chiang Kai-shek and no one feared the giant of China. It was a calm and peaceful nation and more and more was being led to faith in Jesus Christ. Then what happened? Russia, exporting her revolution, took over the government of China, and made China Communist. But God's hand is still stretched out. God still lives and He still governs the nations of the earth, for Russia could face no enemy so bitter as Communist China. China, with her great hordes, looks with longing eyes to those vast expanses in the north and in the east. Some day there will be a great war fought between Russia and China. Why? Because of God's hand in human history. What once was a peace-loving and Christian-tempered nation with a great Christian leader, is now a government dedicated to the destruction of Russia. Every man, woman, and child of her 800,000,000 population follow that harsh singleness of destructive purpose. According to His foreknowledge and counsel God moves among the nations of the world today as He did centuries ago.

We see the predestinarian sovereignty of God in our individual lives, as well as in the lives of the nations of the world. It was according to the foreknowledge and the elective purpose of God that we were begotten. No infant has any part in its own beginning. We had no choice. We had no part at all in our birth. It came in a sovereign choice of almighty God. It is thus in all our lives. There is a purpose and a plan of God for every life. It fits into the beautiful mosaic of God as He writes the human story.

How do I know that God has a plan? Because in all the years that I have been a pastor I have observed that there is a plan of God for every life. When a man is in the will of God, he is happy, at peace; he has an infinite sense of fulfillment. He may be in the middle of the mission field. He may be half starved to death. He may be surrounded by bitter and vicious enemies. But if the man is in the will of God, he has perfect peace and rest. However, if a man is outside the will of God for his life, no matter how he may succeed, no matter how famous or rich he may become, that man is fundamentally miserable, restless, and unhappy. There is a great Sovereign above us who directs in all of the affairs of men. That same mighty Sovereign has a will for you. When you are in that plan and purpose, you have joy unspeakable, full of gladness and glory. When you are outside of that plan and purpose, you are miserable enough to die every day of your life.

One day, in Africa, I sat at the side of the executive secretary of the Foreign Mission Board at a meeting of missionaries. A young doctor was giving his report of the work of the physicians in the nation. As I sat there and listened, the executive secretary turned to me and said, "Take a good look at that young man, for I have something to tell you about him." After the meeting was over, the executive secretary said, "You noticed that young doctor?" I said, "Yes." He said: "He belongs to a very wealthy family in America.

When he graduated with his Doctor of Medicine degree, he was sought by some of the finest clinics in the north and east, offering him a large salary. He is a brilliant young man, but he felt called of God to be a medical missionary. So we appointed him and you heard him this morning. His salary could be thousands of dollars in America, but instead his salary is $1,000 a year." What a marvelous dedication when a man gives himself to the will of God! Money, fame, or success have nothing to do with happiness. God is sovereign and He made us for a definite purpose. When we give ourselves to that plan, our hearts are filled with the presence of the glory of God. This is the sovereign grace of Him who presides over all time, history, and life.

The Lord says He is the One who declares the end from the beginning and from ancient times and things that are yet to be done; "My counsel shall stand, and I will do all my pleasure." The tragedy of human life is this: if I refuse and spurn the will of God, He raises up someone else, but He does His work. O that all of us might have a yielded heart, and be willing to obey God and to do what He has laid upon our souls to do. We will never be happy any other way.

WHAT THE DOCTRINAL TRUTH MEANS TO US

What is the ultimate and final meaning for us of this glorious doctrine? First, we in Christ shall ultimately triumph. We will not lose. We read in 1 Corinthians 15:

> For he must reign, till he hath put all enemies under his feet. The last enemy that shall be destroyed is death. (vv. 25,26)

Hebrews 10:37 avows, "For yet a little while, and he that shall come will come, and will not tarry." We often look at the headlines and watch the flow of history. There are many times when we think that we have lost the battle, that the whole world is turning into darkness. There is a great and mighty Sovereign who sits above the skies in whose hand even the world is as a small dust in the balance and He guides all times and history. He will not fail. The day is coming when the kingdom of this world shall be the kingdom of our Lord and of His Christ. He will reign forever and ever. We will be joint heirs with Him. We will not lose.

Second, this doctrine assures us of our certain, final, and absolute salvation. We will not fail of that ultimate goal. Peter writes, "We are elect according to the foreknowledge of God." The Lord knew me before I was born and He wrote my name in the Lamb's Book of Life before I came from my mother's womb. We are elect to an inheritance incorruptible, undefiled, that fadeth not away, and reserved in heaven for us who are kept by the power of God. God has given eternal life to those who look in faith to Him. In John 10 we find:

> My sheep hear my voice, and I know them, and they follow me:
> And I give unto them eternal life; and they shall never perish, neither shall any man pluck them out of my hand.
> My Father, which gave them me, is greater than all; and no man is able to pluck them out of my Father's hand.
> I and my Father are one. (vv. 27–30)

When a man looks in faith to Jesus Christ, the Lord saves him forever. We may fall, make mistakes, and sin, but we will never fall out of the grace, love, mercy, care, and tender remembrance of God. The apostle says in Romans 8:

> For I am persuaded, that neither death, nor life, nor angels, nor principalities, nor powers, nor things present, nor things to come,
> Nor height, nor depth, nor any other creature, shall be able to separate us from the love of God, which is in Christ Jesus our Lord. (vv. 38,39)

What does this doctrine of the sovereignty of God mean to us? We will be able to say "And we know that all things work together for good to them that love God, to them who are the called according to his purpose" (Rom. 8:28). If I am a child of God, the things that happen to me are things in which God is working for my good. There are not any accidents in God's time. He sees all things that happen and knows about them before they occur. The Lord orders everything for the blessing and good of His people. Some day, according to His infinite and unfailing promise, He will deliver us without spot and blemish in the presence of the great glory where we shall see Him as He is, face to face, and be like Him, resurrected, immortalized, and redeemed by the love, the grace, the mercy, and the atoning death of the crucified One.

32

Marred More Than Any Man

> Behold, my servant shall deal prudently, he shall be exalted and extolled, and be very high.
>
> As many were astonied at thee; his visage was so marred more than any man, and his form more than the sons of men:
>
> So shall he sprinkle many nations; the kings shall shut their mouths at him: for that which had not been told them shall they see; and that which they had not heard shall they consider. (Isa. 52:13–15)

The prophet in 52:13, having said that the servant of God (Isaiah's word for the coming Messiah Prince), should be greatly exalted and extolled and be very high, now continues with an astonishing announcement: The throngs "were astonied at thee; his visage was so marred more than any man, and his form more than the sons of men." There are many passages in the Old Covenant that depict the suffering of the coming Prince Messiah. In Psalms we read:

> My God, my God, why hast thou forsaken me? why art thou so far from helping me, and from the words of my roaring? . . .
>
> I am poured out like water, and all my bones are out of joint: my heart is like wax; it is melted in the midst of my bowels . . .

For dogs have compassed me: the assembly of the wicked have
enclosed me: they pierced my hands and my feet.
I may tell all my bones: they look and stare upon me . . .
They part my garments among them, and cast lots upon my
vesture. (22:1,14,16-18)

Other prophecies such as Isaiah 53 depict the terrible suffering of
our Lord.

Those who watched His suffering were astonished at Him, for
His visage was so disfigured, marred more than any man, and His
form more than the sons of men. The reality of that prophecy in
the life of our Lord brings tears to our eyes. Our Lord was misused
and mistreated unbelievably. His beard was plucked out, a crown
of thorns was pressed on His brow, and He was scourged and
beaten.

In studying Roman crucifixion I learned that often the criminal
was killed by the fierceness of flagellation. Our Lord was scourged
by the hands of Roman soldiers. They nailed Him to the tree and
then raised Him up. The jarring of the cross as it fell into its place
in the ground must have torn the tendons in His hands and feet. So
disfigured and marred was the Son of God that when the Roman
soldiers came to Him and saw that He was dead, they did not break
His bones as was the normal Roman procedure. But as an after-
thought, it seems, one of the Roman soldiers took a spear and
thrust it into His heart. When the spear was withdrawn, there
flowed out blood and water. The cardiac sac in which the heart
beats caught the blood. It separated the red corpuscles from the
limpid serum and it looked like blood and water. What an unthinkable and unbelievable trauma that the Son of God should be
so marred and disfigured!

One time I heard of an American soldier in World War I in
France who was critically injured by the bursting of a bomb that
fell in front of him. He lost the use of one of his limbs and was
greatly disfigured. The saddest part of his loss was the destruction
of his memory. His boyhood, his family name, who he was, and
where he was from, were blotted out of his broken mind. For days
and years after he would go wherever people gathered, and lifting
up his sightless eyes and disfigured face, he would cry, "Does

anyone know who I am?" It is thus with our Lord. His visage and form were more disfigured than any of the sons of men.

Who Is This?

Second Corinthians 5:21 says, "For he hath made him to be sin for us, who knew no sin; that we might be made the righteousness of God in him." God made Him to be sin for us and Habakkuk says of the Lord God, "Thou art purer of eyes than to behold evil" (Hab. 1:13a). When the Son of God was made sin, God turned His face away. The whole earth was black and dark.

> Well might the sun in darkness hide
> And shut His glories in,
> When Christ, the mighty Maker died
> For man, the creature's sin.

The angels were present at the nativity of our Lord when He was born, they were present at His temptation and ministered to Him, they were present in Gethsemane when He prayed in agony, and they were present at the tomb. Yet our Lord was dying. Where were the angels? He could have asked for twelve legions of angels and they would have come. Why did not just one come? Because the hand of the Father held them back. God made Him to be our sin.

Mary, is this the child to whom you gave birth? Is that the lovely son, Jesus? The apostle John, looking at our Savior on the cross, heard His voice addressed to him saying: "John, take her away. It is too much for My mother to look upon such suffering and agony and death." From that moment, John took her to his own home that she might not see Him suffer and die.

There is no more pathetic story than the one of an American soldier who returned from World War II. He had been deeply hurt and seriously wounded, but he looked forward to coming home and to being with his young bride-to-be. As the soldier stepped off the train and onto the platform, his bride-to-be with her mother and father were there waiting for him. When the young woman saw him she started toward him, then she stopped. She looked in amazement and then in horror. She turned and buried her face in the arms of her mother and cried, saying, "I cannot bear to look at him." The family walked away with that young girl and left the soldier standing alone on the platform.

THE CHRIST WE PREACH

They who looked upon Him were astonished and the kings of the earth shut up their mouths at Him. This is the Savior of whom we preach. This is the Christ of our love, worship, and adoration. How different from what one might expect. This is the Prince of Glory. The earth points to its kings and emperors. With what pride do the armed forces of the world point to their great conquerors and dictators. To what and to whom do we point? We see a gentle, yielded, humble, suffering Lord Jesus.

"He shall not cry nor lift up, nor cause his voice to be heard in the street. A bruised reed shall he not break, and the smoking flax shall he not quench: he shall bring forth judgment unto truth." John 3:17 reads, "For God sent not his Son into the world to condemn the world; but that the world through him might be saved."

If we look at the One on the cross, and if God gives us the spirit of understanding, then we are saved. I have often thought that if a man could hear the agonizing cries of his mother in travail when he was born, he would love his mother more. If we could see the suffering of our forefathers in agony and blood, we would cherish our liberty and freedom more. If a man will look at the Prince of Glory, made sin for us on the cross, he could not help but love Him more.

> Were you there when they crucified my Lord?
> Were you there when they crucified my Lord?
> Oh, sometimes it causes me to tremble, tremble, tremble.
> Were you there when they crucified my Lord?
>
> Were you there when they nailed Him to the tree?
> Were you there when they nailed Him to the tree?
> Oh, sometimes it causes me to tremble, tremble, tremble.
> Were you there when they nailed Him to the tree?
>
> Were you there when they laid Him in the tomb?
> Were you there when they laid Him in the tomb?

Oh, sometimes it causes me to tremble, tremble, tremble.
Were you there when they laid Him in the tomb?

Were you there when He rose up from the grave?
Were you there when He rose up from the grave?
Oh, sometimes I want to shout glory, glory, glory.
Were you there when He rose up from the grave?

This is what God has done for us.

Let this mind be in you, which was also in Christ Jesus:
Who, being in the form of God, thought it not robbery to be equal with God: But made himself of no reputation, and took upon him the form of a servant, and was made in the likeness of men:
And being found in fashion as a man, he humbled himself, and became obedient unto death, even the death of the cross. (Phil. 2:5–8)

33

The Suffering Savior

Who hath believed our report? and to whom is the arm of the
LORD revealed? (Isa. 53:1)

In our study of Isaiah we have come to a Holy of Holies in the
prophetic ministry of those who spoke of the glorious coming of
our Lord. When the Lord opened their minds to understand the
Scriptures, He showed them in the prophets how Christ should
suffer. For example, we read in Luke 24:

> Then opened he their understanding, that they might understand
> the scriptures,
> And said unto them, Thus it is written, and thus it behoved
> Christ to suffer, and to rise from the dead the third day.
> And that repentance and remission of sins should be preached in
> his name among all nations, beginning at Jerusalem. (vv. 45–47)

The passage in our text is, beyond any other in the Old Testament, quoted in the New Testament presenting Jesus as the
suffering Savior of the world making atonement for our sins.
When we read Isaiah 53 we should feel like someone entering a
holy and heavenly sanctuary. We must tread softly in His presence, speak quietly, for the Lord is there, and kneel reverently

before Him who suffered so traumatically for our sins.

In this incomparable prophecy it is hard to believe that Isaiah lived 750 years before the day of the cross. We would think that Isaiah was standing by the cross. As the prophet writes of the atoning grace that saves us from our sins and the tears and sobs of the Son of God, he speaks of His sufferings in three ways: first, suffering in His body, second, suffering in His heart, and third, suffering in His soul.

THE ATONEMENT OF OUR LORD AS HE SUFFERED IN HIS BODY

We read in Isaiah 52:

> Behold, my servant shall deal prudently, he shall be exalted and extolled, and be very high.
> As many were astonied at thee; his visage was so marred more than any man, and his form more than the sons of men . . .
> So shall he sprinkle many nations; the kings shall shut their mouths at him: for that which had not been told them shall they see; and that which they had not heard shall they consider. (vv. 13–15)

The throngs were astonished at the bodily suffering of our Lord. His visage was marred more than any other man. This was the atoning suffering of our Lord in His physical frame. An all-night vigil began with the Passover Supper, at which the Lord instituted the memorial of the breaking of bread and the drinking of the cup. It was followed by the words of our Lord that are found in John 14–16 and the high-priestly prayer found in John 17. He said in John 16:6, "But because I have said these things unto you, sorrow hath filled your heart." Then we read in John 14:

> Let not your heart be troubled: ye believe in God, believe also in me.
> In my Father's house are many mansions: if it were not so, I would have told you. I go to prepare a place for you. (vv. 1,2)

The story continues beyond the Brook Kidron on the other side of Moriah and at the base of Mt. Olivet in the Garden of Gethsemane, where Jesus was arrested. He was arraigned before Annas, then Caiaphas, then the Sanhedrin, and finally delivered into the hands of the Roman soldiers before Pontius Pilate. He was tried before Herod the ruler of Galilee and then He was returned to

Pilate who condemned Him to be executed by crucifixion. All
night long the Lord was brought from one trial to the other, and
condemned by them all. Finally, under the aegis of the Roman
procurator, Pontius Pilate, He was delivered to the Roman soldiers
to be crucified. The Roman soldiers apparently were delighted in
taking a despised Jew and marring His body. So they beat Him with
Roman rods, a whip made of nine knotted cords attached to a
handle. Often the felon who was being crucified died under the
heavy blows of those brutal Roman soldiers. Our Lord was so
beaten, so scourged, and so much blood had fallen from His back,
that when they placed the cross on Him to bear it to the place of
crucifixion, He staggered and fell beneath the weight of the cross.
They compelled a passerby, Simon of Cyrene, to bear the cross of
Christ. Finally they came to the hill of the skull. In Latin it is
called "Calvary," in Hebrew it is called "Golgotha," and there
they crucified Him.

So sorrowful was the scene that the Lord said to John, "Take my
mother away, lest she look upon it." His suffering and death were
hidden from the face of His mother. The sun refused to shine, lest
the earth look upon it. God held back the angel hosts in heaven,
lest the angels look upon it. The Father Himself turned His face,
lest He look upon it.

THE SUFFERINGS IN HIS HEART

We read in Isaiah 53: "He is despised and rejected of men; a man
of sorrows, and acquainted with grief: and we hid as it were our
faces from him; he was despised, and we esteemed him not" (v. 3).
He was outcast by men, denied by His own, tortured and nailed to
the tree, but the hurt in His heart was the hardest to bear. It is the
heart that was broken for me. Let us progress in the depths of that
hurt to His heart.

First, those to whom He belonged, His own people, rejected
Him. John wrote in John 1:11: "He came unto his own, and his
own received him not." These who should have loved and welcomed Him, should have treasured His presence, and should have
adored all that He said and did are the ones who hated Him the
most bitterly. The Pharisees hated the Herodians, but they hated

Jesus more. They joined with the Herodians to encompass His destruction. The nation hated the Romans, but they hated Jesus more and delivered Him into the hands of the Romans that He might be crucified. The Pharisees, scribes, Herodians, and elders all hated the unwashed sinners, but they hated Jesus more because He ate with them and preached the gospel to them. It is almost unthinkable how the tender, loving, mild, and gentle Jesus should have been so hated, despised, and cruelly treated by these He called His own.

Second, we look at the Jewish trial. One came up to Him, smote Him on the face, and said: "Ha, You who are a prophet, what is my name? Who smote You?" Another came and spat in His face and said, "Ha, You who are a prophet, who spits in Your face?" Another came and tore out His beard and said, "Ha, You who are a prophet, call my name." They ridiculed and mocked Him.

In the Roman trial, when Pontius Pilate delivered Him to death, the brutal, rude Roman soldiers said: "So, He is a King. A King must have a crown." They wove for Him a crown of thorns and pressed it on His brow. "A King must have a robe." They found a cast-off piece of purple cloth and shrouded His shoulders with it. They also said, "A King must also have a scepter." They found a stick, a reed, and placed it in His hand. "And a King must have adulation," and they bowed in mockery before Him and said, "Hail, King of the Jews." Finally, taking Him to a garbage dump, to a place of a skull where other felons had died and dead animals were thrown, there they nailed Him to a tree. As though His sufferings were not enough in His being nailed to the cross, they gambled for His garments, casting lots as to who would take each of the five pieces of clothing. Then, sitting down in contempt, they watched Him die.

I have often thought of the text which is the theme of the apocalypse, Revelation 1:7. It says, "Behold, he cometh with clouds; and every eye shall see him, and they also which pierced him: and all kindreds of the earth shall wail because of him."

John was there and saw their hard faces and cruel hands. He saw the Roman soldiers press the crown of thorns on His brow, mock

Him, ridicule Him, and finally nail Him to the tree. That is why I think John wrote Revelation 1:7, "And they also which pierced him."

Zechariah 13:7 says that God will "smite the shepherd, and the sheep shall be scattered." Both Matthew and Mark record the fact that the disciples forsook Him and fled. They also turned their backs upon Him and He died alone. How could such a thing be, that when the Lord is suffering and dying they all forsake Him and flee? The hurt in His heart was the hardest to bear.

A few years ago I heard a story that I feel is one of the saddest stories I have ever heard. An American soldier from the Midwest was seriously wounded in the conflict in Vietnam, and having been nursed back to health, he came home. When he reached San Francisco, he called his father and mother and said, "Mom and Dad, I have come home." And you can imagine how happy those parents were. The boy said: "Mom and Dad, I have a friend. He has been with me in the war and I am bringing him along. Is that all right?" They replied: "Yes, son. We would love to have him." He said: "But he has been wounded. You do not realize how badly he has been hurt. He has to be cared for. He has one eye that is gone, an arm that is gone, and a leg that is gone." "Well," said the father and mother, "we do not know about that. Son, we could not take care of a boy like that. There are government hospitals to take care of boys with such extensive injuries. We will help you take the lad to a hospital and there they can take care of him." The boy replied, "All right, I will be seeing you soon." The next day the father and mother received a call from a morgue in San Francisco, which said: "We think we might have your son. Do you have a son from the Vietnam war by this name and is this your address?" "Yes," they said. So they went and identified the lad. The boy took his life the night before in a cheap hotel in San Francisco. When the couple looked upon his face, they immediately recognized him as being their son, but as they looked more closely they saw he had one eye gone, one arm gone, and one leg gone. "He is despised and rejected of men . . . and we hid as it were our faces from him; he was despised, and we esteemed him not." The hurt in His heart was the hardest to bear.

HE SUFFERED IN HIS SOUL

". . . when thou shalt make his soul an offering for sin . . . (God) shall see of the travail of his soul, and shall be satisfied" (Isa. 53:10b–11a). The theological word for satisfaction is "propitiation," which means "to make satisfaction," "to render favorable and acceptable."

Thus far we have been discussing the suffering in His body. I can comprehend the pain of having nails driven through hands and feet. I can understand the sufferings of having been scourged. I can understand the hurt a man would bear in His heart when those who should have loved Him, hated Him; and when those who should have stood by Him, despised Him; and when those to whom He had opened His heart forsook Him and fled. I can understand that. I cannot enter into the deep, unfathomable mysteries of His soul being offered for our sins, and God looking upon the travail. The word "travail" is used to describe the pain a woman feels in childbirth and is said to be the most agonizing pain in the world. That suffering of our Lord for us I cannot comprehend.

Some of our great seminaries have libraries of more than 100,000 books. One can read all 100,000 of them and not be able to understand the mystery of God making His soul an offering for our sins.

In my doctoral work I studied the subject of the Atonement for three years. When I took the examination at the end of three years of study, I still was amazed at the mystery of the atonement of Christ for our sins, when God made His soul an offering. In the beautiful ritual of the Greek Catholic Church, there is a reference to "Thy unknown sufferings." That is all that we can say.

When the Bible presents the atonement for our sins, I can follow it pretty well. For example, a man who is a sinner is brought to the high priest, and he is told to slay a lamb. He puts his hands over the head of the animal and confesses his sins. The high priest takes the animal, slays it, and pours out its blood at the base of the altar. When the nation had sinned, once a year the high priest would take an innocent animal, slay it, carry the blood into the Holy of Holies, and there sprinkle it on the mercy seat in atonement for the sins of the people.

In Hebrews 10 the author says that the blood of bulls or goats could not suffice to take away our sins, only a body which God prepared for the Son of Glory. Incarnate with a body, He was offered unto God, a sacrifice for us. I can understand that.

But I cannot comprehend this:

> Yet it pleased the LORD to bruise him; he hath put him to grief. when thou shalt make his soul an offering for sin, he shall see his seed, he shall prolong his days, and the pleasure of the LORD shall prosper in his hand.
>
> He shall see of the travail of his soul, and shall be satisfied: by his knowledge shall my righteous servant justify many; for he shall bear their iniquities. (Isa. 53:10,11)

There is something further in His sufferings that I cannot understand. That is when God bore our sins away in the suffering of our Lord. All I can do is to bow. All I can say is, "Thank You, Jesus." All I can do is offer myself to Him.

> Was it for crimes that I have done
> He groaned upon the tree?
> Amazing pity! grace unknown
> And love beyond degree!
>
> But drops of grief can ne'er repay
> The debt of love I owe;
> Here, Lord, I give myself away —
> 'Tis all that I can do.

This is the miracle of miracles. There is no man who can honestly gaze upon the suffering Lord and not be affected. There is something about the Lord's dying on the cross that makes a man pause. He is hushed, quiet. To us who have looked in faith to the Son of God, there is something about the gift of His life and the pouring out of the crimson of His life upon the earth that brings a flood of power and the consciousness of forgiveness.

> There is a fountain filled with blood
> Drawn from Immanuel's veins,

And sinners plunged beneath that flood
Lose all their guilty stains.

The dying thief rejoiced to see
That fountain in his day.
And there may I, though vile as he,
Wash all my sins away.

E'er since by faith I saw the stream
Thy flowing wounds supply,
Redeeming love has been my theme
And shall be till I die.

34

The Cross and the Crown

Yet it pleased the LORD to bruise him; he hath put him to grief:
when thou shalt make his soul an offering for sin, he shall see his
seed, he shall prolong his days, and the pleasure of the LORD shall
prosper in his hand.

He shall see of the travail of his soul, and shall be satisfied: by his
knowledge shall my righteous servant justify many; for he shall bear
their iniquities.

Therefore will I divide him a portion with the great, and he shall
divide the spoil with the strong; because he hath poured out his soul
unto death: and he was numbered with the transgressors; and he
bare the sin of many, and made intercession for the transgressors.
(Isa. 53:10–12)

In chapter 53 we find bound together the humiliation and
exaltation of our Lord. Typical of the prophets as they spoke of His
coming, Isaiah wrote:

He was oppressed, and he was afflicted, yet he opened not his
mouth: he is brought as a lamb to the slaughter, and as a sheep
before her shearers is dumb, so he openeth not his mouth . . .

Therefore will I divide him a portion with the great, and he shall
divide the spoil with the strong. (vv. 53:7,12a)

The same marvelous depiction of our Savior as being humble

and exalted is found in the apostles. Typical of the presentation is the passage of Scripture found in Philippians:

> Let this mind be in you, which was also in Christ Jesus:
> Who, being in the form of God, thought it not robbery to be equal with God:
> But made himself of no reputation, and took upon him the form of a servant, and was made in the likeness of men:
> And being found in fashion as a man, he humbled himself, and became obedient unto death, even the death of the cross.
> Wherefore God also hath highly exalted him, and given him a name which is above every name:
> That at the name of Jesus every knee should bow, of things in heaven, and things in earth, and things under the earth;
> And that every tongue should confess that Jesus Christ is Lord, to the glory of God the Father. (2:5–11)

In Revelation John says:

> And when I saw him, I fell at his feet as dead. And he laid his right hand upon me, saying unto me, Fear not; I am the first and the last.
> I am he that liveth, and was dead; and, behold, I am alive for evermore, Amen; and have the keys of hell and of death. (1:17,18)

> And I beheld, and I heard the voice of many angels round about the throne and the beasts and the elders: and the number of them was ten thousand times ten thousand, and thousands of thousands;
> Saying with a loud voice, Worthy is the Lamb that was slain to receive power, and riches, and wisdom, and strength, and honour, and glory, and blessing.
> And every creature which is in heaven, and on the earth, and under the earth, and such as are in the sea, and all that are in them, heard I saying, Blessing, and honour, and glory, and power, and unto him that sitteth upon the throne, and unto the Lamb for ever and ever. (5:11–13)

THE SUFFERING LAMB

Our highest imagination cannot enter into the glory nor comprehend the exaltation from whence He came. The immeasurable distance between the glory of our Lord in heaven and the shame to which He descended in earth is beyond human understanding. He was made in the form of a man who is composed of the dust of the ground. He became a servant. Finally, our Lord was sentenced to execution in a death reserved for criminals and felons. He was raised between the heaven and the earth as though both heaven and earth rejected Him.

As though abuse were not vile enough, the cruel jeering crowd covered Him with spittle. They also plucked out His beard. Going further, they crowned Him with thorns, and as though the thorns were not agonizing enough, He was pierced through with a Roman spear. It was the earth's saddest hour and it was humanity's deepest, darkest day. At 3:00 P.M. it was all over. The Lord of life bowed His head and the light of the world flickered out.

Tread softly around the cross, for Jesus is dead. Repeat the refrain in hushed and softened tone. The Lord of life is dead. The lips that spoke forth Lazarus from the grave are now stilled in the silence of the death. The head that was anointed by Mary of Bethany is bowed with its crown of thorns. The eyes that wept over Jerusalem are glazed in death. The hands that blessed little children are nailed to a tree. The feet that walked on the waters of blue Galilee are fastened to a cross. The heart that went out in compassionate love and sympathy for the poor and the lost of the world is now broken. He is dead.

The infuriated mob that cried for His crucifixion gradually disperses. He is dead. The passersby who stopped just to see Him, go on their way. He is dead. The Pharisees, rubbing their hands in self-congratulation, go back to the city. He is dead. The Sadducees, breathing sighs of relief, return to their coffers in the temple. He is dead. The centurion who was assigned the task of executing Him makes his official report to the Roman procurator, "He is dead." The soldiers who were sent to dispatch the victim, and seeing the man on the center cross was certainly dead, broke not His bones but pierced Him through. He is dead. Joseph of Arimathaea and Nicodemus of the Sanhedrin go to Pontius Pilate and beg the Roman governor for His body because He is dead. Mary, His mother, and the women with her are bowed in sobs and tears. He is dead. The eleven apostles, like frightened sheep, crawl into eleven shadows to hide from the pointing finger of Jerusalem and they cry that He is dead. Wherever His disciples meet, the same refrain is sadly heard: He is dead. It would be almost impossible for us to enter into the depths of despair that gripped their hearts. Simon

Peter, "the Rock," is a rock no longer. James and John are "sons of
thunder" no longer. Simon the Zealot is a zealot no longer. Jesus
is dead. The hope of the world has perished with Him.

He Is Alive!

Then men stopped dead in their tracks. A message leaps from
mouth to mouth like liquid fire. An angel says, "He is alive!" Mary
Magdalene says, "I have seen the Lord!" Simon Peter is filling
Jerusalem with the bold and courageous announcement: "He is
alive, He is alive!" All up and down the highways of Judaea, along
the shores of Galilee, beyond the coasts of the great Mediterra-
nean, on the road to Athens and Rome, in every poor man's
cottage and in every rich man's palace, there is that glorious news:
"He is alive, He is alive!"

> Lift up your heads ye sorrowing ones,
> And be ye glad of heart.
> For earth's saddest day and earth's gladdest day,
> Calvary's day and Easter day are just one day apart.

The bitter seed brought forth a beautiful and precious flower.
The cross magnifies our exalted and risen Lord. Every point in that
crown of thorns is now a diamond in His diadem. The crimson of
His life that was poured out stained His royal robe with purple.
The iron nails of the cross and of the spear are now the rod of His
scepter by which He will rule the nations of the world. The wood
of the cross is His identity with all humanity. The most sacred spot
in the earth is Mount Calvary where He died. The cross itself is the
symbol of the Christian faith and our hope in the world that is to
come.

> If in Flanders' fields poppies grow,
> It will be between crosses row on row.

If He is alive, where is He now? There are almost two thousand
years of the record of His living. Is there proof? Is there evidence?
Had every man in the Roman Empire seen Him walk out of that
grave, had Caesar and all of his officers witnessed the resurrection
of Christ on the first day of the week, had Josephus, Tacitus, and
Suetonius recorded in their historical annals the eyewitnesses of

the living Lord, it would not be proof as corroborated as the evidence that we have today in our very lives.

How We Know He Lives

First, we know His presence by His healing grace and His saving power. The only healing is divine healing. A surgeon may sharpen his scalpel and cut, but only God can heal. Jesus is the Great Physician. In how many sick rooms, darkened in despair, have we seen health, life, and length of days given in the gracious and healing hands of our living Lord!

Second, He is alive because He bows down His ear to hear His children when they pray. Without number are the times when we laid before our blessed Lord those decisions, problems, and hurts for which we were not equal in our lives. We told Him all about it. He, who was tried in all points such as we, has bowed down His ear in sympathy and understanding to hear His children when they pray. He is alive. I know Him in answered prayer.

Third, the ableness of His might to regenerate, to save, to deliver, to forgive, and to make new men and women can easily be seen. I see His power in the glorious conversions that daily are brought to God, trophies of grace under His saving hand. They are a Simon Peter, a Paul the persecuting blasphemer of the early Christians, an Ignatius who was fed to the lions in the Roman colosseum, a Billy Sunday, and a George W. Truett. Christ moves in saving power today to save you and me as He did yesterday; He is able just the same.

Fourth, He lives as He walks in grace and blessing among His churches. In Revelation 1 we read:

> And I turned to see the voice that spake with me. And being turned, I saw seven golden candlesticks;
> And in the midst of the seven candlesticks one like unto the Son of man, clothed with a garment down to the foot, and girt about the paps with a golden girdle. (vv. 12,13)

Christ walks among His people, visiting in His churches. There have been times without number when seated in my pulpit chair, I have bowed my head with tears overflowing in the sense of the presence of the power of Christ in this holy place. Our Lord can be found in the midst of His churches.

Fifth, He lives in the victory that He has brought to us over death. "Be not afraid, for I have the keys of the grave and of death." Lest one might think that those keys lie in some other hand, He avows that He possesses the key to our lives and to our deaths. I shall not die until He wills my death. Flame or sword, famine or plague cannot touch me until He appoints the time. Nor am I to cringe before the visage of that pale visitor, death, for our Lord went to the cross and there He destroyed our enemy death and forever brings victory and triumph out of the tomb. There is no sting in death nor victory in the grave, for Christ has made death for us our entrance into heaven. When I die will be in His all-powerful choice. Death to the Christian holds no terror, for death is but a homegoing to be with Jesus.

"Yea, though I walk through the valley of the shadow of death, I will fear no evil: for thou art with me." The hour of our death is to be our greatest day. It is our moment of triumph, when earth recedes and heaven draws near, first the cross and then the crown.

> O precious cross,
> O glorious crown,
> O resurrection day,
> Ye angels from the stars come down,
> And bear my soul away.

This is the victory Christ has brought us in His precious, nail-pierced hands.

35

The Lamb of God

Who hath believed our report? and to whom is the arm of the
LORD revealed?

For he shall grow up before him as a tender plant, and as a root
out of a dry ground: he hath no form nor comeliness; and when we
shall see him, there is no beauty that we should desire him.

He is despised and rejected of men; a man of sorrows, and
acquainted with grief: and we hid as it were our faces from him; he
was despised, and we esteemed him not.

Surely he hath borne our griefs, and carried our sorrows: yet we
did esteem him stricken, smitten of God, and afflicted.

But he was wounded for our transgressions, he was bruised for our
iniquities: the chastisement of our peace was upon him; and with his
stripes we are healed.

All we like sheep have gone astray; we have turned every one
to his own way; and the LORD hath laid on him the iniquity of
us all.

He was oppressed, and he was afflicted, yet he opened not his
mouth: he is brought as a lamb to the slaughter, and as a sheep
before her shearers is dumb, so he openeth not his mouth.

He was taken from prison and from judgment: and who shall
declare his generation? for he was cut off out of the land of the living:
for the transgression of my people was he stricken.

And he made his grave with the wicked, and with the rich in his death; because he had done no violence, neither was any deceit in his mouth.

Yet it pleased the LORD to bruise him; he hath put him to grief: when thou shalt make his soul an offering for sin, he shall see his seed, he shall prolong his days, and the pleasure of the LORD shall prosper in his hand.

He shall see of the travail of his soul, and shall be satisfied: by his knowledge shall my righteous servant justify many; for he shall bear their iniquities.

Therefore will I divide him a portion with the great, and he shall divide the spoil with the strong; because he hath poured out his soul unto death: and he was numbered with the transgressors; and he bare the sin of many, and made intercession for the transgressors. (Isa. 53:1–12)

The mighty prophet begins by stating that he will tell us a revelation from heaven that is so unbelievable, that one can hardly believe God said it. The announcement is so marvelous that unless the Spirit of the Lord reveals it to a man, he could never encompass its magnitude.

Who hath believed our report? and to whom is the arm of the LORD revealed? (Isa. 53:1)

Then he begins with his prophecy of the coming Christ Messiah:

For he shall grow up before him as a tender plant, and as a root out of a dry ground: he hath no form nor comeliness; and when we shall see him, there is no beauty that we should desire him. (Isa. 53:2)

THE LORD'S LOWLY ORIGIN

The prophet is saying that the prospect of a glorious king arising from the background of the origin of the incarnate Son of God was almost unbelievable. When Isaiah refers to His growing up as a tender plant, he is speaking of the same prophecy he mentioned in Isaiah 11:1, "And there shall come forth a rod out of the stem of Jesse, and a Branch shall grow out of his roots." The prophet is describing the stump of the house of David. The kingdom has been destroyed and the king and his lineage are of the past with nothing left but a stump. The prophet says that out of that stump — the destroyed house of David — there shall grow a tender, little plant and the root will give birth to new life. What an amazing thing, that a root will grow out of a stump!

The timing of when Christ would come out of Israel was in the fulfillment of prophecy. The nation was in servitude and was a festering sore in the life of the Roman Empire. Our Lord was crucified in A.D. 33 and in A.D. 66 the destructive rebellion against Rome took place under the legions of Titus. The national religion was a farce and was led in temple worship by the Sadducees. To me the Sadducees were atheists since they were rationalists of the first order. Religion was imposed by the formal and ritualistic Pharisees who fastened upon the people burdens they could not bear. Yet out of that came the glorious incarnate Son of God. He was born in Bethlehem and grew up in a despised town called Nazareth, a town of such impure reputation that a godly man in Israel said, "Can any good thing come out of Nazareth?"

The Lord's Unattractive Form

The prophet next says that in Christ Himself there was no personal grandeur that we should desire Him. He was a peasant. He dressed like a peasant, lived like a peasant, and walked like a peasant. When He was brought before Herod Antipas the tetrarch of Galilee, there was no admiration on the part of the king. In contempt and disgust, Herod Antipas sent Him back to Pontius Pilate. Can you imagine standing in the presence of Jesus Christ, the Son of God, and looking upon Him in contempt and disgust?

When Pontius Pilate, examining the Lord Jesus before His crucifixion, heard that He called Himself a King, he incredulously looked at that peasant crowned with thorns, buffeted, mocked, and despised and said, "Art thou a King?" How our values are turned around!

The prophet in the next verse describes the reception of the Son of heaven:

> He is despised and rejected of men; a man of sorrows, and acquainted with grief: and we hid as it were our faces from him; he was despised, and we esteemed him not. (Isa. 53:3)

The prophet means by "acquainted with grief" that grief was the companion of our Lord. When He walked, He walked alone. His words were flung into His teeth as the people paraded up and down in front of His cross. They reminded Him of the words He had spoken during His ministry. When our Lord turned in His hour of greatest need to those who should have befriended Him, the Book says that all His disciples forsook Him and fled.

THE LORD BORE OUR GRIEFS

The prophet writes in the next three verses an incomparable description of the vicarious, atoning death of our Lord who is suffering in our stead and for our sins:

> Surely he hath borne our griefs, and carried our sorrows; yet we did esteem him stricken, smitten of God, and afflicted.
>
> But he was wounded for our transgressions, he was bruised for our iniquities: the chastisement of our peace was upon him; and with his stripes we are healed.
>
> All we like sheep have gone astray; we have turned every one to his own way; and the LORD hath laid on him the iniquity of us all. (Isa, 53:4–6)

Our Lord did not deserve any stripes. The stripes that were laid so heavily upon Him should have fallen on us. We are the ones who sin and deserve the punishment, but we do not receive it.

The prophet mentions a mystery that no man can enter into: "the LORD hath laid on him the iniquity of us all." The sins of the whole world were heaped upon His soul. In a way that is known only to God, the Lord saw the travail of His soul and was satisfied. For His sake God forgives us. It is not because we are lovely or righteous or deserving that God is merciful to us. God is gracious to us and forgives us for His sake.

THE SUFFERING SERVANT'S ATTITUDE

In the next verse the prophet describes the attitude of the suffering servant. How did He bear it when He was cursed, spat upon, reviled, blasphemed, and finally nailed to a tree? Did He answer with bitter recrimination? "He opened not his mouth."

> He was oppressed, and he was afflicted, yet he opened not his mouth: he is brought as a lamb to the slaughter, and as a sheep

before her shearers is dumb, so he openeth not his mouth. (Isa. 53:7)

Only twice did our Lord speak. When He stood before the Sanhedrin, the high priest said, "I adjure thee by the living God, that thou tell us whether thou be the Christ, the Son of God." Christ replied: "Thou hast said . . . Hereafter shall ye see the Son of man sitting on the right hand of power, and coming in the clouds of heaven." The only other place He spoke was when Pilate asked Him officially, "Art thou a king?" He said, "I am a king." Other than that, He never spoke. When He was nailed to the tree, the only sound that was heard was the sound of the ringing hammers, driving in the nails through His hands and feet.

An experience I can never forget was my visit to the largest meat packing plant in the world, the Armour Company in Chicago, Illinois. The plant was an enormous facility. First I visited the slaughterhouse for the cattle. Oh, the sound of the moaning and the lowing of the cattle as they were led to the slaughterhouse. Then I visited the slaughterhouse for the swine, and what a loud squealing of the hogs as they were led to slaughter. Then I visited the slaughterhouse for the sheep and lambs. The room was as silent as death. The man with the long knife plunged it into the jugular vein and the sheep or lamb would watch the last crimson blood pour out. There was not a sound, not a cry. The only sound that I heard was the sound of the machinery as it pulled the carcass around.

Then the prophet describes something that is amazing:

He was taken from prison and from judgment: and who shall declare his generation? for he was cut off out of the land of the living: for the transgression of my people was he stricken. (Isa. 53:8)

No one in His generation could understand why He was cut off out of the land of the living. There was not one who understood that it was for the transgression of His people that He was stricken. That is why, when the Lord was raised from the dead, He took the Scriptures and taught His disciples that it behooved Christ to suffer, and that remission of sin should be preached in His name.

Then the prophet writes words that are enigmatic and seemingly meaningless until we understand them in their fulfillment.:

> And he made his grave with the wicked, and with the rich in his
> death; because he had done no violence, neither was any deceit in
> his mouth. (Isa. 53:9)

For 750 years those words were meaningless. In the days of Roman
crucifixion, the one who was crucified was left on the cross as a
lesson to a would-be runaway slave or a would-be criminal. The
body was left on the cross until it decayed and fell of itself to the
ground in pieces. It was a cruel and awesome sight. However, the
Jews had a law against leaving a body unburied, so in the days of
the Lord in Judah the criminal's body was buried in an unclean
place.

Those were enigmatic words for 750 years. The Scriptures were
fulfilled, for His body was not left on the cross to decay, nor was He
cast into an unclean place. But a rich man, Joseph of Arimathaea,
and his affluent friend, Nicodemus, carefully and tenderly took
the body of our Lord from the cross, wrapped it in a winding sheet
with one hundred pounds of aloes and myrrh, then lovingly and
prayerfully laid His body in the rich man's tomb. Who would have
thought that such a detail could have been written by the prophet
750 years before it took place? How beautifully God reveals the
things of His Son to us!

His Work After Death

The rest of Isaiah 53 concerns the work of our Lord after His
death. We would suppose that when He was in the grave that was
the end. No, for His death was the beginning. In this great
prophecy by Isaiah nothing is spoken of the life of our Lord before
His death except His suffering. The great work of our Lord,
according to the prophet Isaiah, is done after His death:

> Yet it pleased the LORD to bruise him; he hath put him to grief:
> when thou shalt make his soul an offering for sin, he shall see his
> seed, he shall prolong his days, and the pleasure of the LORD shall
> prosper in his hand. (Isa. 53:10)

The great, mighty kingdom of God shall come through the
leadership of Jesus Christ, the Son of God:

He shall see of the travail of his soul, and shall be satisfied: by his knowledge shall my righteous servant justify many; for he shall bear their iniquities. (Isa. 53:11)

We are washed from our sins in the knowledge of the gracious gospel of the Son of God. He never came so much to preach the gospel as He came to die that there might be a gospel to preach.

Therefore will I divide him a portion with the great, and he shall divide the spoil with the strong; because he hath poured out his soul unto death: and he was numbered with the transgressors; and he bare the sin of many, and made intercession for the transgressors. (Isa. 53:12)

"And made intercession for the transgressors" refers to the glorious intercessory ministry of our Lord in heaven. Romans 5:10 describes it magnificently: "For if, when we were enemies, we were reconciled to God by the death of his Son, much more, being reconciled, we shall be saved by his life." We are forgiven by His atoning death. We are cleansed by the blood of the cross and are kept saved by His life in heaven. No one is able to pluck us out of our Lord's hand.

Then Isaiah closes the prophecy with a coming triumph of our Lord in the earth. "Therefore will I divide him a portion with the great, and he shall divide the spoil with the strong" (Isa. 53:12a). The kingdom of God is in the hands of the great Sovereign of the universe. Do not ever be discouraged by the clouds that cover the face of the earth, for the Lord God omnipotent reigns. The day is ever nearer when He shall be King of the hosts in heaven and of His redeemed in earth. The whole world shall be filled with the knowledge of our glorious Lord like the waters cover the sea. What a privilege to belong to the household of faith, to be numbered among the children of God!

36

The Gospel of Isaiah

Ho, every one that thirsteth, come ye to the waters, and he that hath no money; come ye, buy, and eat; yea, come, buy wine and milk without money and without price.

Wherefore do ye spend money for that which is not bread? and your labour for that which satisfieth not? hearken diligently unto me, and eat ye that which is good, and let your soul delight itself in fatness.

Incline your ear, and come unto me: hear, and your soul shall live; and I will make an everlasting covenant with you, even the sure mercies of David.

Behold, I have given him for a witness to the people, a leader and commander to the people.

Behold, thou shalt call a nation that thou knowest not, and nations that knew not thee shall run unto thee because of the LORD thy God, and for the Holy One of Israel; for he hath glorified thee.

Seek ye the LORD while he may be found, call ye upon him while he is near:

Let the wicked forsake his way, and the unrighteous man his thoughts: and let him return unto the LORD, and he will have mercy upon him; and to our God, for he will abundantly pardon.

For my thoughts are not your thoughts, neither are your ways my ways, saith the LORD.

For as the heavens are higher than the earth, so are my ways higher than your ways, and my thoughts than your thoughts. (Isa. 55:1–9)

These verses in Isaiah 55 describe the call of our Lord in the marketplace. When we think of God in the temple, in the sanctuary, or in the center of our worship hour, we see Him where people usually think of Him, but God in the marketplace selling His wares is an amazing depiction of our Lord.

I remember visiting a large city in the Middle East where there were those who were walking up and down the streets selling water. Their call in Arabic was translated "O thirsting one, water!" "Ho, every one that thirsteth, come ye to the waters."

There are two different features, however, of the wares and the merchandising that God offers. First, what God offers satisfies. There is no emptiness in what He gives. It is full, abundant, and overflowing. Second, God says that if the buyer has no money, then there is no cost or price — it is absolutely free.

God Argues for His Merchandise

Then the Lord argues His case. He says, "Wherefore do ye spend money for that which is not bread? and your labour for that which satisfieth not?" Why take your life and exchange it for things that are empty and sterile and that bring unhappiness? The Lord has an overflowing gift. Why buy something that has no fullness, joy, and happiness in it? Our Lord said:

> Whosoever drinketh of this water shall thirst again:
> But whosoever drinketh of the water that I shall give him shall never thirst; but the water that I shall give him shall be in him a well of water springing up into everlasting life. (John 4:13b,14)

How true is God's description of the vain and empty rewards of the things we seek in this world.

One time I preached for a convocation of our Southern Baptist fellowship in Reno, Nevada. Reno is one of the most unusual places I have ever preached. The people there are searching, hoping, and grasping. The casinos never close; they are open twenty-four hours every day in the week, and every week in the year. They are thronged with thousands of people. At 4:00 A.M. or 4:00 P.M. the gambling houses are still jammed with hungry-hearted, wanting people.

One of the ministers with me said: "Look. You will never see a smile." Another minister said to me: "I have been invited to go to Lake Tahoe on the Nevada side of the lake to be a chaplain and minister there. You do not realize how desperately they want and need us because of the high suicide rate." On the dresser in my hotel room there was a little placard giving the name, address, and telephone number of a chaplain. If one needs a chaplain, he is there on duty.

The reward of the world is no different. Probably the most pampered and petted of all of the great literary figures of the earth was Lord Byron. He was a nobleman, a lord. He was famous over the whole civilized world and was adored and worshiped by the literary generation to which he belonged. He was exalted and praised, but Lord Byron wrote these words:

> My days are in the yellow leaf;
> The flowers and fruits of love are gone;
> The worm, the canker, and the grief
> Are mine alone.

The title of that poem is "On My Thirty-Sixth Yearday," after which he soon died.

Bobby Burns, the bard of Scotland, was loved by the people, and received much praise and adoration. He gave his life to the world in dissipation. These are his words:

> But pleasures are like poppies spread —
> You seize the flow'r, its bloom is shed;
> Or like the snow falls in the river —
> A moment white — then melts forever.
> Or like the rainbow's lovely form,
> Vanishing amid the storm.
> Or like the borealis race that flit,
> E'er, you can point their place.

In Jefferson, Texas, the hotel displays the register book which the front desk used many years ago. The register shows the signature of Jay Gould who was the richest man in the world at that time. In signing his name, Jay, he drew a picture of a bluejay then wrote "Jay Gould." He was a wealthy and powerful railroad tycoon who spoke of his life like this: "I suppose I am the most miserable man in the world."

If one were looking for a candidate for suicide, he could go to Reno or to Las Vegas. Or he could go to Hollywood, for there is much emptiness in the rewards of the world.

THE BESEECHING, ENTREATING WORDS OF THE LORD

The words of Isaiah the prophet are evangelistic. He uses the word "come" three times in the first verse of the fifty-fifth chapter. Then in the second verse we see "hearken." In the next verse we see "incline," then in the next one we see "hear." In the following verse we see "seek ye," and in the next we see "call upon him." Then in verse 7 we see "return." Like the apostles of Christ, Isaiah is always evangelistic and heart-moving. Never does he call to ritual, ceremony, or form, as had been the custom. The Israelites had a temple, a tabernacle, an altar, a laver, lampstands, tables of shewbread, and incense, but these accouterments of ceremonial worship are not mentioned by the prophets. The call is always to the heart to believe, to forsake sin, to seek pardon. Isaiah says that our righteousnesses are as filthy rags in God's sight. The plea is to come just as we are. God has for us an abounding grace and an abundant pardon.

When we come before the Lord, how could we ever have enough money to buy the grace and mercy of God? How could we ever think that we could be good enough or righteous enough to inherit or merit the abounding mercies of God? If His mercies are mediated to us, they must be given in His grace, in the fullness of His abounding love. It is a gift of God.

The last invitation of the Bible in Revelation 22:17 is, "And the Spirit and the bride say, Come. And let him that heareth say, Come. And let him that is athirst come. And whosoever will, let him take the water of life freely." Paul says: "For by grace are ye saved through faith; and that not of yourselves: it is the gift of God" (Eph. 2:8).

A beautiful illustration of God's free gift can be seen in a story I read a long time ago. In one of the great cities of America, a ragged newspaper boy on an early Sunday morning was selling his wares.

As he walked down the street he came to a beautiful home in the heart of the city. The little boy, looking through the tall fence, wandered through the gates of the extensive grounds and was overwhelmed by the beauty of the home. He found himself on the porch and, to his great surprise, he was ringing the doorbell. The big businessman, Mr. Lowry, opened the door and saw the boy. The boy blurted out, "Mister, do you have any children?" The big man replied: "No, my wife and I have no children." The boy said, "Oh, mister, I wish I was your boy so I could play on this lawn and nobody would make me get off and I could live in this beautiful house and nobody would throw me out." The man was amused. He called for his wife, and Mrs. Lowry came down the graceful steps and stood by her husband. The man turned to his wife and said, "Honey, would you like to have a little boy?" She said, "Yes." The little boy, seeing sympathy and hope in the eyes of the big man and his wife, said, "Oh, mister, if you would let me be your little boy, I would give you everything that I have." The tycoon asked, "Son, what do you have?" The boy counted out his remaining papers and reached in his pocket and counted out thirteen pennies which he offered to the man. The husband and his wife looked at each other. He asked the boy if he had a home, a father, or mother. The boy said, "No." Then the man said, "Son, where do you sleep?" The boy answered, "On the streets." "Where do you live?" The boy again said, "On the streets." Then the wife said to her husband, "Honey, let us take him in." They took in that boy. True to his promise, the lad offered the man the papers and pennies. The kindly man looked down at the lad and said: "Son, you keep it. I have more than enough for us both."

What impressed me most about that story was that we come before God and offer our little nothingness to Him. God says: "Salvation is not for sale. One does not buy it. It is a gift from heaven. I have more than enough for us both." We come to be children of God by grace and by adoption. The Lord opens wide the door, and we as sinners are welcomed in. We are given the name of our Lord and we are adopted into the family of God.

Oh, the abounding grace of the love of God for those of us who are sinners! All we need do is come to Him.

37

The Ways of God and of Man

Seek ye the LORD while he may be found, call ye upon him while he is near:

Let the wicked forsake his way, and the unrighteous man his thoughts: and let him return unto the LORD, and he will have mercy upon him; and to our God, for he will abundantly pardon.

For my thoughts are not your thoughts, neither are your ways my ways, saith the LORD.

For as the heavens are higher than the earth, so are my ways higher than your ways, and my thoughts than your thoughts. (Isa. 55:6–9)

Our ideas of salvation are different from God's ideas and thoughts. As we read Isaiah 55 we see a comparison of how a man thinks about sin and salvation, and how God thinks about it. It is easy for us to do that because we are people and we know our thoughts. We all pretty much think alike. From the revelation of God in the Holy Scriptures, we know how God thinks and how He responds to sin.

How Man and God Differ in Their Concept of Sin

First, men categorize sin. We say that some sins are little and some are big. We say that some of them are venial and forgiven, while others are mortal and damn us. Some of them are trifles and are to be overlooked. Others are awesome.

In God's sight, however, there are no categories of sin. Sin damns and destroys, and sin is sin. However man may delineate sins, to God they are all dark and damning.

James 2:10 reads, "For whosoever shall keep the whole law, and yet offend in one point, he is guilty of all." When a man sins, in God's eyes he is guilty of every sin. Why? Because God's thoughts are not our thoughts and God's ways are not our ways. We look at sin one way, but God looks at sin another way. Though a man may look upon himself as being righteous and may walk in his own integrity, God knows his heart and life. There is no man that does not sin. Sin brings with it a separation and an alienation from God.

Our thoughts differ from God's thoughts concerning the corollary that attends sin. Someone else's thoughts may be dark and damnable, but ours are not. All of us have the attitude that God should not be offended particularly by what we do, for there are extenuating circumstances and reasons for what has befallen us and what we do. Our sins should be overlooked and categorized as trifling.

But what does God do? He says, whatever the sin, it carries with it an inevitable penalty. For, you see, the world reflects the character of God. The created universe is but the work of His hands. It is put together in law and law carries with it inevitable penalty. There is no law without a penalty in its violation. The whole world (including us in it) is representative of those laws in the character of God. There are planetary laws, gravitational laws, mechanical laws, thermodynamical laws, chemical laws, physical laws, governmental laws, anatomical laws, and civil laws. All of these laws are grounded in His character.

A man who sneers at gravitational laws and walks off a ten-story building into blank space comes down in splattered death. He does not break the law, he just illustrates it.

Consider an anatomical law. Our body has to follow certain chemical lines, so a man ridicules God's laws of anatomy and asks for a vial of strychnine. He swallows the strychnine and dies in horrible convulsions.

There are governmental laws. The Bible plainly says that government and law are of God. Society is impossible without it. An anarchist actually believes in the destruction of the human race. So a man stands before the judge and says, "I realize I have broken the law, but it is a trifle and I am expecting to be dismissed." The judge sternly replies: "Sir, I must uphold the law and you must obey the law, for without my upholding the law and your obeying the law, we would be swept away by terror, murder, rape, and robbery. For that is what the law is."

So it is with God's moral law. When we break God's moral law, it carries with it an inevitable penalty, for the Lord God welded the two together.

However a man may think, God does not think like a man. We, with eyes of our modern Christian ethical standards, sometimes judge those people who lived thousands of years ago. But we must remember that they lived according to a norm in their day.

Let us look at the days of David who lived one thousand years before Christ. An Oriental monarch was absolute. He did as he pleased. He was above the law, above the people, and above all castigation. When David saw Bathsheba bathing, he took her. He was an Oriental monarch and could do as he pleased. When Uriah, her husband, was returned from the war, David sent him into the heart of the battle that he might be slain. David did as he had absolute right to do. But this was man's judgment, not God's.

Jezebel said to Ahab: "So you want Naboth's vineyard. I will get it for you." A legal trial was conducted, Jezebel produced witnesses, and Naboth was condemned to death. He was stoned and the ground drank up his blood. Ahab went down to Naboth's vineyard to possess it. But that was man's judgment, not God's. Then the story follows that God appeared to Elijah the prophet and said, "Get up and go down to Naboth's vineyard." Elijah confronted Ahab and Ahab the king looked at Elijah and said, "So you found me, O my enemy?" Elijah replied: "In the place where the dogs licked up the blood of Naboth shall the dogs lick up your blood. Jezebel your wife shall be eaten by dogs by the wall of Jezreel."

How does one escape God? I have often heard men say: "How harsh, how judgmental. A forgiving God would not damn like that." But God says that His ways are not our ways, for the purpose of the law is that we might be brought to Jesus to know the wrong of our sin.

We teach our children that fire burns and that pins stick. The child learns. The penalty teaches the youngster. So it is when we go down the road of life. We see a flashing red signal and hear a bell ringing, for a train is coming. The railroad company is not our enemy to flash the sign and ring the bell, but it is done to protect us and spare our lives. If a bridge is out, the highway department builds a barricade across it. The barricade keeps us from being destroyed.

So it is with God. Someone said there are five hundred references in the New Testament to hell. That is, there are five hundred signs that God has placed along our road of life saying in His Word: "This way leads to hell. Stop. Look." When man disregards them, there is nothing left but judgment, death, and damnation.

How Man and God Differ in Their Concept of Salvation

How do we differ from God in our thoughts on salvation? Man may think of the great judgment as a weighing of the good and the bad. If the good outweighs the bad, he will be saved. If the bad outweighs the good, he will be lost. So man decides he must do good to add to that side of the scales. He reforms and attempts to cut out the things he is doing that are wrong. Sometimes he decides he is going to be altruistic. He will perform good works with his money and time. Or he will come to the place where he will practice self-discipline like Martin Luther. In order to commend himself to God, Martin Luther beat himself in an attempt to get rid of his sin and to commend himself to God. Finally man may enter into all kinds of religious rituals to save himself: belief in baptism, in masses, communions, confessions, vespers, and chants.

Now, what does God think about salvation? First, He says, "All [your] righteousnesses are as filthy rags" (Isa. 64:6). That is, there is nothing we can do that does not have with it the overtone of our fallen nature. I am not only fallen in my physical body and am dying, but I am fallen in all of my faculties — my mind, emotions, and will. Even in my prayers I lack.

Second, God says we are dead in trespasses and sins. Funeral directors may prepare the body of the deceased, comb the hair, prepare the face, place fine-looking clothing on the corpse. But the corpse is dead. However one dresses the body, it is dead. A corpse cannot raise itself to life, neither can a man who is dead in trespasses and sin quicken himself.

If a poor man who is a sinner becomes rich, then he is a rich sinner. If a man who is uneducated is sent to school, then he is an educated sinner. God says that the changing of the clothes, the changing of the house, and the changing of the bank account do not change the man.

How do we wash the stain of sin out of our lives? From this moment on we pledge to live perfectly and above sin if it is possible. What shall we do with our years that have already passed?

> Could my tears forever flow,
> Could my zeal no languor know,
> These for sin could not atone —
> Thou must save, and Thou alone:
> In my hand no price I bring,
> Simply to Thy cross I cling.

God's Way of Salvation

How can God save us and at the same time uphold His law? The answer is found in what the Bible calls "Good News," the gospel. It is this: God Himself took our sins, bore our iniquities, and paid the penalty in His own body on the tree. He became incarnate, and as the incarnate Prince of glory He was able to bear the penalty for all our iniquities. We cannot bear it. We are dying. Our parents may have been saintly, but they also faced age, senility, and death. Those who love us would give their lives for us, but they cannot save us. The only One who is able and mighty to save is God incarnate. "And the LORD hath laid on him the iniquity of us all. With his stripes we are healed." He bore the penalty for everyone, and for His sake, God pardons and forgives us.

38

Deathbed Repentance

Seek ye the LORD while he may be found, call ye upon him while he is near. (Isa. 55:6)

The background of the appeal in our text is evident. There may come a time when a man cannot find God because it is too late. He has passed forever the open door of grace. When could that be?

Satan has a statement he often whispers in a man's heart. It says: "You have plenty of time; they are trying to rush you; do not give your heart to Jesus now. Put it off to some other day, some other time." That is what Felix did in Acts 24:35, "And as he reasoned of righteousness, temperance, and judgment to come, Felix trembled, and answered, Go thy way for this time; when I have a convenient season, I will call for thee." Satan continues to whisper that thought today.

There is something else that Satan whispers. It is: "Why miss the joys and pleasure of the world? You would give them up if you became a Christian. If you are going to give them up, do it at the end of your life, but right now enjoy all the pleasures of sin for a season. Maybe on your deathbed there will be time to spare. Between now and then you can enjoy all the pleasures of the world." God has something to say to you who are listening to that siren voice of Satan.

What God Says

God says that no man has any mortgage on tomorrow. We do not know what tomorrow may bring. We read in James 4:14, "Whereas ye know not what shall be on the morrow. For what is your life? It is even a vapour, that appeareth for a little time, and then vanisheth away."

There is an old Talmudic story of a young man who went to the rabbi and asked, "Rabbi, how long may I put off my repentance and be saved?" The old rabbi replied, "Son, you can put it off until the day of your death." Then the young man asked, "But Rabbi, when will it be that I die?" The rabbi answered, "Then you must repent now and get right with God now." So it is with us. We do not know what any tomorrow may bring.

God says that Satan deceives us when he persuades us that we are having a good time in the world, and that we will have to give up joy and happiness if we become a Christian. He whispers that especially into the hearts of young men and women. God answers: "I am come that they might have life, and that they might have it more abundantly." God says the full and rich life is in Christ, not in the world.

A man stood up to testify and said: "When I became a Christian, I gave up many things. I gave up the liquor bill. No longer do I fall into delirium nor am I terrified by hallucinations nor do I have a dark, heavy hangover. I gave that up when I became a Christian. I also gave up the wrecking of my home and the leading of my children down to hell. I gave up gambling my check away and leaving my family in want. I gave up my dirty and foul mouth and my evil mind. I gave up the squandering of my life and salary. Now I am free of my chains and slavery and I am free in Jesus Christ. It cost me much. I gave up much to become a Christian."

This is so true. We give up the world's tears, despair, darkness, sin, filth, chains, slavery, and death, and we walk out free into the love of the grace of God. All who have accepted Jesus as Savior have found Him unfailingly true.

What does God say about putting off our repentance and acceptance of Christ until — hopefully — our deathbed? God says that our whole life belongs to Christ:

> And one of the scribes came, and having heard them reasoning together, and perceiving that he had answered them well, asked him, Which is the first commandment of all?
> And Jesus answered him, The first of all the commandments is, Hear, O Israel; The Lord our God is one Lord:
> And thou shalt love the Lord thy God with all thy heart, and with all thy soul, and with all thy mind, and with all thy strength: this is the first commandment.
> And the second is like, namely this, Thou shalt love thy neighbor as thyself. There is none other commandment greater than these. (Mark 12:28–30)

The strength of our heart, mind, and soul belongs to God.

A man with a lovely wife and two darling little girls went off into sin and the world and left his family. The wife moved to the edge of town, rented a hovel of a house, and took in washing to support herself and her family. The girls grew up, and she gave them the finest education she could. They became beautiful young women. Some years later her husband came back home. He knocked at the door and the wife went to answer it. As he stood there, she first didn't recognize him, but then realized it was her husband. He was diseased and his life was ruined. He had come back home and asked her to take him in. She cared for him until he died. We cannot help but admire a woman like that. But I doubt if there is anyone, anywhere, who would say, "That man did a noble deed." There is something on the inside of us that says that the man did a horrible thing.

Are you doing that? Are you giving your life to the devil and to sin and then at the end of the way casting at God's feet a hull and a shell? We must realize that the strength of a man's life, his finest thoughts, and all that he is belongs to God. Man should give his heart to Christ in his greatest strength and serve the Lord all the days of his life. We belong in strength to Him.

A MAN'S CHARACTER SETS

Character sets and has a way of hardening. In Ecclesiastes 11:3

we read, ". . . and if the tree fall toward the south, or toward the north, in the place where the tree falleth, there it shall be." When a man has lived a certain way, somehow character solidifies. That is why there are so few aged men and women who are converted. I pleaded with an aged man one time who faced inevitable death and his reply to me was, "Somehow I just cannot believe." He died in unbelief. When a man continues to say no to the Spirit of God, he becomes hardened to His call.

A famous English physician studied hundreds of cases of deathbed repentance. He made notes of them through the years of his practice. He recorded the cases in which the man recovered. The physician reported that in a lifetime of observation, of the hundreds of men who recovered and lived, only one continued in the faith. That has also been my experience.

In the city of Dallas a famous businessman was ill in the hospital. I went to see him. He said to me: "The doctors say I will surely die. Will you kneel down by my side and pray? Tell God that if He will spare my life, I will serve Him all the rest of my days. You will see me in every service at your church. I will be a faithful servant of God." I knelt by his side and, holding his hand, I told God for him that if the Lord would spare his life, he would serve Him the rest of his days. He said, "Amen." God heard the prayer and blessed that man. He was given strength and length of days.

I never saw him in my congregation. He never even bothered to attend church, much less give his heart and life in service to Jesus. I buried him not long ago. He died outside the faith, without God and without hope.

We need to serve God *now*.

We need to repent *now*.

We need to be saved *now*.

Deathbed repentance is vain and futile.

39

The Humble of Heart

> For thus saith the high and lofty One that inhabiteth eternity, whose name is Holy; I dwell in the high and holy place, with him also that is of a contrite and humble spirit, to revive the spirit of the humble, and to revive the heart of the contrite ones. (Isa. 57:15)

The spiritual sentiment found in Isaiah 57:15 is repeated often in the Scriptures. In Isaiah 66 the prophet writes of the same lofty thought again:

> Thus saith the LORD, The heaven is my throne, and the earth is my footstool: where is the house that ye build unto me? and where is the place of my rest?
> For all those things hath mine hand made, and all those things have been, saith the LORD: but to this man will I look, even to him that is poor and of a contrite spirit, and trembleth at my word. (Isa. 66:1,2)

The thought in the text is staggering beyond imagination. God who dwells in infinity also dwells in the narrow confines of the human heart. It is inconceivable that God, who fills the universe, should also dwell in the confines of a small, human heart. I can comprehend somewhat of the infinitude of God by looking into the starry heavens. I can certainly comprehend the iniquity of the human heart. But I cannot comprehend how one can be encompassed in the other.

THE GREATNESS OF GOD IN RESPECT TO SPACE

We look first at the description of God as being great in space. God who does "dwell in the high and holy place." Wherever that is, there is God. He is here, He is there, He is in the farthest outreaches of space and beyond the barriers that separate us and the distances we cannot even find. In the infinitude of the heavens above us, God is and dwells. Such truth staggers the thought and imagination of how vast is the abode of the Almighty. We need to have the measuring rod that John saw in the angel's hand.

Men have tried to speak of the distances of God's infinitude. Scientists first used the measurement of miles and said that infinitude is billions of miles, then trillions of miles, then quadrillions of miles. Then the measuring rod became useless. A method of study of the velocity of a cannon ball over a period of twenty-four hours was then invented. Using that as a measurement, they found that it would take so many months, years, and centuries to reach a goal until it finally became a useless and clumsy instrument. Eventually man turned to the measuring rod of heaven itself, the velocity of light, speeding 186,300 miles per second. From the earth to the sun is eight minutes and seven seconds for·92,000,000 miles. But once again, measuring God's infinite home, astronomers found in light years that the universe continues millions, billions, trillions, and quadrillions of light years beyond. Ah, the vastness of God's universe in which He dwells.

An illustration that approaches what our text means when it speaks of God who dwells both in the high and lofty place and also in the human heart, is this: as vast as the starry heavens are, and as infinite are those unbounded and immeasurable distances, at night I can encompass it in the small circle of my eye. A shepherd watching over his flock can lie on the ground and look up into God's infinite sky. He can capture the great infinitude of the Lord's handiwork in the small pupil of his eye. So it is of the magnitude of the infinite God who dwells in infinite space, but who also makes His home in the human heart.

The Greatness of God in Respect to Time

The text speaks of the great and mighty God in time. He inhabits eternity. Here again, language staggers under the weight of the magnitude of the burden laid upon it. God dwelt in eternity in the aeons and ages before creation, and will dwell in the great consummation of the aeons that are yet to come. He is ageless and unchanging.

The tall, graceful Sears Building is located in Chicago. It is the highest man-made structure in the world, towering a quarter of a mile high above the streets of the city. The thickness of a nickel placed on top of that vast building would be relative to the age of man compared to the age of creation itself. Yet creation is but a small part of the eternity before and the eternity that shall follow after. In all of the ageless aeons, God dwells.

The Greatness of God in Respect to Character

He is described also as the great God of character, whose name is holy, or *kadosh*. *Kadosh* literally means "separate." It seems as though our understanding of what is holy is almost based on our understanding of what is not holy. Impurity we understand, and God is not impure. Iniquity we understand, but God is not iniquitous. Pride and deceitfulness we know, but God is not proud and deceitful. God is *kadosh*, separate from sin. He is of such purity that Habakkuk says He cannot look upon iniquity. When Paul writes that God made Jesus to be sin for us, then we understand the cry of the cross, "My God, my God, why hast thou forsaken me?" The sun refused to shine, the light of the world went out, and God turned away His face, for He is of purer eyes than to look upon iniquity. Yet the mighty God who inhabits eternity, the infinite majesty that fills all space, the Lord's pure character that cannot bear to look upon iniquity, dwells in a sinful heart.

The Humble of Heart

God dwells in those who are of a contrite and humble spirit.

What is a humble man? A humble man is one who has a true evaluation of himself. A man who is proud and lifted up forgets that he is made of the dust of the ground and that he lives in the presence of a great and lofty God. In his spirit, being full of pride, the exalted man lifts himself up. He is not humble.

Men who live in an intellectual world often are anything but humble. They are filled with the pride of the intellectual and academic achievements of their lives. An astronomer, looking into the vast heavens, can easily forget the God who made him. The evolutionist forgets that matter cannot originate or organize itself. The surgeon can sometimes forget that only God can heal. A metaphysician can easily forget that above all we see and know there is an intelligence and genius beyond us. The intellectual lifts himself up in pride as though he knows more than God. He scoffs in ridicule at those who bow before the name of the great and mighty Lord.

A man can be proud and lifted up in his own self-esteem. He magnifies his own self-importance; therefore, he is hurt at some slight and supposed injury. He is offended when his opinions are not taken with deep sincerity. He lives a life of unhappiness. He is proud in his heart, uplifted in his spirit, and has an overweening estimation of his own importance.

How wonderful it is when the man can look upon himself as he is: made of the dust of the ground, when he can say in the presence of his great Creator, "Lord, make me and use me." Thus, without a spirit of jealousy, he can watch others exalted while he may be debased; he can see others introduced to stand up while he must remain seated and unrecognized; he can watch others pass him by in success and praise; he can listen to the words of appreciation he covets for himself; and he can rejoice in the advancement of other people. God dwells in the heart of that humble man.

God dwells in the heart of a contrite man. For example, I am on my way to the Lord with a little bundle. My little bundle is composed of tears, trials, troubles, sobs, cares, anxieties, frustrations, and disappointments. I am on my way to lay them at the feet of the mighty God. A philosopher stops me along the way and asks: "What have you in your little bundle? Let me see." I open my bundle before him and he says, "What, do you dare bring those fragments of wretchedness before the great and high God?" My heart is smitten. I remember He told me to do this. It was He who said in Matthew 11:28, "Come unto me, all ye that labour and are heavy laden, and I will give you rest." He who runs this universe, who guides the great planets in their orbits, who takes care of the starry galaxies of infinitude, is the One who bows down to hear our prayers, to see our tears, and to look through our little bundles of trials and troubles.

Again I am on the way to appear before the great and high God, this time to lay something at His feet. The philosopher stops me and says, "What do you have in your hand that you are to lay at the feet of God?" I open my hand and there is an important personal request. He says: "What? Do you not understand that the mighty God runs this universe by law? Do you suppose He will suspend His inexorable law at your foolish request?' Then I remember the time Joshua prayed to God and God stopped the sun and the moon in answer to his request. I remember that Elijah asked God to pour fire out of heaven upon the earth and He did it. Then I remember the request of Hezekiah that God turn the shadow on the sundial of Ahaz back ten degrees — and it was done. I remember what He said to me in Matthew 19:26, "But with God all things are possible." And there are many other illustrations we could use.

Two men went up into the temple to pray. One was proud, lifted up his head, and said to God, "I thank Thee that I am not like other men." But the publican, standing afar off, would not so much as lift up his head, but beat upon his breast and cried, saying, "Lord, be merciful to me a sinner." The Lord Jesus said, "The Mighty came down and made His home in the heart of that contrite and praying man."

Revelation 3:20 says, "Behold, I stand at the door, and knock: if any man hear my voice, and open the door, I will come in to him, and will sup with him, and he with me." Open the door of your heart and the great God of the universe will come in.

40

The Barrier Between

Behold, the Lord's hand is not shortened, that it cannot save;
neither his ear heavy, that it cannot hear:
But your iniquities have separated between you and your God,
and your sins have hid his face from you, that he will not hear. (Isa.
59:1,2)

There are three characteristics in this prophetic message from
Isaiah that describe our most holy faith.

The prophecy is first moral and ethical. True religion is
grounded in the character of almighty God. Such a statement
today sounds trite, because people think of the Christian religion
as being moral and ethical. But to have said something like this in
the ancient world would have been to make an unbelievable
announcement, for in the ancient world, religion was separated
from morality.

If we would have visited a temple in ancient Egypt, we would
have seen that it was surrounded by a wall and inside was the court.
As we entered the outer courts, there would have been an altar
where the sacrifices were burned. Just beyond would have been a
laver where the priest washed his hands. Behind the laver would
be the sanctuary with its door leading into a holy place. As we en-

tered in, we would have noticed the sacred furniture, and just beyond, the veil. Pulling the veil aside we would have found a sacred ark. But we would be astonished at what we saw. The object of adoration of the ancient pagans was a stork, a crocodile, a cat, or a cow. This was the heart of the religious faith of the ancient world.

Now let us go to the great temple of Jehovah in Jerusalem. Around the Jewish temple there would be a wall and, on the inside, the court. That is familiar. In the outer court we would have found the altar. That is familiar. Beyond the altar we would find a laver where the priest washed his hands. That is familiar. Just beyond would be the sanctuary and the inner door. We go inside and there would be the holy place with its beautiful furniture. That is familiar. Just beyond that we would see the veil, separating the holy place from the Holy of Holies. That is familiar. Behind the veil would be an ark. That is familiar. But when we look in the ark we see the Ten Commandments of the living God written by His finger on two tables of stone. The heart of the religion of almighty God is always moral and ethical. It has to do with righteousness and godliness.

THE CHRISTIAN RELIGION IS SOTERIOLOGICAL

Second, our faith is a presentation of a God of mercy, pardon, salvation, and forgiveness. Our great God is able to save and is able to answer prayer. The heart of God in mercy and in pity is open to the sons of men. The message is always one of repentance, forgiveness, and salvation.

Isaiah 1:18 says, "Come now, and let us reason together, saith the LORD: though your sins be as scarlet, they shall be as white as snow; though they be red like crimson, they shall be as wool." Ezekiel 33:11 says, "As I live, saith the Lord GOD, I have no pleasure in the death of the wicked; but that the wicked turn from his way and live: turn ye, turn ye from your evil ways; for why will ye die, O house of Israel?" The great God in heaven who cannot bear to look upon impurity and iniquity is a God of salvation and of answered prayer.

Then why are we not all saved? Why are so many lost? Why is it that some of our prayers are not answered and it seems God does not hear us? Because of our sins:

> Behold, the LORD's hand is not shortened, that it cannot save; neither his ear heavy, that it cannot hear:
> But your iniquities have separated between you and your God, and your sins have hid his face from you, that he will not hear. (Isa. 59:1,2)

THE CHRISTIAN RELIGION IS JUDGMENTAL

Third, our faith is judgmental. It has in it a penalty and judgment when we turn our backs on God and when we defy His sacred commandments. We would think that the man who chose to say no to God, who chose to be defiant of the laws of God, chose to do so because there was something better. But God Himself says:

> But the wicked are like the troubled sea, when it cannot rest, whose waters cast up mire and dirt.
> There is no peace, saith my God, to the wicked. (Isa. 57:20,21)

When a man turns from God and in defiance follows his own sinful ways, there is no rest and no peace, nothing abiding but trouble.

We mention first the open and flagrant transgressions, the carnal and gross sins. The man turns his back on God and follows his own willful ways. In judgment God says that there will be no peace, no rest, but trouble.

A man gives himself to greed. Money, affluence, success, and rewards are his goals. He thinks if he can just have so much he will be satisfied — and he gains his desires. Then he sets his goals again and again, but he is never satisfied; he is never at rest, never at peace. If he owned the world, he would covet the moon and the stars besides.

A doctor said to his surgeon friend: "So you have no time for God, and your Sundays are spent in your profession in order to make money. You shall be the richest surgeon in the cemetery." The surgeon soon died of a heart attack. The man who gives himself to greed wants more and more and he is never satisfied. Neither is a man content who gives himself to selfish ambition to rise over others, disregarding love, friendship, and compassion. There is no rest, no peace.

A man covets praise. It sounds like music to his ear when he is complimented. A little praise makes him want more praise. There is no rest, no peace.

A man gives himself to lust, to evil and burning passions, and there is trouble. He has intimate relationships with one after another and is not satisfied. He goes from one to the other and gives himself to a life of lust and evil passion. There is no rest, no peace.

A man gives himself to anger, bitterness, bearing a grudge. Like the troubled waters of the sea, casting up mire and dirt, the heart and life are destroyed. God says, "Let not the sun go down on your wrath." Settle your grievances before you retire. To hate and to be full of anger is to be restless.

King Saul of Israel, returning from the battle of the Philistines, heard the women of Israel singing, "Saul hath slain his thousands, but David his tens of thousands." From that moment on, Saul was jealous of David. He never found rest or peace. The last years of his reign were destroyed by envy and jealousy. The Bible says, "But the spirit of the Lord departed from Saul, and an evil spirit from the Lord troubled him" (1 Sam. 16:14). There is no peace, but a life of troubled restlessness.

In Ezekiel 28 we read that it was pride that lifted up the heart of Satan and God cast him down to hell. It is when one lifts himself up in self-esteem that there is no rest, no peace.

Drugs and drink offer no rest. To get a kick from drugs the intake has to be more than the last time, then more and more. There is no rest, no end.

Psalm 7:11 says, "God judgeth the righteous, and God is angry with the wicked every day." The holiness of God burns against sin. The Lord has declared war against iniquity forever. There is never an armistice. The one who gives himself to the defiance of God breaks the great order of God's universe and violates the great character of the Almighty. He consigns himself to trouble, restlessness, and unhappiness.

MORAL, RESPECTABLE, LAW-ABIDING TRANSGRESSORS

We turn now from gross and carnal sins to respectable transgressions. A man may say: "I am no violent murderer. I am no drug addict. I am no gross sinner living in a promiscuous world." He is a respectable transgressor. God says that he too must repent. The man does not repent. God says he must have faith in Christ. The man does not believe in Christ. God says he must give his heart in faith to the Lord Jesus. The man refuses and turns his back upon the overtures of grace. He spurns the blood of the covenant that sanctified our Savior. He follows his own way and finds there is no rest, no peace.

The man says: "I will go to church and attend the services." "No peace," says God. He adds, "But I will take the sacraments; I will bow." "No peace," says God. The man continues: "But You do not understand. I will walk as an upright citizen." God says, "No peace." The man implores: "But I will go even further. I will take part in the fine civic enterprises of my community. I will make my contribution and walk in and out before the people as an upstanding man." But God says, "There is no rest, no peace." Outside of Christ, the man is troubled and his heart finds no peace.

One day he buries one of his best friends, and as he turns from the open grave his heart cries within him. That day will come for him and he is not ready to die. He has not made peace with God. When that hour comes, will the time be triumphant for him? He is troubled. He lives in a lonely world when he grows older. The days multiply and the tokens of an ultimate knocking at his door inevitably appear. There are crow's-feet around his eyes, and there is gray in his hair. He loses the strength and zest of young manhood. He is troubled. What will become of him and his soul? When he stands before God, what will he say?

If you had been asked the question twenty years ago, some of you would have said: "Oh, in twenty years I will surely have become a Christian, for I am just putting it off until some other time, some more convenient season. But I intend to respond. I do not plan to be lost. I do not mean to be damned. I am going to be saved." The man is almost in the kingdom, he is almost persuaded. Then he turns aside.

> "Almost" cannot avail.
> "Almost" is but to fail!
> Sad, sad, that bitter wail,
> "Almost," but lost!

God is able to save and is ready to hear. All I must do is to come and bow in His presence. I must confess my sins and ask God to be merciful and forgive my transgressions.

41

The Light of the Lord

> Arise, shine; for thy light is come, and the glory of the LORD is risen upon thee.
>
> For, behold, the darkness shall cover the earth, and gross darkness the people: but the LORD shall arise upon thee, and his glory shall be seen upon thee.
>
> And the Gentiles shall come to thy light, and kings to the brightness of thy rising.
>
> . . . for the LORD shall be thine everlasting light, and the days of thy mourning shall be ended. (Isa. 60:1–3,20b)

When the consummation of the age comes, the marvelous prophecies named in these verses will come to pass. Let us look at three ways the prophecy will unfold.

WHAT THE PROPHETIC TEXT MEANT TO ISRAEL

We speak first of the prophecy as the prophet meant it in his day and time for his people. The prophetic message is addressed to millennial Israel. We can imagine what a prophecy like this meant to a people who were in Babylonian captivity, and who were slaves in a foreign and alien land.

There was a time when there was light in the homes of Israel,

279

and there was darkness in all of Egypt. There was a time when the light of God's spiritual blessings shone brightly among His chosen people and the entire world beyond lay in gross darkness. Under the smile of heaven Israel prospered. As the days multiplied into years, the nation turned aside from the Lord, began to worship strange and foreign gods, and began to pattern their life after the life of the world. God's judgment was swift and terrible. They were cast into slavery and captivity. They were visited by the iron hand of destruction. They fell from the glory of the kingdom that was Solomon's into servitude and slavery of King Zedekiah. God's chosen people exchanged the golden beauty of their Solomonic temple for the ashes and ruin of a destroyed and abandoned city. In slavery they languished and wept in Babylon. The prophet Isaiah brought this incomparable revelation to a people desperate for divine help.

Our text in Isaiah 60 is the reason I am a premillennialist. I believe that in God's time every promise He has made to Israel He will faithfully fulfill. No word of the Lord will ever fall to the ground, but in His time His chosen people will be returned to their land. A nation will be born in a day, for they will look upon Him whom they pierced. There will be a great mourning, as the mourning at Hadadrimmon when the people wept over the slaughter of good King Josiah and his army. In that day a fountain of cleansing will be open for Israel. They will look into the face of their Messiah God and the whole kingdom will be placed in their hands. Israel will be the leader of the nations of the earth to whom the Gentiles will come in the brightness and glory of their shining. What an incomparable prophecy! The whole earth be marvelously, gloriously blessed!

A LIKE PROPHETIC PATTERN FOR THE CHURCH

Second, the prophecy is addressed to the mystic body of Christ, His church. As there was a dispensation for Israel, so there is a new dispensation for those who belong to the mystical body of Christ called His church.

When Jesus was born in Bethlehem, Simeon the old prophet lifted up his voice in heavenly vision and said that the child was born for a light to lighten the Gentiles, and for the glory of Israel.

This new age of grace is a mystery. When we translate the Greek word *musterion* into English, the word is "mystery" in our language. But mystery to us refers to a riddle. The word *musterion* in the Bible always refers to a "secret," a "mystery that can be revealed." This *musterion* was a secret God kept in His heart until He revealed it to His holy apostles. The secret was that there would be another dispensation. In this new dispensation there would be a mystical body of Christ composed of both Jew and Gentile — all the people, families, and tribes of the world who would look in repentance and faith to Him. To that mystical body of our Lord is this glorious millennial promise and appeal addressed.

The history of the church and what I see today in the church trouble me. The church is His body and is made of those who are the elect of God. I am troubled by what I see and read, for the church is not always the church. It often becomes something else. There are times when the church rises in power, when the presence of God moves in saving grace in its midst, when it is glorious in its witness and testimony to the Lord. There are other times when the church descends to the dismal damps, when it chills the bone, when it loses its power and fellowship with God. There are dark pages of history that record the life of the church of the past, and we often can see emptiness and sterility in the church of today's world.

I see from God's Word two things. First, I see that there is an invisible church in the visible church, an elect in the church. There are those who are justified, who are born again, who are regenerated, who belong to the body of Christ. That church is the mystical church of our Lord. Often I am asked, "Are all the members of your church saved?" I am not to judge. That belongs to God alone. I can only look at the fruit of these who profess a Christian devotion. Then my answer has to be, "No, they are not all saved." When I look at the visible church, I am disturbed and troubled. A large part of it repudiates the faith completely. Some parts of the church are nothing but a preview of atheism and denial. I am troubled until I understand that in the visible church there is an invisible congregation. There is an elect in the membership and God knows those who belong to Him.

Second, I learn from God's Word that this mystical church will be caught away in the Rapture to meet our Lord in the air. Out of the denial and poor witness of the visible church in this earth there is a true assembly who will be caught up to meet our Lord in the air.

Savanarola was one of the greatest preachers of all time. When I was in Florence I wanted to visit the little cell in St. Mark's where Savonarola lived and studied the Bible. I wanted to stand in the pulpit in the great cathedral where he preached the Word of God. I wanted to go to the square in Florence where he was hanged and where his body was burned. As I went to those places, I relived that day when the people came from Rome and stood before the mighty preacher who was behind bars. They read the paper to him of excommunication and execution. The paper closed with this sentence: "I hereby separate thee from the church militant and from the church triumphant." Savonarola replied, "Sir, you can separate me from the church visible, and from the church militant, but you cannot separate me from the church triumphant, the church in heaven." By one spirit we are all baptized into the body of Christ. We are joined to our Lord forever.

The Prophecy Is Addressed to a Local Church

I am reminded that the word "church" in the Bible is almost always used to refer to a local congregation. Paul writes of the churches (plural) of Macedonia, or the churches (plural) of Achaia, or the churches (plural) of Judaea. However, we can apply this text to a local church, and we will be in the spirit of the text, "Arise, shine; for thy light is come, and the glory of the Lord is risen upon thee."

If the Holy Spirit is in your heart, when you come together in worship, then the power of His presence is openly displayed. You have an inner, secret life, one of prayer and intercession. When you come together in worship your secret devotion to the Lord is openly seen. You love the Lord in your heart, and when you worship with other Christians you praise His Name. Oh, how Christians exalt together in the songs and words that lift up our blessed Jesus! We have a secret concern for the lost, and when we come together openly, such compassion for souls is seen and felt. The Holy Spirit moves in the service, and God answers our prayers.

42

The Spirit of Jesus

> The Spirit of the Lord GOD is upon me; because the LORD hath anointed me to preach good tidings unto the meek; he hath sent me to bind up the brokenhearted, to proclaim liberty to the captives, and the opening of the prison to them that are bound;
>
> To proclaim the acceptable year of the LORD, and the day of vengeance of our God; to comfort all that mourn;
>
> To appoint unto them that mourn in Zion, to give unto them beauty for ashes, the oil of joy for mourning, the garment of praise for the spirit of heaviness; that they might be called trees of righteousness, the planting of the LORD, that he might be glorified. (Isa. 61:1–3)

Do you sense and feel with me the incomparable announcement of the prophecy in Isaiah 61? Whoever the prophet describes in the text must be a glorious prince from heaven. He must be God come down among men.

Let us look now at Luke 4:

> And he came to Nazareth, where he had been brought up: and, as his custom was, he went into the synagogue on the sabbath day, and stood up for to read.
>
> And there was delivered unto him the book of the prophet Esaias. And when he had opened the book, he found the place where it was written,

> The Spirit of the Lord is upon me, because he hath anointed me to preach the gospel to the poor; he hath sent me to heal the brokenhearted, to preach deliverance to the captives, and recovering of sight to the blind, to set at liberty them that are bruised,
>
> To preach the acceptable year of the Lord.
>
> And he closed the book, and he gave it again to the minister, and sat down. And the eyes of all them that were in the synagogue were fastened on him.
>
> And he began to say unto them, This day is this scripture fulfilled in your ears. (vv. 16–21)

This is the text our Lord read when He preached His first great message in Nazareth, and the text is as fresh and pertinent now as it was then.

ANOINTED TO PREACH

When a pastor is anointed in the power of the Lord, a congregation is blessed. A minister of a church has many responsibilities and duties, He is an administrator, an organizer, a visitor, a money-raiser, and a counselor, but the most outstanding feature that should characterize the minister of the church is that he is a preacher anointed of God, a prophet-spokesman from heaven. The congregation should constantly pray that he be just that. However many other assignments he has, first and above all he should be an anointed preacher of the grace and love of God in Christ Jesus.

Why does the prophet name the poor? Because they are so often overlooked, forgotten, and neglected. How easy it is to pass them by. The most tender quality about Jesus is that He ministered to the poor and common people. They crowded around Him, and His words were water of life and salvation to their souls.

CHRIST HEALS THE BROKENHEARTED

When we break a bone, the physician can easily splint and bind the bone until it heals. But who is able to bind up the fractured heart? When the spirit is cowed and the heart is crushed and life is wretched, when there is seemingly no strength left to fight in the battle of life, we need someone. The doctor may tell you to take a long journey, but how do you leave your heart? When you get off the plane ten thousand miles away, you carry your spirit and heart with you. Finally, life becomes a burden almost too difficult to carry. There is a tendency on the part of people not to be associated with those who are down in spirit. What a Friend is Jesus who can bind up the brokenhearted!

The prophet speaks of the captives and those in prison. They are behind iron bars and stone walls and are slaves to sin. God is their deliverer, to deliver them from sin to salvation, from wrong to right, from selfishness to service, and from hell to heaven.

"The recovering of sight to the blind" is a reference to sin. Sin blinds a man's eyes. Sin never pays off. To be stumbling and staggering in the world of sin is to be like a man groping in the darkness of midnight.

The prophet continues, "To proclaim the acceptable year of the LORD." What a herald of salvation was the announcement of the great jubilee year of God! Whether it be a Mary or a Martha lamenting over the loss of their brother Lazarus, or whether it be a leper who is thrust away because he is unclean, the day of salvation is here. The light of the glory of God is shining down. This is the acceptable year of the Lord. Rejoice and be glad!

I would have thought that when our Lord read His text and offered Himself as the Savior of human hearts, the people with one accord would have opened their arms and hearts to receive Him, that they would have bowed down and worshiped Him. But we read that when they heard the Lord's message they were filled with wrath. They rose up in anger and thrust Jesus out of the city. They led Him to the brow of the hill upon which their city was built that they might throw Him to His death.

In Norfolk, Virginia, attending a session of our Southern Baptist Convention, I sat in the auditorium awaiting the arrival of the President of the United States. It was the first time the Chief Executive Officer of the United States had ever been invited to speak to our assembly. The Secret Service and local police had sealed off the center of the city. Every driver of a vehicle who sought to drive down a street was stopped and asked his destination. For hours all of the area around the auditorium was sealed off. Before anyone was allowed to enter the auditorium, he had to present the badge of registration which was affixed to his clothing and a special ticket to the officers. If anyone was carrying anything, he had to place the item on a table for inspection. The great hall looked like a rendezvous of the police department. Uniformed officers and plainclothesmen were standing everywhere. The throng waited in anticipation. Finally, followed by a great troop and escorted by other men, the President of the United States appeared. He came with great dignity into the vast arena. Then he was escorted to the platform and, amid the standing ovation of the people, he was finally able to present his address. Never have I heard a finer address than that delivered by the then President of the United States. His words were appropriate and warm in feeling and tone. When he finished, even though the political complexion of the convention was mixed, the convention arose with one accord in great appreciation and applauded as our Chief Executive was escorted from the platform and from the building.

As I contemplated on the President's appearance and address, I could not help but compare the reception of the President of the United States amid the applause and ovations of the people to the reception of the Prince of Glory from heaven. When the President appeared, we stood. When he spoke, we applauded. But when our Lord came from heaven and announced the most glorious news the world had ever heard, the people were seized with wrath. In anger they thrust Him from their midst.

We All Crucified Jesus

The Scriptures say, "He came unto his own, and his own received him not" (John 1:11). What was the matter with our Lord? Why were the people so furious and what were their thoughts against Him? They said, "This man forgives sins." "He heals on the Sabbath day." "He receiveth sinners and eats with them." "Destroy this temple, and on the third day I will raise it up." "He says he is Christ, a King. That is treason." Because of these sayings, they hated Him and delivered Him to be crucified.

But you say: "Judas did that. He betrayed Jesus, not I. The Jews delivered Him to be crucified, not I. The Roman soldiers drove those nails through His hands and feet, not I." We all crucified

Him. We all had a part. Our sins pressed the crown of thorns on His brow and our sins drove those great nails through His hands and feet. If you want to see the blackness of sin, look at Jesus hanging on the cross. If you want to look on the depravity of human nature, look at the Savior nailed to the tree. We did this to the Prince of Glory; we crucified our Lord.

When the Lord read the text, He stopped in the midst of the second verse. Any man, anywhere, can repent of his sins and be saved. But there is coming a time when the books will be closed and we will all stand at the judgment bar of almighty God. Then we will confront Him face to face.

Revelation 1:7 says, "Behold, he cometh with clouds; and every eye shall see him, and they also which pierced him: and all kindreds of the earth shall wail because of him. Even so, Amen." There is another day, another chapter coming. Now I have the open door to be saved, to come to Him in repentance, but there is coming a day when I will be forced to stand before Him and be judged. What will happen to me then? How I need an advocate, a pleader, an intercessor!

43

The Terrible Tribulation

Who is this that cometh from Edom, with dyed garments from Bozrah? this that is glorious in his apparel, travelling in the greatness of his strength? I that speak in righteousness, mighty to save.

Wherefore art thou red in thine apparel, and thy garments like him that treadeth in the wine vat?

I have trodden the winepress alone; and of the people there was none with me: for I will tread them in mine anger, and trample them in my fury; and their blood shall be sprinkled upon my garments, and I will stain all my raiment.

For the day of vengeance is in mine heart, and the year of my redeemed is come.

And I looked, and there was none to help; and I wondered that there was none to uphold: therefore mine own arm brought salvation unto me; and my fury, it upheld me.

And I will tread down the people in mine anger, and make them drunk in my fury, and I will bring down their strength to the earth. (Isa. 63:1–6)

This passage is startling and awesome. Whatever its meaning, the prophecy carries an abounding deliverance for God's people and a crushing defeat for God's enemies. This Scripture prophesies the great day of the vengeance of almighty God against those who reject His overtures of grace and mercy.

Isaiah 63:7–19 and chapter 64 belong together. Isaiah 63:7 should be a part of chapter 64. The first section is the announcement of the deliverance of God's people in the day of judgment and wrath. The second half is a beautiful prayer of Isaiah in contrition and confession, looking forward to that day of intervention and deliverance.

ISAIAH AND DANIEL

What is described here in Isaiah is found also in Daniel 9. Daniel is in Babylonian captivity, and while there he reads the prophecy of Jeremiah where God said that after seventy years of desolation He would intervene, that He would judge the Babylonians, deliver His people, and set them free. The passage in Daniel states:

> In the first year of his reign I Daniel understood by books the number of the years, whereof the word of the LORD came to Jeremiah the prophet, that he would accomplish seventy years in the desolations of Jerusalem.
> And I set my face unto the Lord God, to seek by prayer and supplications, with fasting, and sackcloth, and ashes:
> And I prayed unto the LORD my God, and made my confession, and said, O Lord, the great and dreadful God, keeping the covenant and mercy to them that love him, and to them that keep his commandments;
> We have sinned, and have committed iniquity, and have done wickedly, and have rebelled, even by departing from thy precepts and from thy judgments:
> Neither have we hearkened unto thy servants the prophets, which spake in thy name to our kings, our princes, and our fathers, and to all the people of the land. (9:2–6)

That is exactly what is happening in Isaiah. The great prophecy is stated in the first part announcing the intervention of God, then the beautiful prayer follows in verse 7 through Isaiah 64.

ETERNAL HATRED TOWARD ISRAEL AND JUDAH

Why does God use Edom? Edom in this passage is taken as a symbol of those who hate God, who reject His overtures of grace and mercy. Edom has been the eternal enemy of the people of

God. The story of their years is a story of bitterness and hostility.

In Amos 1 a judgment is pronounced upon Edom because Edom allied herself with Tyre when the armies of Tyre overran Israel. Edom followed that army with unspeakable ruthless atrocities against the people of the Lord. The entire prophecy of Obadiah is against Edom in which Edom is described as one who has cut off the escape of Israel and has taken the people of God into slavery.

In 2 Chronicles 28 we read how Edom invaded Judah and ravished the people of the Lord. In Psalm 137 we see how Edom is watching the Babylonians destroy the city of Jerusalem and burn the holy temple with fire. Edom hates the people of God. So deeply did that bitterness enter into the memory of the nation that in Malachi 1:3 the Scripture says, "And I hated Esau [Edom]." That is the passage quoted in Romans 9 when Paul discusses election. In the bloodbath that overwhelms Edom, we have a symbol of the destruction of all of God's enemies.

Edom means "red." Isaiah 63:1 describes a victorious conqueror. Verses 1–4 constitute one of the best examples in the world of men who preach and teach but who refuse to face the reality of God.

For example, many say that in Isaiah 63:1 the person who is glorious in apparel and whose garments are dyed red with blood is our Lord who has poured out His blood on the cross for our sins that we might be saved. There is nothing wrong with the preaching of Christ and His blood, but that is not meant in our text. The answer is given in this same chapter: "Where did you get that red that dyes your garments?" He replies: "It is the blood of My enemies that I have trampled in My fury. I have stained My garments in battle, for the day of vengeance is in My heart."

God says, "I have trodden the winepress alone." Two symbols are used here to describe the fury of God. First, He will "make them drunk in my fury." This refers to the cup of God's wrath. One of the most startling passages in Jeremiah is when God says, "Take the wine cup of this fury at my hand, and cause all the nations, to whom I send thee, to drink it" (Jer. 25:15). Jeremiah carried that cup of the judgment of God to the nations of the earth.

When they refused to drink it God said, "Ye shall certainly drink" (Jer. 25:28). No nation will escape the judgment of almighty God.

THE CONQUERING KING RETURNS
FOR HIS WORK OF VENGEANCE

Second, the Lord treads His enemies in the fury of His judgment and their blood flows out. Then the blood stains his garments. We are not familiar with that image, for when we buy grape juice today the juice has been squeezed out at a processing plant. In Isaiah's day men put the grapes in a large vat called a winepress. A man stomped on the grapes in the vat, and as he stomped, the juice ran out and was gathered. As he trod the grapes, the rich, red juice stained his garments until he looked red all over. That is the image here. The Lord God is trampling out the enemies of God in the winepress of the fury of the day of vengeance.

Notice another thing. He says: "I have trodden the winepress alone; and of the people there was none with me. . . . And I looked, and there was none to help; and I wondered that there was none to uphold: therefore mine own arm brought salvation unto me; and my fury, it upheld me. And I will tread down the people in mine anger, and make them drunk in my fury" (Isa. 63:3,5,6). Do you see what the prophet says? God's people will be isolated in the end time. There will be no one to help. When God looked down from heaven and saw His people separate and apart, He alone helped them.

Let us read this passage out of the *Living Bible* and we will see more clearly the isolation of God's people:

> "Who is this who comes from Edom, from the city of Bozrah, with his magnificent garments of crimson? Who is this in kingly robes, marching in the greatness of his strength?"
>
> "It is I, the Lord, announcing your salvation; I, the Lord, the one who is mighty to save."
>
> "Why are your clothes so red, as from treading out the grapes?"
>
> "I have trodden the winepress alone. No one was there to help me. In my wrath I have trodden my enemies like grapes. In my fury I trampled my foes. It is their blood you see upon my clothes. For the time has come for me to avenge my people, to redeem them from the hands of their oppressors. I looked but no one came to help

them; I was amazed and appalled. So I executed vengeance alone; unaided, I meted out judgment. I crushed the heathen nations in my anger and made them stagger and fall to the ground." (Isa. 63:1–6)

If you want to know tomorrow's news, read the Bible. God says that His people will be increasingly isolated and Israel today is isolated. She has very few friends. Even those who once championed her in the United Nations now seek her excommunication. Nations are turning their backs upon the people of God, the Jews of the world. The enemies of Israel are the enemies of the Christian. Do not think that a Mohammedan loves a Christian. Do not think that a Communist loves a Christian. We are becoming increasingly isolated, just as the Bible says.

THE TRIUMPHANT CHRIST IN THE GREAT TRIBULATION

This prophecy in Isaiah 63 is the prophecy of the awesome battle of Armageddon. It is the prophecy of the intervention of Christ when He comes, the warrior to deliver His people in the earth.

We look at two instances in Revelation that refer to this prophecy of Isaiah 63. In Revelation 14 we read:

> And another angel came out from the altar, which had power over fire; and cried with a loud cry to him that had the sharp sickle, saying, Thrust in thy sharp sickle, and gather the clusters of the vine of the earth; for her grapes are fully ripe.
> And the angel thrust in his sickle into the earth, and gathered the vine of the earth, and cast it into the great winepress of the wrath of God.
> And the winepress was trodden without the city, and blood came out of the winepress, even unto the horse bridles, by the space of a thousand and six hundred furlongs. (vv. 18–20)

A furlong is one-eighth of a mile. One thousand six hundred furlongs total 200 miles. The blood of the battle of Armageddon will cover that much distance.

Revelation 9 says that the king of the east (China) has an army of 200,000,000 men at that great battle. The carnage is so great that the blood is to the bridles of the horses by a space of 1600 furlongs. From Bozra to Megiddo is exactly 1600 furlongs, or 200 miles.

The great rendezvous of the nations of the world will take place there.

The second reference in Revelation is found in the nineteenth chapter and is the same as Isaiah 63, describing the intervention of God in human history:

> And I saw heaven opened, and behold a white horse; and he that sat upon him was called Faithful and True, and in righteousness he doth judge and make war.
>
> His eyes were as a flame of fire, and on his head were many crowns; and he had a name written, that no man knew, but he himself.
>
> And he was clothed with a vesture dipped in blood: and his name is called The Word of God.
>
> And the armies which were in heaven followed him upon white horses, clothed in fine linen, white and clean.
>
> And out of his mouth goeth a sharp sword, that with it he should smite the nations: and he shall rule them with a rod of iron: and he treadeth the winepress of the fierceness and wrath of Almighty God.
>
> And he hath on his vesture and on his thigh a name written, KING OF KINGS, AND LORD OF LORDS.
>
> And I saw an angel standing in the sun; and he cried with a loud voice, saying to all the fowls that fly in the midst of heaven, Come and gather yourselves together unto the supper of the great God;
>
> That ye may eat the flesh of kings, and the flesh of captains, and the flesh of mighty men, and the flesh of horses, and of them that sit on them, and the flesh of all men, both free and bond, both small and great.
>
> And I saw the beast, and the kings of the earth, and their armies, gathered together to make war against him that sat on the horse, and against his army.
>
> And the beast was taken, and with him the false prophet that wrought miracles before him, with which he deceived them that had received the mark of the beast, and them that worshipped his image. These both were cast alive into a lake of fire burning with brimstone.
>
> And the remnant were slain with the sword of him that sat upon the horse, which sword proceeded out of his mouth: and all the fowls were filled with their flesh. (vv. 11–21)

What does that mean for us? God's grace does not continue forever in His overtures of love to the nations of the world. A time is coming when God will say it is enough. Judgment will fall. God will not sit on His throne forever and listen to a government like Russia that flaunts their blasphemies into His face and kills those who trust in His name. Nor will God sit on His throne and look in indifference upon a China that has destroyed the visible church of Jesus Christ. Nor will God look upon the nations of the earth that turn aside from His message and name. The wicked and all the nations that forget God shall be turned into hell. Men who stand in the pulpit and preach a petty, sentimental God have never read the Bible. God judges sin and the nations of the world. We are facing that judgment now.

When the quadrennium convention of the Church of the Nazarene met in Dallas, I read the address of their superintendent: "Nowhere has crisis been more continual than in the Middle East. The uneasy truce presently existing could be broken at any moment. The worldwide energy crisis has thrown this area into an even more critical position, since the largest petroleum reserves are located there. A struggle for this prize could well trigger the final holocaust. Small wonder that Billy Graham recently declared that 'many world leaders will admit in private that they believe the world stands on the very edge of Armageddon.'" There is a limit to the patience of God and there is a limit to the day of grace.

Not always does God strive with a man. In the many years that I have been a pastor, I have become increasingly aware that there are some men who say no to God for the last time and God leaves them alone; they are never saved and are eternally without God.

There is a time, a place that marks the destiny of men to glory or despair. There is a path that crosses the hidden boundary between God's mercy and God's wrath. If I am ever to be saved, I must be saved now. If I am ever to repent, I must do it now, for tomorrow may be too late. The day of judgment inevitably comes.

44

For Those Who Love God

For since the beginning of the world men have not heard, not perceived by the ear, neither hath the eye seen, O God beside thee, what he hath prepared for him that waiteth for him. (Isa. 64:4)

We are going to consider four incontrovertible absolutes that our eyes see and that can be confirmed by what we know in the earth. We know these absolutes by seeing and by our senses — touch, taste, sight, or hearing.

Four Incontrovertible Absolutes

First, existence is an incontrovertible absolute. I know that I am. I know that you are. I know that we together live in a created universe.

Thomas Carlyle once was exclaiming about a female philosopher who rejected all truth except one. She said, "I accept one thing, the universe." Thomas Carlyle exclaimed, "Egad, she had better!" This is an incontrovertible fact that we are and we are in a universe. That carries with it mathematical truth, astronomical truth, chemical truth, physical truth, biological truth, and truth of every kind. We know, and our eyes and senses confirm the fact of the universe.

Second, the planet earth is unique in all of God's vast creation. There is nothing and none like the planet earth in the universe. Scientists and astronomers continue to try to find life on other planets. Lately we have been reading about Mars. All I can observe is this: If men say there is life on Mars, they are going to have to redefine what "life" is. Imagine life without air, atmosphere, or water. Mars, like the moon and millions of other planets, is barren and sterile. But the planet earth is set apart and unique among all the planets of creation. If for no other reason, Jesus lived here, was born here, and died here. This world and this earth drank up His atoning blood. It was from this earth that He ascended back into heaven and from which some day He shall victoriously return.

Third, the universality of death is an incontrovertible absolute. There is no escaping death in any area of existence or creation. Even the stars burn out. Some day our sun will burn itself out and the whole created universe will collapse in sterility and darkness. Everything that we know faces one inevitable, inexorable conclusion — death.

Fourth, another incontrovertible absolute is the moral sensitivity of all mankind. There is no family, no tribe, no people, nor any nation so degraded but that they have a moral code of what is right and what is wrong. What they think to be right and what they think to be wrong may be strange to us, but everyone has some moral sensitivity.

When Charles Darwin went around the world, he came to the tip of South America and found a group of islands called Tierra del Fuego. He wrote that he had found in those islands a tribe so degraded that they had no moral sensitivity. He said, "I have found the missing link between the animal and the man, for these Tierra del Fuegans are without sensitivity." Some Christians in England read Darwin's statement and sent missionaries to Tierra del Fuego. Soon they reported that the Tierra del Fuegans were noble in their life and virtuous in their deportment. They had been won to Christ and were now disciples of the Lord. When Charles Darwin learned of the evangelization of the Tierra del Fuegans, he himself became a subscriber and a faithful contributor to the Church Missionary Society of London, England, who sent out the missionaries. There are no people in the world who have ever lived or ever shall live in whom that spirit of moral discernment is not present.

THE WORLD UNSEEN

The four incontrovertible absolutes we have named are things that we see with our eyes and can verify with our senses. But there is another world, another dimension. Aristotle wrote of the physical world when he wrote the treatise, *Physics*. He added a volume called *Metaphysics*, that is, the world beyond what a man can see, beyond the physical. There is an unseen world that the senses cannot touch.

For example, we can examine a brain, but we cannot examine a mind. We can measure impulses of the nervous system, but we cannot measure thought. We can dissect a cadaver, but we could never dissect a soul. We can verify and categorize the organs of the physical frame, but we could never find or categorize a conscience. There is another world beyond our physical senses which has nothing to do with our physical senses. As a silver coin is unlike the bread that it buys, so there is no relation between the physical of this world and that dimensional unseen world beyond. But the unseen world is no less real.

For example Paul, in quoting the verse in Isaiah 64:4, says it like this: "But as it is written, Eye hath not seen, nor ear heard, neither have entered into the heart of man, the things which God hath prepared for them that love him" (1 Cor. 2:9). You have heard that verse repeated a thousand times, and usually it is read by itself. To stop there is to stop in the middle of what the apostle is saying. The next verse says, "But God hath revealed them unto us by his Spirit: for the Spirit searcheth all things, yea, the deep things of God" (v. 10). There are marvelous realities that the senses of sight, sound, and touch can never know. But the apostle avows that they are revealed to us by the Holy Spirit of God, for the Holy Spirit searches the deep things of God and opens them to our hearts and view.

As we have discussed four incontrovertible absolutes that we can verify by our physical senses, let us now look at four deep phenomena that are revealed to us by the Holy Spirit, things that we could never know by our physical senses unless God revealed them to us.

WE ARE CREATED IN GOD'S IMAGE

First, we are created in the image of God for the glory of the Lord. A man is not a fortuitous concourse of atoms. His life is not an accident that happened in the course of human development, but he is a creation of God formed by the hands of the Almighty, made in His likeness and in His image for a definite God-called, God-assigned, and stated purpose. What a marvelous revelation God has made for us in Genesis 1 and 2! We are not accidents, we are not the products of blind, impersonal forces, but we are the creation of the hands of God placed in this earth for a purpose — the glory of our Lord. I know of nothing more degrading than for men to say that we are nothing but blind results of forces that are also impersonal and blind. I know of nothing more noble than to teach that we are made in the likeness and image of God and are placed in this world with a definite plan and purpose in the mind of God.

Can you imagine an angel from heaven, who stands in the presence of God, being compelled to be a black spider or a rattlesnake? It would be degrading. Can you imagine a majestic, soaring eagel that rises up to the blue of the sky being persuaded to believe that he is a worm? So many of our young people are being taught today that they are animals with no purpose, no plan, and no God-likeness, but that human beings are the result of blind generations of evolution. What a degrading doctrine! When these young people are taught that they are animals, then we seem to be surprised that they act like animals. One of the revelations of God is that we are made in His likeness, after His image. There is nothing so noble and uplifting as a revelation of the Spirit of the deep things of God telling us where we came from, why we were made, and the great plan and purpose God has for us.

When I marry a couple I say: "In the beginning, when God made the first man and placed him in the Garden of Eden, He said, 'It is not good that man should live alone.' He made for him an helpmate, the last and crowning creation, the woman. There in the paradise of Eden God hallowed and sanctified our first home." How uplifting is the revelation of the Spirit of God! The Lord intends us to soar, to be like Him, created in His likeness.

GOD INCARNATE SAVES US

Second, the Holy Spirit reveals to us the incarnate God in Christ Jesus our Lord. It was God who loved us, God who in atoning grace came to make sacrifice for us. It was God who washed our sins away in the blood of the cross. It is God who will raise us from among the dead, who will set us at the right hand of glory on high. This Jesus is God in human flesh. This is a revelation that comes from the Holy Spirit, for no man can know, or receive this revelation of himself. It has to come from the Spirit of God, a revelation of the Lord to us, unveiling and uncovering Jesus Christ who died for our sins.

In John 16 we read:

> Howbeit when he, the Spirit of truth, is come, he will guide you into all truth: for he shall not speak of himself; but whatsoever he shall hear, that shall he speak: and he will shew you things to come.
>
> He shall glorify me: for he shall receive of mine, and shall shew it unto you. (vv. 13,14)

When we magnify the Holy Spirit of God, we are doing the opposite of that, for the Holy Spirit of God magnifies and presents the Lord Jesus.

In John 6:44 the Lord says, "No man can come to me, except the Father which hath sent me draw him: and I will raise him up at the last day." This is a revelation of God to us, that Jesus is the Christ the Son of God, the incarnate God, and that in Him we have forgiveness of sins and hope of heaven. Some might think it unreasonable and irrational that God should become man and die in His grace and love for us. But as stupendous as that revelation is, it has been accepted by the greatest minds of all time, Jew and Gentile alike. The first Christians were Jews and in the centuries since many Christian Jews have given much to the Christian church.

GOD CHANGES US

Third, we see the miracle of the new birth. Can the leopard change his spots? Can the Ethiopian change his skin? Can a man who has given his life to sin ever be saintly in his deportment? Can a man who knows nothing but wrong or violence be a humble child of heaven? It is a miracle what God is able to do in the heart of a man.

I once buried the wife of a faithful member of our church. The husband brought me a poem he had given his wife on their thirty-fifth wedding anniversary. He pointed out a phrase; "She has taken the material of me and made not a tavern, but a temple." He said: "I was on the road downhill beginning to frequent the bars. She won me to Jesus and I could never thank her enough." The ableness of God to change a man is a miracle. He is a new creation accomplished by the regenerating power of the Holy Spirit revealed to us.

GOD HAS A KINGDOM FOR HIS REDEEMED

Fourth, we see a coming kingdom. Isaiah 42:4 declares, "He shall not fail nor be discouraged, till he have set judgment in the earth: and the isles shall wait for his law." When we read the headlines and look at the depravity of human nature, can it ever be that there will be a kingdom of holiness and righteousness in this earth? We cannot see it with the eye, nor can we conceive of it in the heart as we look at our present world, but by the eyes of faith in the revelation of the Holy Spirit of God we can see and believe. God has revealed to us that there will yet be a millennial kingdom in this earth where we now live.

The last chapter of Genesis speaks of the end of Joseph's life. Before Joseph died, he gathered his brethren around him and said, ". . . God will surely visit you, and ye shall carry up my bones from hence" (Gen. 50:25). When God delivered Israel, they carried with them the bones of their brother Joseph. They buried him in the land of promise in Canaan. At the blowing of the

302 Isaiah: An Exposition

trumpet, at the last day, Joseph will rise in that millennial kingdom and will be a fellow heir in the presence of the great and coming King. What God has said of Joseph, He says of you.

Paul writes in 1 Corinthians 15:

> Now this I say, brethren, that flesh and blood cannot inherit the kingdom of God; neither doth corruption inherit incorruption.
>
> Behold, I shew you a mystery; We shall not all sleep, but we shall all be changed,
>
> In a moment, in the twinkling of an eye, at the last trump: for the trumpet shall sound, and the dead shall be raised incorruptible, and we shall be changed.
>
> For this corruptible must put on incorruption, and this mortal must put on immortality.
>
> So when this corruptible shall have put on incorruption, and this mortal shall have put on immortality, then shall be brought to pass the saying that is written, Death is swallowed up in victory?
>
> O death, where is thy sting? O grave, where is thy victory? (vv. 50–55)

Death is mighty but Jesus our Lord is mightier still. He will certainly triumph. This is the revelation of the Holy Spirit who lays before us the deep things of the Lord. There is a coming kingdom, a millennial reign of our living Lord. In that kingdom we will have a part. O glorious, golden tomorrow!

45

The Millennial Kingdom

For, behold, I create new heavens and a new earth: and the former shall not be remembered, nor come into mind.

But be ye glad and rejoice for ever in that which I create: for, behold, I create Jerusalem a rejoicing, and her people a joy.

And I will rejoice in Jerusalem, and joy in my people: and the voice of weeping shall be no more heard in her, nor the voice of crying.

There shall be no more thence an infant of days, nor an old man that hath not filled his days: for the child shall die an hundred years old; but the sinner being an hundred years old shall be accursed.

And they shall build houses, and inhabit them; and they shall plant vineyards, and eat the fruit of them.

They shall not build, and another inhabit; they shall not plant and another eat: for as the days of a tree are the days of my people, and mine elect shall long enjoy the work of their hands.

They shall not labour in vain, nor bring forth for trouble; for they are the seed of the blessed of the LORD, and their offspring with them.

And it shall come to pass, that before they call, I will answer; and while they are yet speaking, I will hear.

The wolf and the lamb shall feed together, and the lion shall eat straw like the bullock: and dust shall be the serpent's meat. They

303

shall not hurt nor destroy in all my holy mountain, saith the Lord.
(Isa. 65:17–25)

All of God's creation is involved in the future. We are born into
this world. What do the days ahead hold for us? What is the future
of the world? Will sin, death, and the grave be our inheritance
forever? Is that the future to which we look? Will the course of
human history forever be as the centuries past, a story of
bloodshed, war, violence, and terror? Will the planet earth go on
in its course until finally it falls into the sun and is burned up into a
cinder? Or will it finally be that the sun goes out and the earth
eventually becomes a dead planet in eternal night and darkness?
What is the future of our own life and of this world?

Without exception, the prophecy of the Old Testament and the
revelation of the New Testament is that there lies ahead for us and
for our world a golden age, a millennial kingdom when God's will
is done in earth as it is in heaven, when the King Messiah sits upon
His throne and rules in this earth as now He rules over the angelic
hosts in glory. Of that promise of a kingdom that is to come, Isaiah
writes more than any other prophet. A part of that marvelous
revelation is found in our text. There are six things in this revelation that describe the coming millennial kingdom. We will discuss
them in succession.

The Kingdom Will Be Established by God

First, the coming kingdom will be established in this earth not
by the genius of men but by the intervention of almighty God.
Look at the personal pronouns in our text:

> For, behold, I create new heavens and a new earth.
> . . . be ye glad and rejoice for ever in that which I create: for,
> behold, I create Jerusalem a rejoicing.
> . . . And I will rejoice in Jerusalem, and joy in my people.
> And it shall come to pass, that before they call, I will answer; and
> while they are yet speaking, I will hear.
> . . . They shall not hurt nor destroy in all my holy mountain,
> saith the Lord. (vv. 17–19,24,25)

Anyone sensitive to the Word of God can not but be sensitive to the
emphasis of those personal pronouns. The Lord's kingdom will be

established not by the means of ableness of men but by the intervention of God from heaven, by the coming of the Lord.

For many years the theology of a large number of theologians was that the kingdom would come by the preaching of the gospel. The sin of nature and man would be taken away through the preaching of the gospel of Christ. That doctrine is contrary to the Word of God. Such teaching is certainly contrary to the experience and history of men. After two thousand years of gospel preaching, there are more unbelievers and infidels in the world than there were two thousand years ago. There is more crime, more violence, more terror, and more fear in the world today than there ever has been. The sinful condition of the world today is according to the Word of the Lord, for in 2 Timothy 2 and 2 Timothy 3 Paul, by inspiration, says that wicked men shall wax worse and worse. There always has been a faithful remnant and God will not disappoint them. The kingdom is coming, not by the keenness of man, but by the coming of the Lord and the intervention of almighty God.

JERUSALEM WILL BE THE CAPITAL OF THE WORLD

Second, we read that the capital of the millennial world will be Jerusalem. In Amos, Isaiah, Ezekiel, Jeremiah, and in the rest of the prophets, we read that the people of the Lord, the Jews who had been scattered, will be back in the land. God will gather His chosen people home. In that millennial day, Jerusalem will be the capital of the whole world.

If I could summarize the consummation of the age briefly, I would do it like this: at the end times, there will be three great movements.

There will be an upward movement which will include the resurrection of the dead and the rapture of the church when those who have fallen asleep in Christ, the Old Testament saints and the New Testament redeemed, are called forth at the sound of the trumpet and are raised in the glory of the likeness of Christ. They will be taken upward in the rapture of the church into the New Jerusalem, into the city of God.

There will be a downward movement which will be the perdition of those who reject Christ, who spurn His overtures of mercy, who do despite unto the Spirit of grace, and who tread under foot the blood of the covenant. God will take out of His kingdom all that is offensive, all that hurts and destroys.

There will be a forward movement which will be into the earthly millennial kingdom of God. Those who are alive on the earth will go through a great judgment. First, there will be a judgment of Israel which is meticulously outlined in Ezekiel 20. Those who turn to God in repentance and faith among Israel will enter into the millennial kingdom. There will be a judgment for the Gentiles which is identified and characterized in Matthew 25. Those Gentiles who have accepted the Lord Christ as their Savior will enter into the millennium. No one will enter the millennium who is not saved. The whole earth will live in glory and in peace.

In Isaiah 2 we read:

> The word that Isaiah the son of Amoz saw concerning Judah and Jerusalem.
> And it shall come to pass in the last days, that the mountain of the Lord's house shall be established in the top of the mountains, and shall be exalted above the hills; and all nations shall flow into it.
> And many people shall go and say, Come ye, and let us go up to the mountain of the Lord, to the house of the God of Jacob; and he will teach us of his ways, and we will walk in his paths: for out of Zion shall go forth the law, and the word of the Lord from Jerusalem.
> And he shall judge among the nations, and shall rebuke many people: and they shall beat their swords into plowshares, and their spears into pruninghooks: nation shall not lift up sword against nation, neither shall they learn war any more. (vv. 1–4)

The whole world will be one united family in Christ. It will be filled with the knowledge of the Lord, with peace and glory, and with joy and happiness.

Weeping and Crying Will Be Banished Forever

Third, there will be no more hurt, no more crying, and no more weeping. The Book of Revelation states that the source of our weeping and crying will have been taken away. Satan will be bound and cast into the bottomless pit.

One time when I walked to my car from the church, the guard met me. He said: "I received a telephone call and placed the number on the windshield of your car. The caller was a woman who seemed to be in great trouble." I took the number and called. On the other end of the line a woman said: "You do not know me. I do not belong to any church, but for many years I set the type for your 'Pastor's Pen' that you publish in the church paper. I felt that I got to know you really well. We have just been told by the doctor that my husband has a tragic and terminal illness. I just thought that maybe you would pray for me and for him in our hour of sorrow." In the Lord's kingdom there will be no more crying and weeping, no distress and breaking of heart.

Life Without Sickness and Age

Fourth, there will be no sickness and age in heaven. We read in Isaiah 33:24, "And the inhabitant shall not say, I am sick." That is an astonishing prophecy. Then we read in Isaiah 35:

> Then the eyes of the blind shall be opened, and the ears of the deaf shall be unstopped.
> Then shall the lame man leap as an hart, and the tongue of the dumb sing. (vv. 5,6)

There will be no one who is sick and no one who grows old. The only one who will die in the millennial kingdom is the one who, reaching the age of accountability at one hundred years, shall rebel against God. But for Christians, their days shall be as the days of a tree.

In the beginning, God never meant for us to die. Man was created to live forever and the first men lived long. Adam lived 930 years. Methuselah lived 969 years. God said to Adam, "In the day that thou eatest thereof, thou shalt surely die" (Gen. 2:17). That day the Spirit died. In the day of the Lord (and a day of the Lord is one thousand years), the physical frame died. But in the millennium we will not grow old and we will not die.

The Curse of Sin Will Be Removed Forever

Fifth, there shall be the Edenic recreation of this world. The wolf and the lamb will feed together. The lion will eat straw like the bullock.

God never intended for the animals to eat each other, to prey and stalk each other. God never planned that animals would be carnivorous and bloodthirsty. He made His world beautiful and gentle. It is going to be that way again. The entire animal world will be at peace with each other.

The vegetable world will be recreated. The reason that the earth brings up briers, thorn, and weeds is because the earth is cursed. God said that when the man sinned, "Cursed is the ground for thy sake; in sorrow shalt thou eat of it all the days of thy life; thorns also, and thistles shall it bring forth to thee" (Gen. 3:17,18). The Lord never intended that. He intended for the earth to be fruitful and beautiful. In that Edenic world Isaiah says in Isaiah 55:13, "Instead of the thorn shall come up the fir tree, and instead of the brier shall come up the myrtle tree." In Isaiah 35 he says,

> The wilderness and the solitary place shall be glad for them; and
> the desert shall rejoice, and blossom as the rose.
> It shall blossom abundantly. (vv. 1,2a)

The world will look like a beautiful garden with flowering trees and beautiful blossoming vegetation everywhere. The serpent will be harmless, without fangs, without poison, a creature meek and mild. The earth will be so fertile, so prolific, so rich that the serpent will find its food just eating on the ground. There shall be none to make them afraid.

One will not have to worry about a burglar at the door. He will not live in dread and fear nor walk down the streets of the city in the dead of the night and be afraid. The world will be beautiful, fertile, quiet, and at peace. None will be afraid.

THE CONSUMMATION OF THE AGE

Sixth, the best part of the millennial kingdom will be the loving nearness of our great King, the Lord Christ Messiah.

When the Lord came the first time, everyone was disappointed. The Jews were disappointed because they expected their Messiah to deliver them from the Roman yoke. The disciples were disappointed because one thought that he would sit on His right hand as prime minister, the other would sit on His left hand as chancellor, and the rest of them would have prominent cabinet positions. They were looking forward to a glorious reign and to being exalted and lifted up with power and influence. When the road finally led to Golgotha, Mark says that they all forsook Him and fled. When our Lord came the first time, seemingly everyone misunderstood and was disappointed. They did not understand that atonement first had to be made for our sins, for it is blood that washes away sin. But there is also the exaltation that follows. In Philippians 2, when Paul describes the descent of our Lord and His suffering on the cross, he says:

> Wherefore God also hath highly exalted him, and given him a name which is above every name:
> That at the name of Jesus every knee should bow, of things in heaven, and things in earth, and things under the earth;
> And that every tongue should confess that Jesus Christ is Lord, to the glory of God the Father. (vv. 9–11)

Can you imagine a whole world loving Jesus, bowing in adoration, and remembering that He died for us? "I am here because of His blood, His sacrifice." What a world, what a millennium, when we all bow, loving our Lord.

The Messiah Jesus will be a great King who is sensitive to our every need. "Before they call, I will answer; and while they are yet speaking, I will hear" (Isa. 65:24). Grace on top of grace, overflowing grace, grace for grace, flowing like streams in the desert from the throne of the omnipotent King. Before they even ask, He will answer. Before they call, He will hear.

These are marvelous mysteries of the golden age before us. These miracles are no greater than these that we see wrought by the hand of God around us day by day. The stars in their courses, the beautiful earth, and our souls and bodies are miracles in it all. The Lord created all of His world in the beginning and He is the same almighty God who will recreate the world and restore its Edenic and pristine beauty in the end.

46

The Birth of Spiritual Children

> Before she travailed, she brought forth; before her pain came, she was delivered of a man child.
> Who hath heard such a thing? who hath seen such things? Shall the earth be made to bring forth in one day? or shall a nation be born at once? for as soon as Zion travailed, she brought forth her children.
> Shall I bring to the birth, and not cause to bring forth? saith the LORD: shall I cause to bring forth, and shut the womb? saith thy God. (Isa. 66:7–9)

The text of the message is: "For as soon as Zion travailed, she brought forth her children." That imagery of birth is used with profound significance in the Word of God. In John 3, when our Lord was speaking to Nicodemus, He said to him, "Ye must be born again." He added to it further: "Verily, verily, I say unto thee, Except a man be born of water and of the Spirit, he cannot enter into the kingdom of God" (John 3:5). Then yet again He said, "Marvel not that I said unto thee, Ye must be born again" (John 3:7). Birth is a profound imagery in the Holy Scriptures, and it is so used here in our text.

The mother is Zion and the man child that is born is the

spiritual and true Israel of God. The birth is miraculously rapid, sudden, and immediate. The rapidity of the birth is astonishing: "Who hath seen such things . . . shall a nation be born at once?" Months, years, maybe centuries of longing, waiting, crying, agonizing, and travailing, then in a great and marvelous intervention of God, a nation is born in a day.

GOD'S WAY OF WORKING THROUGH THE AGES

In the climactic verse of Revelation 22:20 we read, "He which testifieth these things saith, Surely I come quickly." The Lord did not mean that tomorrow He would return, but at the consummation of the age, after the passing of the tribulation, these things will come immediately, and will occur rapidly and quickly. So it is in God's dealing through the ages. There is a passage of time and God's people, the faithful remnant, cry and agonize, pray and plea. Then, when the fullness of vehemence rises to God, there is a marvelous and miraculous deliverance. God seems to work like that, for as soon as Zion travails, immediately there is the birth — the man child is born, the nation is regenerated, revival comes, and there is deliverance from His blessed hands.

The children of Israel cried in Egyptian bondage, and when the height of their crying was beyond what God's ears could bear, He sent Moses to deliver the people from the bondage of Egypt.

So it was in the days of Ahab and Jezebel. To the 7000 who remained faithful to Jehovah in their crying to God, the prophet Elijah suddenly appeared. On Mount Carmel he led Israel out of its apostasy back to God in a great revival.

In the days of Manasseh, for whose depravity God refused to deliver Judah, the wicked king brought the nation down to depths of sin and idolatry it had never known before. Then Josiah arose. He found the book of the law in the temple. In the great revival movement that followed, Daniel, Ezekiel, and Jeremiah came to know the Lord.

It was so in the days of the Babylonian captivity. After seventy years of agonizing and weeping on the banks of the rivers of Babylon, Cyrus the Persian, Zerubbabel, Ezra, and Nehemiah suddenly delivered the people and rebuilt the wall and temple in Jerusalem.

It was so in the days of the Roman bondage. The religion of the people was formal and barren and sterile. They finally crucified the Lord Prince of Glory in heaven. But out of their bondage, suddenly, like a great rushing, mighty wind, the Holy Spirit was poured out from God in heaven and the great age of the grace of the Christian faith was begun.

It was so in the days of the Inquisition. God's faithful martyrs were burned at the stake and torn on the rack. Suddenly Martin Luther stood on his feet where he had been kneeling. Like a thunderbolt from heaven the Word came to his soul that the just live by faith, not by liturgy. The great Reformation was launched.

We Can Always Look for the Mighty Intervention of God

All of these events are harbingers of how it will be at the end time. There is tribulation, agony, and crying of the people of God, then suddenly the consummation of the age and Jesus has come. God seems to work that way, therefore it is right for us to expect and pray for the intervention of God from heaven. These great revelations in the Book and the great doctrines in the Scriptures are not just for a moment, but they apply to all time. They are like God Himself. They never change. They are applicable in every situation, and it is so in this doctrine.

A musician astonishes the world with his beautiful music on an organ, on a piano, or any other musical instrument. What lies back of the beautiful performance is travail, hours and days of work and practice.

The same is true in medicine. A great surgeon or a fine doctor brings healing to people, but back of that medicinal ministry are years of toil and travail.

A like sacrifice can be found on the athletic field. The men who so nobly carry the banner of their city or state or school or nation are crowned with success. But back of it are years of hard work and practice.

The same travail is to be found in the political freedom of a nation. Behind the blessings that we enjoy lie the blood and sacrifice of the soldiers who laid down their lives for us. Therefore, it is not strange that we see that same doctrine in the church. Out of the travail, suffering, and sorrow of our Lord salvation is born. We are taken as a people out of His side. We were born in His blood, in His sorrows, in His sufferings, in His tears and sobs, and in His death. The same travail is true in the church that continues today.

Paul wrote in Colossians 1:24, "Who now rejoice in my sufferings for you, and fill up that which is behind of the afflictions of Christ in my flesh for his body's sake, which is the church." How could such a thing be? Was his atonement not complete when He died for us on the cross? It was complete. "It is finished," He cried. There remains no more sacrifice for sins. Then what could Paul mean? He means that as Christ died for us that we might be redeemed and saved from our sins, there remains for us a suffering, a travailing in the church that it might live, be vibrant, and have the moving Spirit of God in it. There is no spiritual blessing that will come to us without that travail and agony in prayer and burden of heart.

WHY THE TRUE CHURCH BOWS IN TRAVAIL

The church must travail and must agonize in prayer because of the worldliness of its members. I preside over the church as its moderator. I also shepherd the flock as an undershepherd. I see everywhere the fact that the hearts of my own people are out there in the world. The service of God becomes incidental, never central and dynamic. Satan oversows the sowing of the Lord. The coils of that serpent have surrounded and enclosed the whole earth and that includes us. How do we break that hold of Satan on our lives and the call and the blandishments of the world? There is no way to have freedom from Satan but to plead before God. The church bows in travail because of the hardness of the world and the difficulty of winning people to Jesus. More than fifty years ago Billy Sunday, the colorful evangelist, said, "It is harder to win a fifteen-year-old boy at the end of my ministry than it was to win a seventy-year-old man at the beginning of my ministry." If Billy Sunday said that more than fifty years ago, what would he say if he lived today? It is difficult winning people to Christ and getting them out of the world and into the grace of our Lord Jesus.

The church bows in travail because of the tragedy of the lost. However one wishes to say it — philosophically, academically, theologically, culturally, politically, scientifically, historically, or personally — this is the one crude, harsh fact of human history and human life: a nation is lost without God. A state is lost without God. A city is lost without God. A family is lost without God. A life is lost without God. The human soul is lost without God. That causes us to bow in travail before the Lord.

The church bows in travail because it is God's purpose to work the fullness of grace in our lives. Without travail, that fullness of grace is never achieved. When our first parents fell, the Lord turned to the woman and said, in Genesis 3:16b, "In sorrow thou shalt bring forth children." Then He said to the man, "In the sweat of thy face shalt thou eat bread, till thou return unto the ground; for out of it wast thou taken: for dust thou art, and unto dust shalt thou return" (Gen. 3:19). Does God have a reason for that? He does. If we could buy a child at a department store, we might acquire the youngster indifferently. But a child does not come from a department store. The child is nurtured beneath the mother's heart. The birth of a child is accompanied by pain, labor, and travail. It is an unusual mother and an unusual father who would take the child of their love and then leave that child on a doorstep. There is a purpose of God in the way a child is born and there is no less purpose for us in our spiritual birth when we come through prayer, tears, intercession, and travail. Such agony is the way God has of placing upon us those beautiful and precious graces that so marvelously live in the life of our Lord.

In travail, tears, intercession, and prayer the church is cemented together. How could I be full of critical grudges, bitterness, and hatred when I am kneeling, praying and pleading with God for lost souls? How could the church be rent and separated when it is agonizing before God for the outpouring of the Spirit of revival? It is to us as it was to the congregation of the Lord in Jerusalem when He said, "Tarry till you see the promise of my Father." In one place, with one accord, they were praying to God and the great visitation came. Our common sacrifice, our common praying, our common travailing before God binds us together as a people as nothing else in the world will.

The sharing of the burden centers our souls upon the main purpose in the worship of our Lord. What is the tremendous blessing we receive when we assemble ourselves in the house of the Lord? Could it be litany, decorum, eloquence, or magnificent speech? Such accouterments are incidental. Even the architecture of the building is trifling and peripheral. We could meet in a barn on a sawdust floor and have God with us just as powerfully and as gloriously. The blessing in worship centers our hearts upon the main thing which is love and compassion, sympathy and understanding, intercession and pleading, asking God to save the lost and to build us up in the faith of our wonderful Savior.

How the Church in Travail Appears

If we saw a church in travail, how would it look? What would it be doing? According to the Word of the Lord, a church in travail would be burdened for the lost. Romans 10:1 reads, "Brethren, my heart's desire and prayer to God for Israel is, that they might be saved." In Romans 9:3 we read, "For I could with that myself were accursed from Christ for my brethren, my kinsmen according to the flesh." If there is no burden of heart, no longing, crying, and praying for people to be saved, we will not see a church in travail and we will not see people born into the kingdom of God. When Zion travailed, children were born into the kingdom. If we find a church in travail, it will be a church with a burden on its heart that the people might be saved.

Such a church will have a new kind of praying; not formal, cold, or removed, but it will be a church begging God in agonizing tears. It is tragic not to be able to bring fruit before our Lord.

> Must I go, and empty-handed?
> Must I meet my Savior so?
> Not one soul with which to greet Him —
> Must I empty-handed go?

Where is concern for the lost in the church and in the pulpit today?

Where is that seeking, compassionate note? I cannot remember when I have seen a congregation bowed before the Lord weeping because of their burden for the lost. The agonizing for souls has left us, but the great doctrine is forever. It does not change, for as soon as Zion travailed she brought forth her children. Without travail, people are not born into the kingdom of God. As we were saved in the love and sufferings of our Lord, so the gospel of grace that is mediated to others is intellectual and academic until it assumes blood, life, agony, care, tears, burden, and prayer from us who minister the grace of the Lord before His blessed throne of love. O God in heaven, grant to us that seeking note, that compassionate spirit, and that heart that cares!